Abstracts *of* Bucks County Pennsylvania

LAND RECORDS

1684-1723

Compiled by
Charlotte D. Meldrum

HERITAGE BOOKS
2008

HERITAGE BOOKS
AN IMPRINT OF HERITAGE BOOKS, INC.

Books, CDs, and more—Worldwide

For our listing of thousands of titles see our website
at
www.HeritageBooks.com

Published 2008 by
HERITAGE BOOKS, INC.
Publishing Division
100 Railroad Ave. #104
Westminster, Maryland 21157

Copyright © 1995 Charlotte D. Meldrum

All rights reserved. No part of this book may be reproduced or transmitted in any form or by any means, electronic or mechanical, including photocopying, recording or by any information storage and retrieval system without written permission from the author, except for the inclusion of brief quotations in a review.

International Standard Book Numbers
Paperbound: 978-1-58549-393-7
Clothbound: 978-0-7884-7273-2

CONTENTS

Introduction v

Map of Bucks And Part of Philadelphia Counties, taken from Holme's "Map of the Improved part of the Province of Pennsylvania." vi

Land Records 1

Index 131

INTRODUCTION

Bucks County was one of Pennsylvania's original counties. In 1685 its boundary with Philadelphia County ran along the east side of Potquessin Creek from its mouth on the Delaware River northwest to near its source and continued in the same direction along the west side of Southampton and Warminster townships. The Delaware River formed its southeast and northeast boundaries while its northwest boundary was determined by Indian treaties. See Thomas Holme's *Map of the Improved Part of the Province of Pennsylvania in America* on the following page.

For a thorough discussion of the complex history of the administration of the land under William Penn see Donna Bingham Munger, *Pennsylvania Land Records. A History and Guide for Research.* Published by Scholarly Resources, Inc. (1991).

In this work we have included references to all persons found in the records. Our primary goal was to reveal information useful to genealogical research. We have eliminated the proforma legal requirements and also the specific descriptions of the metes and bounds of the tracts - all for reasons of economy. The omission of specific descriptions of the boundaries is indicated by ellipsis (...). Dates shown include acknowledgement (Ackn:), registration at the court (Reg:) or recordation (Rec:). Witnesses are indicated by "Wit:." The reader is invited to acquire complete copies of the records through the county court or by ordering microfilm through a local Family History Center (LDS).

F. Edward Wright
Westminster, Maryland
1995

Deed Book A, Vol. I

P. 1. Deed. John Ackerman of Falls of Delaware, Bucks Co., PA, yeoman, for £3.2.6 per year grants to Richard Ridgway, a tailor, a parcel of land containing two rods breadth through the lower side of his lands next adjoining beginning at the River of Delaware ... with lower line of the land of said John Ackerman as now it is run out according to his patent. Wit: Edward Covet, Thomas Rowland, Phineas Pemberton. Ackn: 10th da, 10th mo, 1684. Reg: 22nd da, 11th mo, 1684.

P. 2. Deed. Daniel Gardiner, Bucks Co., shoemaker, for £5 grants to Edward Green of Philadelphia Co. a parcel of land containing 100 acres lying over against Orestonds Island bounded on the upper side with the lands of John Luff and on the lower side with the lands of Leonel Brittain. Wit: Thomas Rowland, Edmond Lovet, Phineas Pemberton. Justices present: John Otter, Edmond Bennett, William Yardley, William Biles. Ackn: 10th da, 10th mo, 1684. Reg: 12th da, 11th mo, 1684.

P. 3. Bond. Francis Rossell and Michael Rossell, both of Bucks Co., milners, stand indebted to John Otter, Bucks Co., yeoman, for £10, to be paid 9th of 6th month next. Wit: Edmond Bennett, John Prallworth, Robert Row. Reg: 22nd da, 11th mo, 1684.

P. 3. Deed. Lawrence Bannor of Falls of Delaware, Bucks Co., for £17 grants to Gilbert Wheeler, of said county a parcel of land containing 250 acres bounded on the east with the lands of Robert Lucas, on the south with William Hiscock, on the west with William Brian, on the north with William Dark. Wit: Thomas Dungan, John Clows, John Pidcock. Justices then present: James Harrison, William Yardley, William Biles. Ackn: 14th da, 11th mo, 1684. Reg: 23rd da, 11th mo, 1684.

P. 4. Deed. Edmond Lovett of Bucks Co., planter, for £10 grants to Abraham Cocks of said county, a parcel of land containing 100 acres bounded on the northwest with the lands of said Edmond Lovett and on the northeast with the lands of Ralph Smith, on the southeast side with lands of William Bennett, on the southwest with the lands of Richard Lundy. Wit: Henry Margerom, Thomas Woolfe. Ackn: 8th da, 4th mo, 1685. Reg: 26th da, 5th mo, 1685.

P. 4. Deed. Edmond Lovett, Bucks Co., for £6.5 grants to Joseph

English a parcel of land containing 50 acres bounded on the southeast, southwest and northwest by the lands of aforesaid Edmond Lovett and the northerly side by lands of John Rowland. Wit: Henry Margaram, Thomas Woolfe. Ackn: 10th da, 4th mo, 1685. Justices present: William Yardley, William Biles, Edmond Bennett, William Beaks, Phinehas Pemberton, cleric, Comitab. Recorded 26th of 5th month.

P. 5. Deed. 10th da, 4th mo, 1685. Israel Taylor of Neshaminy Creek, Bucks Co., chirurgeon, for £10 paid by Christopher Wetherill of Burlington, West New Jersey, tailor, grants a parcel of land containing 150 acres in Bucks Co., beginning at a corner tree by Neshaminy Creek ... said 150 acres which were granted to Christopher Taylor of Tinicomb Island in Delaware River by patent dated 15th da, 5th mo, 1684 and since by bill of sale dated 7th da, 2nd mo, 1685 that Christopher Taylor hath granted to said Israel Taylor. Wit: Nicholas Waln, Phineas Pemberton. Ackn: 10th da, 4th mo, 1685. Phineas Pemberton, Cl. Rec: 27th da, 5th mo, 1685.

P. 6. Deed. 8th da, 7th mo, 1685. Richard Lundy, Bucks Co. to Jacob Tellnor of town and province of New York for £3 and 1000 acres in the woods of Pennsylvania, a tract of 200 acres beginning at the River Delaware, granted by William Penn to Richard Lundy by letters patent dated 26th da, 5th mo, 1684. Wit: William Biles, David Davies. Justices then present: Thomas Janney, William Beaks, William Biles, William Yardley. Ackn: Richard Lundy to William Biles for the use of Jacob Tellnor 9th da, 7th mo, 1685. Phinehas Pemberton, Clericl. Comitatl. Rec: 21st da, 9th mo, 1685.

P. 8. Deed. 5th da, 8th mo, 1685. Anne Millcome, Bucks Co., widow, for natural affection to Philip Conway, son in law of said Anne Millcome, and for other considerations, a tract in Bucks Co. ... which runs along the line of Jeffrey Hawkins ... containing 50 acres. Which parcel is part of a tract granted to said Anne Millcome by letters patents dated 16th da, 5th mo, 1684. Wit: Robert Lucas, John Collins, Luke Brindley. Ackn: 17th da, 8th mo, 1685. Phinehas Pemberton Cleric Comitatus. Rec: 10th da, 9th mo, 1685.

P. 9. Deed. 6th da, 8th mo, 1685. Anne Millcome of Bucks Co., widow, to William Biles, of said County, for £27.10 a parcel of land in Bucks Co., of 200 acres which is part of a tract granted by William Penn to said

Anne Millcome by letters patents dated 16th da, 5th mo, 1684. Wit: Lyonel Brittain, Joseph Wood, William Hiscock. Ackn: 7th da, 8th mo, 1685. Rec: 8th da, 9th mo, 1685.

P. 10. Deed. John Rowland and Thomas Rowland his brother, both of Bucks Co., for £10.15 granted to Samuel Burgess a parcel of land containing 200 acres now in the occupancy of said Samuel Burgess bounded on the northerly side with land of James Hill, on the easterly side with the great Timber Swamp, on the southerly side with piece of vacant land and the land of Randle Blackshaw. Said parcel which was part of a parcel granted by James Claypoole and Robert Turner, Commissioners for William Penn, to said John and Thomas Rowland by letters patents dated 13th da, 7th mo, 1685. Wit: Jonathan Scaife, Richard Ridgway, Phinehas Pemberton. Ackn: 9th da, 10th mo, 1685. Rec: 10th da, 12th mo, 1685.

P. 13. Commission for Recorder Thomas Loyd to Phinehas Pemberton. Commission granted by Thomas Loyd Master of the Rolls to Phinehas Pemberton for keeping the Rolls Office in Bucks Co. 5th da, 2nd mo, 1686.

P. 13. Deed. Griffith Jones of the town and Philadelphia Co., merchant, 3rd da, 8th mo, 1685, for £100 grants a parcel of land in Bucks Co. fronting Delaware River, containing 500 acres, to Thomas Loyd of the town and Philadelphia Co., Gent., Wit: Ann Powell, Pat. Robinson. Ackn: 9th da, 10th mo, 1685 by David Powell, Attorney of Griffith Jones to Thomas Holms for the use of Thomas Loyd. Rec: 4th day of 12th month.

P. 14. Deed. Jeffrey Hawkins of Bucks Co., planter, to Roger Hawkins of said county, planter and brother of Jeffrey Hawkins, for £8.15. A parcel of land in Bucks Co. containing 100 acres bounded on the east with lands of John Wood, on the south with lands of Philip Conway, on the west and north with the lands of said Jeffrey Hawkins. Said 100 acres is part of a tract granted by William Penn to said Jeffrey Hawkins by letters patent dated 4th da, 7th mo, 1685. Wit: Margaret Boare, Lawrance Bannor. Ackn: 10th da, 1st mo, 1685/6. Reg: 1st da, 3rd mo, 1686.

P. 15. Deed. Thomas Wolfe of Bucks Co., planter, to Elizabeth Gibbs of said county, widow for £7.10. A parcel of land bounded on the easterly side with the lands of aforesaid Thomas Wolfe, on the south with the lands of Ralph Smith, on the west with the lands of John Rowland, on the north with part of the lands of Christopher Bennett, in Bucks Co., containing 130 acres. Said tract is part of a tract granted by William Penn to said Thomas Wolfe by letters patent dated 27th da, 11th mo, 1684. Wit: Joseph Wood, David Davies. Ackn: 10th da, 1st mo, 1685/6. Reg: 1st da, 3rd mo, 1686.

P. 17. Patent. 22 March 1681. To John Alsop of Ingestry, Stafford Co., yeoman for £20 a parcel of land containing 1000 acres. Wit: Harbt. Springett, Tho. Coxe, Ben. Griffith. Reg: 1st da, 3rd mo, 1686.

P. 20. Deed. Morgan Drewett, New Castle Co. to Hannah Salter, a widow of said county, for £10 a parcel of land containing 100 acres near Unknown creek to one side of the said Hannah Salter's 10,000 acres near Cohansey, 100 acres purchased of Samuel Cleft adjoining his land having the River of Delaware on the front thereof ... lands of Griffith Jones on the north side ... And obliging me to cause Cassandra my wife to renounce her right of dower. 17th da, 3rd mo, 1684. Wit: Enoch Flower, David Ogden. Ackn: 9th da, 10th mo, 1685. Reg: 1st da, 3rd mo, 1686.

P. 22. Deed. Robert Holgate of Sussex Co., planter, to Robert Heaton, Bucks Co., planter for £20 a parcel of land in Bucks Co. beginning at a post by Neshamany Creek northerly by the lands of Alexander Giles ... southerly by widow Croasdale's land ... containing 250 acres, granted by a patent dated 18th this instant month, 1686. Wit: Thomas Janney, William Yardley, John White. Ackn: 9/4/1686. Reg: 17/2/1686.

P. 24. Articles of Agreement between Thomas Coverdale and Gilbert Wheeler, both of the Falls. Whereas said Gilbert doth let to Thomas Coverdall 100 acres for 12 years. 23 Sep 1685. Wit: Jno. Pidcock, William Bryan, Robt. Blackwell. Rec: 3rd da, 1st mo, 1686.

P. 25-26. Deed. Nicholas Waln of Bucks Co., yeoman to Edmond Cutler of said county, planter for £32 a parcel of land containing 200 acres in Bucks Co., beginning at a tree by Neshaminy Creek then west and by north by the widow Plumley's land ... land belonging to Elizabeth Walmsley ... Granted by patent to Nicholas Waln by letters patent dated

29th da, 11th mo, 1684. Wit: Robt. Hall, John Horner. Ackn: 9th da, 10th mo, 1686. Rec: 13th da, 5th mo, 1686.

P. 26. Bond. Patrick Kelley of West Spring, Philadelphia Co., husbandman, to pay Philip Conway of Warmaster, Bucks Co., the sum of £20 the first of December next. 29th da, 3rd mo, 1686. Wit: Silas Crispin, Tryall Holme, Edmond McVagh. Reg: 13th da, 5th mo, 1686.

P. 27. Deed. James Dilworth, Bucks Co., yeoman, to John Horner, West New Jersey, yeoman, for £20 a parcel of land containing 480 acres, purchased of William Penn. Wit: Nicholas Wallne, John Nicholls. Ackn: 9th da, 4th mo, 1686. Reg: 13th da, 5th mo, 1686.

P. 29. Deed. Nicholas Wallne, Bucks Co. a yeoman to Thos. Stackhouse, Jr. Bucks Co., planter, for £5 a parcel of land containing 50 acres beginning at marked tree of property of Nicholas Waln and Elizabeth Walmsley then south and west of the lands of Nicholas Waln, 5th da, 4th mo, 1686. Ackn: 9th da, 4th mo, 1686. Reg: 9th da, 4th mo, 1686.

P. 30. Deed. Richard Ridgway, Bucks Co., tailor to Philip Conway, Bucks Co., planter for 40 shillings a parcel of land containing 4 acres. Land lying from Delaware River ... part of the Great Timber Swamp and adjoining land known by name Anne Millcome lands, now in possession of William Biles and Philip Conway. Ackn: 9th da, 4th mo, 1686. Reg: 15th da, 5th mo, 1686. Witness: Samuel Overton, Henry Margerum, Henry Greenlaw.

P. 31. Deed. Philip Conway, Bucks Co., planter to Thomas Dickerson, Bucks Co., tailor, for £22. a parcel of land containing 50 acres lying from the Delaware River ... Great Timber Swamp granted to Philip Conway by a deed from Richard Ridgway. Other parcel adjoining land of Annie Millcome. Ackn: 9th da, 4th mo, 1686. Reg: 13th da, 5th mo, 1686. Wit: David Powell, John Coats, William Biles.

P. 34. Patent. To Arthur Cook granted a parcel of land containing 1500 acres lying in and being in Chester Co., by a warrant dated 5th da, 6th mo, 1685 patented 2nd da, 5th mo, 1686. Reg: 15th da, 6th mo, 1686. Wit: James Claypool and Robert Turner.

P. 35. Deed. Daniel Brinson, Bucks Co., planter to John Nicholls and

Elias Nicholls, Bucks Co., brothers, both chapmen, for £105 a parcel of land containing 102 acres land patented to Daniel Brinson 31st da, 5th mo, 1684 adjoining Land of John Accerman. Ackn: 9th da, 7th mo, 1686. Reg: 22nd da, 4th mo, 1686. Wit: William Emley, John Wood.

P. 38. Deed. Andrew Robeson, West Jersey, a merchant to Daniel Jones, Philadelphia, cordwainer, for £100 a parcel of land containing 500 acres, 6th da, Aug, 1686. Granted 10th da, 2nd mo, 1685 recorded in Book A, Folio 99. Land lying on the Delaware River adjoining William Haige ... and Thomas Bowman. Wit: Pat Robeson,, Sr. Reg: 6 Aug, 1686.

P. 41. Letter of Attorney. Daniel Brinson, Bucks Co., to Richard Ridgway, Bucks Co., attorney to convey 102 acres, to John and Elias Nicholls, Bucks Co. Ackn: 19th da, 4th mo, 1686. Reg: 24th da, 4th mo, 1686. Wit: Bartholomew Lugg, Mary Kenway.

P. 42. Deed. James Harrison, Bucks Co., a yeoman, the executor of Ralph Smith, Bucks Co., to Edward Stanton, Bucks Co., a joiner, for £12 a parcel of land containing 110 acres adjoining land of Robert Hall. Ackn: 9th da, 4th mo, 1686. Rec: 9th da, 5th mo, 1686. Wit:; William F. Phillips, Lydia Wharmly.

P. 44. Deed. John Alsop, of Ingestry in Stafford Co., yeoman to Thomas Tunniclift, of Haugton, Stafford Co., for £20 a parcel of land containing 100 acres. Original granted on 20 Mar, 1682. Ackn: 8th da, 7th, 1686. Reg: 12th da, 7th mo, 1686. Wit: William T. Phillips, Lydia W. Wharmly, Peter Littleton, John Gill, Thomas Worrilow, Edward Firth, Phinehas Pemberton.

P. 48. Deed. Jeffery Hawkins, Bucks Co., laborer to John Collins, laborer, and Susanna Collins, Bucks Co., for £9.12.6 a parcel of land containing 110 acres of land dividing the land of Jeffery Hawkins and John Luff, [adjoining] lands of Robert Lucas. Ackn: 8th da, 7th mo, 1686. Reg: 12th da, 7th mo, 1686. Wit: Israel Taylor, Robert Lucas, John Saxby.

P. 50. Commission to Phinehas Pemberton as Clerk of Court. Commission given to Phinehas Pemberton the 21st da, of 5th mo, 1683. Rec: the 14th da, 7th mo, 1686.

P. 51. Deed. Andrew Robeson, of West New Jersey, a merchant to Daniel Jones, of Philadelphia, a cordwainer, for £100, a parcel of land containing 500 acres lying by the Delaware River adjoining land of William Haige to adjoining Thomas Bosman's land, 2nd da, 6th mo, 1686. Ackn: 8th da, 7th mo, 1686. Reg: 20th da, 7th mo, 1686. Wit: Andrew Robeson, Jr. and Pat Robinson, Sr.

P. 54. Power of Attorney. Elizabeth Gibbs, widow, Bucks Co. appoints Edmond Lovett, Bucks Co. to convey 130 acres 8th da, 1st mo, 1686 to Thomas Wolfe, Bucks Co. Reg: 20th da, 7th mo, 1686. Wit: Charles Bringham and Phinehas Pemberton.

P. 55. Power of Attorney. Robert Holgate, Sussex Co. a planter appoints Shadrack Walley, Bucks Co. to convey 250 acres to Robert Heaton. Rec: 20th da, 7th mo, 1686. Wit: William Yardley, John White.

P. 56. Patent. A parcel of land lying in Bucks Co., adjoining Richard Amos' land by Neshaminy Creek ... to Henry Paxson's land containing 500 acres warranted to William Charter. 9th da, 5th mo, 1686. Wit: James Claypoole and Robert Turner.

P. 57. Assignment of Patent. William Carter [Charter] to Robert Carter, yeoman for £10 a parcel of land containing 500 acres lying next to Richard Amos's land and Henry Paxson's land along the Neshaminy Creek. Ackn: 8th 7th mo, 1686. Reg: 9th da, 7th mo, 1686. Wit: Israel Taylor, George Heitt and John Claypoole.

P. 58. Power of Attorney. William Carter, Philadelphia, black maker appoints Israel Taylor, Bucks Co., yeoman to convey to Robert Carter, Bucks Co., yeoman, 500 acres. 9th da, 6th mo, 1686. Rec: 9th da, 7th mo, 1686. Wit: Robert Hudson, Peter White, Edward Carter.

P. 59. Patent. 7th da, 7th mo, 1683. To John Rowland, Pennsbury, a parcel of land standing by Thomas Atkinson's land containing 300 acres. Ackn: 22nd da, 3rd mo, 1686. Rec: 9th da, 7th mo, 1686. Wit: James Claypool and Robert Turner.

P. 60. Deed. Henry Pawlin, Neshaminy, Bucks Co. planter, to William Paxton, of Neshaminy, Bucks Co., planter for £17 a parcel of land containing 150 acres between land of Henry Pawlin and Henry Paxson.

Original granted 17th da, 3rd mo, 1686. Ackn: 9th da, 7th mo, 1686. Rec: 1st da, 8th mo, 1686. Wit: Israel Taylor, Robert Lucas, Phinehas Pemberton and Joseph Wood.

P. 63. Mortgage. 7th da, Sept, 1686. Daniel Jones of Philadelphia, cordwainer to Andrew Robeson, West New Jersey, merchant and Samuel Robeson, his son, for £100 a parcel of land containing 500 acres, standing by the Delaware River adjoining land of William Haigue to ... land of Thomas Bowman. Original granted to Thomas Rudyard 7th da, 6th mo, 1682. Rec: Book A, Vol 1 folio 63. Ackn: 20th da, 8th mo, 1686. Rec: 22nd da, 8th mo, 1686. Wit: Jeremiah Elforeth and Pat. Robinson.

P. 69. Power of Attorney. Andrew Robeson appointed Roger Hawkins, attorney, to receive deed of sale and mortgage dated 8th da, 7th mo, 1686. Rec: 22nd da, 8th mo, 1686. Wit: Jeremiah Elforeth and Pat. Robinson.

P. 70. Bond. Edmund Bennett, Bucks Co., yeoman, bound to James Harrison, Thomas Janney, William Yardley, William Biles, Justices of Peace, for £70 on 20th da, 2nd mo, 1686. Whereof the above bounded Edmund Bennett on the day above written hath in his hands the sum of £35.0.9 being orphanage money appertaining unto James Spencer and Samuel Spencer, children and orphans of his brother, John Spencer, late of Bucks Co., tailor, dec'd, until children are of age to receive it. Rec: 22nd da, 8th mo, 1686. Wit: Abraham Whearly and Phinehas Pemberton.

P. 71. Bond. John Otter is bound unto James Harrison, Thomas Janney, William Biles, William Yardley, Justices of the Peace, in the amount of £70. Whereof John Otter hath in his hands and possession the sum of £35.0.9, being orphanage money appertaining unto James Spencer and Samuel Spencer his brother's children and orphans of John Spencer late of Bucks Co., tailor dec'd. until children are of age to receive it. Rec: 22nd da, 8th mo, 1686. Wit: Abraham Whearly and Phinehas Pemberton.

P. 72. Patent. To Henry Pawlin, a parcel of land consisting of 500 acres, standing by Neshaminy Creek 11th da, 7th mo, 1682. Ackn: 17th da, 3rd mo, 1686. Rec: 22nd da, 8th mo, 1686.

P. 73. Bond. Anthony Tomkins of New Castle Co., bound to George Martin of Kent Co., for the sum of £100 on 13th da, 1st mo, 1686. George Martin appointed Charles Pickering to receive the aforementioned bond. 16th da, 8th mo, 1686. Charles Pickering gave power of attorney to William Yardley to receive bond. Rec: 26th da, 8th mo, 1686. Wit: James Claypool and Robert Turner.

P. 75. Deed. Anthony Tomkins, Duck Creek, New Castle Co., conveyed to George Martin a parcel of land containing 1000 acres of land adjoining land of Robert Turner. 14th da, 7th mo, 1686. Ackn: 20th da, 8th mo, 1686. Rec: 26th da, 8th mo, 1686. Wit: William Biles and Philip H. Lehammany.

P. 76. Power of Attorney. Anthony Tomkins appoints Abraham Wherly to appear in open court for the sale of a certain tract of land containing 1000 acres situated on Neshaminy Creek. Rec: 26th da, 8th mo, 1686. Wit: William Biles and Philip H. Lehammany.

P. 77. Deed. Nicholas Waln, of Neshaminy Creek, Bucks Co., yeoman, to Jedediah Allen, of Shrewsbury, East New Jersey, yeoman, on 20th da, 8th mo, 1686 for £20, a parcel of land containing 230 acres. Rec: 28th da, 8th mo, 1686. Wit: Thomas Janney and Jacob Jenney.

P. 78. Power of Attorney. Jedidiah Allen appoints Robert Heaton, Bucks Co., yeoman, to accept 230 acres from Nicholas Walne. Ackn: 9th da, 8th mo, 1686. Rec: 28th da, 8th mo, 1686. Wit: Thomas Janney and Jacob Janney.

P. 79. Patent. 7th da, 7th mo, 1682. To Robert Holgate, a parcel of land standing on Neshaminy Creek east northerly to land of Alexander Giles, ... to land of widow Croasdale, consisting of 250 acres. Rec: 20th da, 9th mo, 1686. Wit: James Claypool and Robert Turner.

P. 80. Power of Attorney. Edmund Cutler, of Bucks Co., a planter appoints James Dilworth, Bucks Co. to receive conveyance of 200 acres of land from Nicholas Waln, Bucks Co. 7th da, 4th mo, 1686. Rec: 20th da, 9th mo, 1686. Wit: John Cutler and Phinehas Pemberton.

P. 81. Bond. William Hearst, Alice Wigglesworth, Thomas Stackhouse and Nicholas Walln, Bucks Co., are bound to Phinehas Pemberton,

Deputy Register for Bucks Co. for the sum of £300. William Hurst and Alice Wiggleworth, widow and admx. of the estate of Cuthbert Hearst and Mary Hearst. Rec: 1st da, 9th mo, 1686. Wit: John Nicholls and Thomas Wolf.

P. 82. Bond. William Croasdale, John Croasdale, Nicholas Waln, and Robert Heaton all of Neshaminy Creek, Bucks Co., yeomen, are bound unto Phinehas Pemberton in the sum of £212. William Croasdale and John Crosdale to administer the estate of Agnes Croasdale, late of Neshaminy, dec'd. and mother of said John and William Croasdale. Rec: 1st da, 9th mo, 1686. Wit: James Dilworth and Thomas Wolfe.

P. 83. Deed. 22nd da, 7th mo, 1686. Daniel Brinson, a planter, of Crook Horne near the Falls of Delaware, to John Wood, carpenter, of same part, for £250 a parcel of land lying near Falls of Delaware adjoining Widow Ackerman and a parcel of land lying along said creek containing 205 acres. Patent granted to Daniel Brinson dated of 13th da, 5th mo, 1684. Ackn: 8th da, 10th mo, 1686. Rec: 10th da, 10th mo, 1686. Wit: William Biles, David Powell, John Nicholls, William Emley.

P. 86. Power of Attorney. Daniel Brinson, of Stony Brook in West Jersey, appoints Richard Rigway, of Crookhorne, PA, to acknowledge the deed in open court from John Wood. Ackn: 9th da, 8th mo, 1686. Rec: 10th da, 10th mo, 1686. Wit: Xooll Mow and Hugh Stanley.

P. 87. Deed. This indenture 4th da, 9th mo, 1686, between George Martin of Gloster, Kent Co., and Joseph Growdon, of Bensalem, Bucks Co. and Andrew Griscome of Philadelphia. Witnesseth that in consideration of a marriage between said George Martin and Ursula Colliner, Bucks Co., a spinster, a tract of land in Kent Co., aforesaid called Gloster, situated on the west side of Delaware Bay and north side of the Southwest Branch of Duck Creek ... standing near the lands of Francis Whitwell. Rec: 20th da, 10th mo, 1686. Wit: Nicholas Williams and Joseph Milford.

P. 94. Patent. To John Rowland and Thomas Rowland. Land standing by land of James Hill ... 800 acres, granted by two warrants one bearing the date of 30th da, 9th mo, 1682, the other 13th da, 6th mo, 1685. Rec: 20th da, 10th mo, 1686. Wit: Robert Turner and James Claypool.

P. 95. Patent. 30th da, 9th mo, 1682, to Thomas Rowland a parcel of land lying on the east most side of Neshaminy Creek ... to John Rowland's land consisting of 450 acres granted by a warrant dated 12th da, 7th mo, 1684. Rec: 20th da, 10th mo, 1686. Wit: James Claypool and Robert Turner.

P. 97. Bond. Joseph Milnor, blacksmith, John Brock, yeoman, and Luke Brindley, mason, all of Bucks Co. bound unto Phinehas Pemberton, for £40, the 3rd da, 9th mo, 1686. The condition is such that the above Joseph Milnor shall administer the estate of John Falkner, of Bucks Co. Rec: 20th da, 10th mo, 1686. Wit: William Yardley and Enoch Yardley.

P. 98. Deed. Robert Pressinall, of Southampton, for the sum of £7 paid to him by John Baldwin, of Philadelphia Co. a parcel of land containing 125 acres standing by the highway in South Hampton ... to land of George Jackman ... southwest by land of Robert Pressinal. Ackn: 4th da, 1st mo, 1686. Rec: the 10th da, 1st mo, 1686/7. Wit: Robert Hall, Nicholas Walln.

P. 99. Bond. Israel Taylor, Bucks Co., chirurgeon bound to Francis Hough, of Bucks Co., carpenter, for £50 a parcel of land containing 200 acres standing by a way side ... to Thomas Revel's land. Rec: 20th da, 1st mo, 1686/7. Wit: Robert Lucas and Isaac Burges, Phinehas Pemberton.

P. 100. Deed. Anna Salter, of Tacony, Philadelphia Co. to Thomas Lloyd, of Philadelphia, gentleman, for a certain sum of money a parcel of land containing 160 acres of land fronting upon the River of the Delaware and bound southward by the land late of Samuel Clift near the Ferry opposite to Bradlington ... abutting land owned by Griffith Jones. Ackn: 27th da, of 5th mo, 1686. On the 9th da, of 1st mo, 1686, this conveyance was made by William Biles, attorney for named Anna Salter. Rec: 20th da, 1st mo, 1686/7. Wit: David Powell and David Lloyd.

P. 102. Deed of partition. 14th da, 8th mo, 1686. Between William Biles, of Bucks Co. yeoman and Charles Biles of Bucks Co., planter and brother to William Biles, for a yearly rent [did not state amount] a parcel of land lying next to land of William Darks ... containing 172 acres divided equally. Original warrant dated 13th da, 2nd mo, 1683. Ackn:

9/1/1686. Rec: 20/11/1686/7. Wit: Richard Ridgway, John Cuff and Robert Hudson.

Page 105-107. Deed. William Biles, Bucks Co., yeoman, to John Cuff, Bucks Co., yeoman for £5 a parcel of land containing 236 acres lying in Bucks Co., adjoining land belonging to Charles Biles and the line of William Dark. Ackn: 9th da, 1st mo, 1686. Rec: 20th da, 1st mo, 1686/7. Wit: Richard Ridgway, Charles Biles and Robert Hudson.

P. 108. Bond. Charles Pickering, Philadelphia Co. a yeoman, bound to Gilbert Wheeler and John Wood, of Bucks Co., for £150, 17/Mar/1686/7. The condition is Charles Pickering pay £75 of said bond at or upon the 17/Sept next. Rec: 1/3/1687. Wit: John Redman and Pat. Robinson.

P. 109. Deed. Nicholas Walln, Bucks Co. yeoman to John Austin, Bucks Co., ship carpenter, for £23, a parcel of land containing 60 acres lying on Neshaminy Creek ... being part of a parcel of land granted to Thomas Collins, Philadelphia. 27th da, 2nd mo, 1687. Rec: 2nd day, 3rd mo, 1687. Wit: John Nicholls, Samuel Allen and Thomas Rowland.

P. 110. Defeasance. John Hart, Byberry, Philadelphia Co. yeoman sold to John Bordale and Sarah Bordale, Neshaminy Creek, Bucks Co., aforesaid children of Arthur Bordale, dec'd, a parcel of land containing 200 acres being in Byberry, Philadelphia Co. for £1.10 by the 4/10/ next being after the date hereof and £1.10 by the 4th da, 7th mo, 1688 and full payment of £26.10 on or before the 7th mo, 1689. Ackn: 22/1/1687/8. Rec: 20/3/1687. Wit: Robert Dave(?), Robert Rigge and William Rootlidge.

P. 113. Bond. Robert Hall, John White, Robert Carter and Nicholas Walln, Bucks Co. yeoman, bound unto Phinehas Pemberton in the sum of £40. The condition of this obligation is that Robert Hall, et. al., administer the estate of Richard Amor, late of Neshaminy. Rec: 20th da, 3rd mo, 1687. Wit: Samuel Woolidge, William White.

P. 114. Bond. Robert Hall and John White, both of Bucks Co. to Robert Carter and Nicholas Walln, of Bucks Co., yeoman in the consideration of £80. The condition of the bond is to free Robert Carter and Nicholas Walln of their obligations in the administering of the estate of Richard Amor. Rec: 9th da, 4th mo, 1687. Wit: Robert Lucas and Joseph Wood.

P. 115. Patent. To Gilbert Wheeler a parcel of land standing by the River Delaware ... running southwest to land of William Biles ... land of Robert Lucas containing 180 acres and also a small island called Wheelers Island. Patented dated 9th da, 3rd mo, 1684. Ackn: 31st da, 1st mo, 1684. Rec: 9th da, 4th mo, 1687.

P. 116. Patent. To John Green, a parcel of land containing 200 acres lying by the River Delaware, [boundary running to] land of Mordecai Borden ... east to land of William Dungan. Dated the 15th da, 6th mo, 1683. Ackn: 25th da, 5th mo, 1684. Rec: 9th da, 4th mo, 1687.

P. 118. Deed. 1st da, 4th mo, 1681. John Rowland and Thomas Rowland, Bucks Co., brothers to Gilbert Wheeler, Bucks Co., for £15 containing 300 acres of land being part of two warrants, one 13th da, 9th mo, 1682 the other from James Claypoole and Robert Turner dated 11th da, 6th mo, 1685. Ackn: 8th dam 4th mo, 1687. Rec: 12th da, 4th mo, 1687. Wit: Robert Hall, Robert Lucas and John Saxby.

P. 119. Deed. John Greene, Bucks Co., to Thomas Greene, Bucks Co. and Katharine Green, his wife, for 4 shillings, a parcel of land containing 100 acres beginning by the side of the River Delaware then north west to land of John Green ... east to land of William Dungan. Ackn: 8th da, 4th m, 1687. Rec: the 12th da, 4th mo, 1687. Wit: Jonathan Scaife and John Saxby.

P. 121. Deed. John Swift, of Southampton, Pennsylvania, and Henry Pointer, of same place, for £10, a parcel of land containing 100 acres on the northwest side ... Coquest Creek, now called Byberry Creek ... to said John Swift's fence. Ackn: 8th da, 4th mo, 1687. Rec: the 12th da, 4th mo, 1687. Witness: Mark Beterey. Wit: Nicholas Walln and John Saxby.

P. 123. Bond. Thomas Langhorne, Robert Heaton, Thomas Stackhouse all of Bucks Co., yeomen, bound to Phinehas Pemberton for the penal consideration of £523 on 8th da, 4th mo, 1687. The condition of this obligation is that Thomas Langhorne, et. al., to administer the estate of Arthur Bordale, late of Kirkbride in Cumberland, dec'd. Rec: 12th da, 4th mo, 1687. Witness: Nicholas Walln and John Saxby.

P. 124. Bond. Thomas Tunniclift, yeoman of Bucks Co., to Joseph

Milner, of Bucks Co., blacksmith, for £20, on 26th da, 7th mo, 1687. Joseph Milner and Frances Rossil at the special instance and request of the above, bounded for him by recognizance. Ackn: before Justice of Peace in open court 14th da, 7th mo. Thomas Tunnisclift, £20, Francis Rossil £10 and said Joseph Milner. That the said Thomas Tunnisclift shall be of good behavior toward Hannah Overton. Rec: 26th da, 8th mo, 1687. Wit: Thomas Janney, the elder and Thomas Janney, the younger.

P. 125. Bond. Thomas Tunniclift, Bucks Co. bound to Francis Rossil, Bucks Co. for £20 on 26th da, 7th mo, 1687. The condition of said obligation is that Thomas Tunnisclift shall be of good behavior toward Hannah Overton. Rec: 26th da, 8th mo, 1687. Wit: Thomas Janney, the elder and Thomas Janney, the younger.

P. 127. Bond. Mary Beakes, widow, Thomas Janney and William Yardley, yeoman, Bucks Co., bound for the penal consideration of £2,000. The condition of said obligation is that Mary Beakes, et al administer the estate of William Beakes. Rec: the 20th da, 9th mo, 1687. Wit: John Willsford, Richard Ridgway and Stephen Beakes.

P. 128. Bond. Arthur Cooke, Bucks Co., indebted to John Chandler, Bucks Co. for £20, to be paid at 6 per cent interest at or within 6 months of this date. Ackn: 1st da, 9th mo, 1685. Rec: 12th da, 10th mo, 1687. Wit: John Cook, Alex. A. Wood.

P. 128. Deed. Anthony Tomkins, Kent Co., yeoman to Griffith Jones, Philadelphia, merchant, for £50 a parcel of land containing 500 acres lying in Bucks Co. adjoining Robert Turner's land ... 22nd da, Aug 1687. Conveyed in open court by Abraham Whearly, attorney for Anthony Tomkins to Richard Ridway, attorney for Griffith Jones. Rec: the 15th da, 10th mo, 1687. Wit: Saml. Bulkley and Pat Robinson.

P. 132. Deed. Thomas Atkinson, Bucks Co., yeoman, to Joseph Kirkbride, Bucks Co., carpenter, for £35, a parcel of land containing 500 acres, standing by land of Jobe Howell. Rec: 15th da, 10th mo, 1687. On the 14th of the 10th mo, 1687 Robert Done, attorney delivered into court the conveyance. Wit: John Rowland, John Webster and Jean Adkinson.

P. 134. Power of Attorney. Griffith Jones to Richard Ridgway. Rec:

15th da, 10th mo, 1687. Wit: Phinehas Pemberton and Da. Loyd.

P. 135. Deed. Jeffery Hawkins, Bucks Co., laborer, for £5 paid by Daniel Hawkins, son of Jeffery Hawkins conveys a parcel of land containing about 100 acres lying on the west side of the water ... north to John Collins land and east with the land of Thomas Dickerson. Ackn: 14th da, 10th mo, 1687. Rec: 1st da, 11th mo, 1687. Wit: Henry Baker and Roger R. Hawkins.

P. 136. Bond. Alice Dickerson, widow, William Biles and Richard Ridgway, yeoman, Bucks Co., bound unto Phinehas Pemberton in the penal consideration of £250. The condition of this obligation is that Alice Dickerson, et. al., administer the estate of late husband, Thomas Dickerson on or before the 9th mo, of the ensuing year. Rec: 1st da, 11th mo, 1687. Wit: Nicholas Walln and Roger R. Hawkins.

P. 137. Deed. Richard Lundy and wife, Elizabeth Lundy, Bucks Co. are to quit claim to Rebecca Bennet all rights to a parcel of 200 acres bequeathed to Elizabeth Lundy by William Bennett, her father. Ackn: 14th da, 10th mo, 1687. Rec: 1st da, 11th mo, 1687. Wit: Ralph Pemberton and Joseph Mather, Phineas Pemberton.

P. 137. Bond. Joseph Wood, a carpenter, John Wood, father of Joseph Wood, and Jacob Hall, yeoman, Bucks Co., are bound unto Phinehas Pemberton in the consideration of £60 this 29th da, 10th mo, 1687. The condition is such that Joseph Wood, administer the estate of Richard Maubie, Bucks Co., before the last da, 9th mo, 1687. Rec: the 1st da, 11th mo, 1687. Wit: Robert Done and John Saxby.

P. 138. Bond. Shadrack Walley, a yeoman, Bucks Co. and Lydia Walley, Bucks Co., a spinster and sister to said Shadrack, are bound to Phinehas Pemberton (for the use of Roger Haydock) in for £25. The condition is that Shadrack Walley, et. al., administer the estate before the 29th da, 7th mo, 1687. Rec: the 1st da, 11th mo, 1687. Wit: John Clark and John Saxby.

P. 141. Deed. Francis Done, of the Parish of St. Martin in the Fields of the county of Midds, tallow chandler, to Thomas Langhorne. William Wiggins, a citizen, leather seller of London and Edward Samways of said Parish and Thomas Langhorne of Pennsylvania, yeoman, for five shillings, a parcel of land containing 860 acres of land lying upon Neshaminy Creek in Bucks Co. Ackn: the 5th da, Sep, 1687. Rec: the 10th da, 11th mo, 1687. Wit: John Nuttby, Joseph Markes and Arthur Tucker.

P. 141. Deed. 6th da, Sep 1687. Francis Done, of the Parish of St. Martin in the Fields of the county of Midds, tallow chandler to Thomas Langhorne, William Wiggins, a citizen, leather sellar of London and Edward Samways of said Parish and Thomas Langhorne of Pennsylvania, yeoman, for £104, a parcel of land containing 1500 acres bounded on the east by Delaware River ... northward to New Castle ... Ackn: 6th da, Sep, 1687. Rec: 10th da, 11th mo, 1687. Wit: John Nuttby, Joseph A. Markes, Arthur Tooker, John Lover, Sen., Geo. Heathiele and Samuel Borden.

P. 146. Bond. Joseph Kirkbride, Bucks Co. and Robert Lucas, Bucks Co., yeoman, are bound to Arthur Cooke, Thomas Janney, William Yardley and Nicholas Walln for the sum of £24. Joseph Kirkbride has in his possession the sum of £12 being orphanage money belonging to Henry Comly, son and orphan of Henry Comly, Bucks Co., dec'd. Estate to be administered before the 14th da, 10th mo, of next ensuing year. Rec: 20th da, 11th mo, 1687. Wit: William Biles and Phinehas Pemberton.

P. 147. Bond. Joan Huff, widow, Robert Hall and Richard Lundy of Bucks Co., ycomen, are bound unto Phinehas Pemberton for £380. Joan Huff, administratrix of the estate of Michael Huff, to administer the estate before the last day, 1st mo, 1687/8. Rec: 1st da, 12th mo, 1687. Wit: Richard Bassiet and John White.

P. 148. Bond. Joan Huff, Bucks Co., widow bound unto Robert Hall and Richard Lundy, Bucks Co., yeoman, in the sum of £700. Joan Huff, Robert Hall and Richard Lundy at the special instant and request of Joan Huff for the true performance of administering the estate of Michael Huff. Rec: 1st da, 12th mo, 1687. Wit: Richard Basnett and John White.

P. 149. Bond. Elizabeth Dungan, widow, Clement Dungan and William Dungan, Bucks Co. yeoman and sons to said Elizabeth Dungan, all of Bucks Co., bound unto Phinehas Pemberton for the penal sum of £100

13th da, 11th mo, 1687/8. Elizabeth Dungan to administer the estate of Thomas Dungan on or before the last da, 12th mo, 1687/8. Rec: the 1st da, 12th mo, 1687. Wit: Arthur Cooke, Will Yardley and John Cooke

P. 150. Bond. Grace Langhorne, widow, Nicholas Walln and Ezra Croasdale, Bucks Co., bound for the sum of £600 on 12th da, 10th mo, 1687. Grace Langhorne, to administer the estate of Thomas Langhorne. Rec: 1st da, 12th mo, 1687. Wit: Griffith Owen, Thomas Priest, cousin and John Eastburn.

P. 151. Patent. To Richard Hough, a parcel of land containing 500 acres, beginning at the corner of Henry Baker's land and running north ... to Henry Sidewell's land along side of Delaware River by a warrant dated 12th da, 7th mo, 1685. Rec: the 1st da, 12th mo, 1687.

P. 153. Bond. William Biles and Richard Ridgway of Bucks Co., yeoman, bound unto Arthur Cooke, Thomas Janney, William Yardley and Nicholas Walln, Justices of the Peace for Bucks Co. the sum of £129.9.2. William Biles and Richard Ridgway have in their possession £64.9.7, being orphanage money for the son of Henry Comley. Rec: the 6th da, 1st mo, 1688. Wit: Stephen Beakes, Jane Atkinson and Phinehas Pemberton.

P. 154. Bond. Abraham Whearly, Bucks Co., yeoman, bound unto Arthur Cooke, William Yardley, Nicholas Walln, Justices of peace in the sum of £40 to be paid to Arthur Cook, William Yardley, Nicholas Walln, Joseph Growdon, executors. The above Abraham Whearley has in his possession the consideration of £20 being orphanage money of James Spencer and Samuel Spencer, sons of John Spencer, Bucks Co., a tailor. James Spencer and Samuel Spencer being the children of Abraham Whearley's brother, John Spencer. Money to be paid before the 12th da, 1st mo, 1689. Rec: the 12th da, 1st mo, 1689. Wit: John Penquoit and Phinehas Pemberton.

P. 155. Patent. To William Yardley for 1 English shilling the first day of the first month in every year for each 100 acres a parcel of land containing 500 acres lying along the River Delaware running west by the land of widow Powall ... south to land of John Clows, granted by a warrant dated 6th da, 8th mo, 1682. Rec: the 12th da, 1st mo, 1688.

P. 156. Deed. Indenture made the 1st mo, 4th da, 1688 between William Pickering of Neshaminy Creek, Bucks Co., yeoman, and John Penquite of Bucks Co., husbandman for £25 a parcel of land containing 200 acres. Rec: the 16th da, 1st mo, 1688. Wit: John Swift, Edward Carter and Henry Siddall.

P. 158. Deed. Henry Pawlin, Bucks Co., to John Taylor, Bucks Co., for £6.10, a parcel of land containing 50 acres lying along side of Robert Done's land ... Henry Paxson's land. Rec: the 16th da, 1st mo, 1688. Wit: Wm. Beakes, Edward Carter, Thomas Brock. Ackn: 14th da, 1st mo, 1688. Rec: 16th da, 1st mo, 1688.

P. 159. Bond. Richard Wilson, Bucks Co., laborer bound unto Joseph English, Bucks Co., yeoman, in the sum of £40. Richard Wilson to pay unto the William Biles the full sum before 25th da, 1st mo, 1688. Rec: the 20th da, 1st mo, next ensuing year. Wit: John Saxby, James Moon and Phinehas Pemberton. Rec: 20th da, 1st mo, 1688.

P. 160. Bond. Joseph English, yeoman, James Moore, planter, William Biles, yeoman, Bucks Co., bound unto Phinehas Pemberton for the sum of £26. Joseph English, et. al., to administer the estate of Benjamin Weeks and present an inventory before the last day of the 1st mo, next ensuing year and a true accounting before the 1st da, 12th mo, of next ensuing year. Rec: the 29th da, 1st mo, 1688. Wit: Jacob Hall, — Hersent.

P. 161. Patent. 7th da, 8th mo, 1682. To Luke Brindley, a parcel of land containing 138 acres standing on the River Delaware [boundary running] southwest to land of Audry Elred ... north to John Paxson's land ... Richard Hougs land. Rec: 20th da, 1st mo, 1688. Wit: John Saxby and James Moon.

P. 162. Bond. Elizabeth Lucas, widow, and Giles Lucas, son of Elizabeth and Richard Ridgway, yeoman, all of Bucks Co., bound unto Phinehas Pemberton for the sum of £30. Elizabeth Lucas, et. al. to administer the estate of Thomas Staples before the last day of 3rd mo, 1688. Rec: the 12th da, 2nd mo, 1688. Wit: Richard Lundy, Edward Lucas.

P. 163. Bond. Mary Jeffs, Bucks Co., widow, and Jacob Hall, shoemaker bound unto Phinehas Pemberton for the sum of £200. Mary Jeffs, et. al., to administer the estate of Robert Jeffs, before the last day of 3rd mo, 1688. Rec: the 12th da, 2nd mo, 1688. Wit: James Crossly and James Hewworth.

P. 165. Bond. Margery Clows, widow, of John Clows, and Joseph Clows and William Clows, sons of Margery bound to Phinehas Pemberton for the sum of £400. Margery Clows, et. al., to administer the estate of John Clows before the last day of the first month of 1689. Rec: 2nd da, 3rd mo, 1688. Wit: Hannah Falkner and Luke Brindley.

P. 166. Patent. 10th da, 6th mo, 1682. To William Dungan, a parcel of land containing 200 acres standing by the River Delaware [boudary running] north to land of John Tuly. 26th da, 6th mo, 1684. Rec: 2nd da, 3rd mo, 1688.

P. 167. Deed. Joseph English, of the Ferry House, a planter, Bucks Co. to Francis Rossil, Burlington, New Jersey, a millwright, for £3, a parcel of land containing 3 acres lying upon the Cliffs Creek and 2 acres along Kings Road. Ackn: the 13th da, 4th mo, 1688. Rec: 14th da, 4th mo, 1688. Wit: Peter, Thomas Boreman and Thomas Revel.

P. 169. Deed. Jacob Telner, for 200 acres lying along the Delaware River, conveyed to him by Richard Lundy, Bucks Co., hath granted 1000 acres to Richard Lundy, beginning at line of Francis Rossel north ... .land of William Say and Robert Wheeler ... land of Thomas Mayleigh. This being part of the 5000 acres granted by William Penn on 9th da, March, 1682, Book A, Vol. 1, page 192-193. Ackn: 12th d, 2nd mo, 1688. Rec: 14th da, 4th mo, 1688. Wit: Da. Loyd and P. Sonmans.

P. 170. Deed. Joseph English, yeoman, Bucks Co. to Richard Wilson, laborer, Bucks Co., for £20, a parcel of land containing 50 acres lying near the land of Edmond Lovett and John Rowland on the north side. Ackn: 13th da, 4th mo, 1688. Rec: 14th da, 4th mo, 1688. Wit: John Saxby, James Moon and Phinehas Pemberton.

P. 171. Deed. Richard Hough, Bucks Co., yeoman to Henry Margereum, for £25, a parcel of land containing 250 acres patented to said Richard Hough on 30th da, 5th mo, 1687, lying on the Delaware River. Ackn: 13th da, 4th mo, 1688. Rec: the 15th da, 4th mo, 1688. Wit: Joseph Clowes and William Clowes.

P. 173. Bond. William Biles and Richard Ridgway, Bucks Co., yeoman, bound to Phinehas Pemberton for the sum of £100. William Biles, et. al., to administer the estate of Joshua Boare, Bucks Co., before the last day of 6th mo, 1688. Wit: John Shippen, Sam. Beakes and Charles Biles.

P. 174. Deed. John Wood, of the Falls of Delaware, Bucks Co., to Joseph Wood, his son, in preference to his marriage, a parcel of land containing 478 acres along with an island called Woods Island. Said land patented to John Wood 1st da, 5th mo, 1684. Rec: 10th da, 5th mo, 1688. Wit: Jacob Hall, Thomas Peter, John Carter, Robert Jeffes.

P. 177. Lease. 26th da, July, 1681 between William Penn, of Worminghurst, Sussex Co. and James Hill of Beckington in Somerset Co., shoemaker, for 4 shillings, a parcel of land containing 500 acres. Rec: the 1st da, 6th mo, 1688. Wit: John Anderson, Thomas Powell, Ezekiel Wooley, Tho. Robertson.

P. 178. Release. 27th da, July, 1681. William Penn, of Worminghurst, Sussex Co. to James Hill, Buckington, Sommerset Co., a shoemaker, for £10, a tract of land containing of 500 acres lying east of the Delaware River twelve miles north of New Castle town ... Ackn: 27th da, July, 1681. Rec: the 1st da, 6th mo, 1688. Wit: John Anderson, Ezekiel Wooley, Thomas Powell and Thomas Robertson.

P. 182. Deed. William Biles, Bucks Co., yeoman, to Joseph English, of said county and province, yeoman, for £35, a tract of land containing 200 acres, granted to said William Biles, by a deed dated 6th da, 8th mo, 1685. Ackn: 5th da, 5th mo, 1688. The within conveyance delivered by Richard Ridgway, attorney to William Biles in open court. Rec: the 15th da, 7th mo, 1688. Wit: Charles Biles and Samuel Beakes.

P. 183. Deed. Francis Rossel to Joan Huff. Francis Rossell, Bucks Co., millwright, for £5 paid by Joan Huff, widow, Bucks Co., a parcel of land containing 1 acre beginning at a corner hickory tree ... being part of three acres of land of Joseph English of Bucks Co. Ackn: 10th da, 7th mo, 1688. Rec: the 13th da, 7th mo, 1688. Wit: Richard Ridgway, Thomas Colman.

P. 185. Power of Attorney. Joan Huff, widow of Michael Huff, late of the Ferryhouse, Burlington, an innkeeper, appoints Thomas Brock, laborer, to be attorney to review and deliver the conveyance of one acre of land from Francis Rossill. Ackn: 10th da, 7th mo, 1688. Rec: the 16th da, 7th mo, 1688. Wit: Phinehas Pemberton and Edmund B. Bennett.

P. 185. Bond. Abraham Cocks, Anthony Burton and Joshua Hoopes, Bucks Co., yeoman bound unto Phinehas Pemberton, in the consideration of £200. 12th da, 7th mo, 1688. The condition is that Abraham Cocks, et. al., administer the estate of Thomas Woolf, late of Bucks Co., on or before the 10th da, of the 8th mo, 1688. Rec: the 16th da, 7th mo, 1688. Wit: Abraham Wharley and Daniel Garnor.

P. 187. Deed. John Taylor, Bucks Co., blacksmith, for £25 paid by John Smith, Bucks Co., blacksmith, a parcel of land containing 50 acres, lying by the land of Robert Done ... south easterly to line of William Paxton ... to a line of Henry Paxton north to the line of Henry Pawlin. Said land patented 17th da, 3rd mo, 1686. Rec: in the rolls of the office at Bucks, 16th da, 3rd mo, 1688 Book A, Vol 1, folio 158. Ackn: 2nd da, 8th mo, 1688. Rec: the 4th da, 8th mo, 1688. Wit: Joseph Wood, Samuel Burges and Wm. Croasdell.

P. 188. Patent. To Margery Plumly a parcel of land containing 250 acres beginning at the line of Joseph Growdon's land standing by Neshaminy Creek ... to a corner of Nicholas Walln land, west ... the 6th da, 1st mo, 1683. Granted 18th da, 3rd mo, 1688. Rec: the 20th da, 8th mo, 1688. Wit: Wm. Markham and John Goodson.

P. 190. Deed. James Swaffer, Chester Co., carpenter, for 26 shillings, to Richard Wilson, a parcel of land containing 2 acres of land fronting on the creek that runs between the Island called Overton and the main ... bound by the land of Lyonel Brittan and Daniel Gardiner. The land conveyed to the said James Swafer by Richard Ridgway, Bucks Co. 31st da, 11th mo, 1683. James Swafter appointed William Croasdale to be his attorney. Ackn: 6th da, 7th mo, 1688. Rec: the 18th da, 10th mo, 1688. Wit: Samuel Bunting, James Crosley and John Bunting.

P. 191. Patent. To Edward Luft, a parcel of land containing 296 acres in Bucks Co., lying by land of Jonathan Eldridge ... north ... Newtown, Said land granted by warrant the 9th da, 9th mo, 1683 unto Edward Luft. Ackn: the 3rd da, 4th mo, 1688. Rec: 19th da, 10th mo, 1688. Wit: Wm. Markham and John Goodson.

P. 192. Deed. Edward Luff, for £8.10, a parcel of land containing 296 acres, to Henry Margerum, Bucks Co., yeoman. Ackn: 4th da, 4th mo, 1688. Rec: the 19th da, 10th mo, 1688. Wit: Da. Loyd and Nat. Claypoole and Edward Luff.

P. 193. Deed. James Hill, Burlington, New Jersey, a shoemaker, to James Moon, Bucks Co., laborer, for £4, 125 acres. Said parcel is a part of 500 acres granted to James Hill, dated 26th da, July, 1681. Ackn: 13th da, 10th mo, 1688. Rec: 20th da, 10th mo, 1688. Wit: Thomas Lambert, Henry Margerum and Joseph Crop.

Page 195. Bond. James Moon, Bucks Co., a planter and James Hill, Burlington, New Jersey, yeoman, bound unto Phinehas Pemberton and Randolph Blackshaw, in the sum of £100. James Hill, et. al., to administer the estate for Joan Moon, wife of James Moon, containing of 125 acres, until James Moon shall come to the age of 21 years. Rec: the 20th da, 10th mo, 1688. Wit: Thomas Lambert, Henry Margerum and Joseph Crop.

P. 196. Deed. Joseph English, Bucks Co., for £15 to William Biles, Bucks Co., yeoman, 160 acres of land granted to Joseph English by a patent dated 30/8/1687. Ackn: 10/10/1688. Rec: the 20th da, 10th mo, 1688. Wit: Charles Pickering and Tho. Story and Francis Stevens.

P. 197. Deed. Lionel Britton, Bucks Co., blacksmith, for £100 to him from Stephen Beakes, Bucks Co., yeoman, 203 acres standing by the River Delaware ... [boundary] south to land of George Brown ... granted to Lionel Britton the 31/5/1684. Ackn: the 10/8/1688. Conveyance delivered by Samuel Dark, appointed attorney, on 10/8/1688. Rec: the 20/10/1688. Wit: William Biles, Phinehas Pemberton and Phebe Pemberton.

P. 200. Deed. 20 March 1681 William Penn to Thomas Woolrick of Shalford, Staford, yeoman, 100 acres lying within the province of Pennsylvania. Rec: the 22nd da, 10th mo, 1688. Wit: Harbt Springett, Tho. Cox and Ben. Griffith.

P. 201. Deed. 22nd da, Mar, 1681. William Penn, of Worminghurst, Sussex Co. granted to Thomas Woolrich for £25 a parcel of land containing 1000 acres in America with the island contained ... on the east by Delaware River ... bounded on the south ... 12 miles distance from New Castle. Rec: the 22nd da, 10th mo, 1688. Wit: Harbt Springett, Tho. Cox and Ben. Griffith.

P. 204. Release. William Penn, of Worminghurst, Sussex Co. released to Thomas Woolrich, for £20 for the purchase of a parcel of land containing 1000 acres. 22 March 1682. Rec: the 22nd da, 10th mo, 1688. Wit: Harbt Springett, Tho. Cox and Ben. Griffith.

P. 204. Deed. 20 April 1682. William Penn, Worminghurst, Sussex Co. to James Harrison, of Bolton, Lancaster Co., shoemaker, for 5 shillings, 5000 acres lying in Pennsylvania. Rec: the 23rd da, 10th mo, 1688. Wit: Harbt Springett, Tho. Cox and Ben. Griffith.

P. 205. Deed. 20th da, Apr, 1682 William Penn, Worminghurst, Sussex Co., to James Harrison, Bolton, Lancaster, shoemaker for £100 a parcel of land containing 5000 acres including the islands bounded on the east by the Delaware River, twelve miles distant north to New Castle. Rec: the 23rd da, 10th mo, 1688. Wit: Harbt Springett, Tho. Cox and Ben. Griffith.

P. 209. Lease. 20 April 1682 William Penn, Worminghurst, Sussex Co. granted to Thomas Croasdale, Newhey, York Co., for the sum of 5 shillings a parcel of land containing 1000 acres of land lying in the province of Pennsylvania. Rec: the 24th da, 10th mo, 1688. Wit: Harbt Springett, Tho. Cox and Ben. Griffith.

P. 210. Release. 22nd da, Apr, 1682 William Penn, Worminghurst, Sussex Co. granted to Thomas Croasdale, Newhey, York Co., for £20, 1000 acres bounded east by Delaware River ... north of New Castle town ... Rec: the 24th da, 12th mo, 1688. Wit: Harbt Springett, Tho. Cox and Ben. Griffith.

P. 213. Release. William Penn, of Worminghurst, Sussex Co. to Thomas Croasdale for £20, 1000 acres. Ackn: 22 April 1682. Rec: the 24th da, 10th mo, 1688. Wit: Harbt Springett, Tho. Cox and Ben. Griffith.

P. 214. Mortgage. 6th da, 1st mo, 1688/9, Samuel Borden, Bucks Co., yeoman and Samuel Carpenter, Philadelphia Co., a merchant, attorney for Joseph Borden, St. Michaels, Island of Barbados, for £277.10, a parcel of land containing two certain islands in Delaware River lying ... west of Nattinniconk Island, formerly known by Kipps Island ... granted to Peter Allricks, 15/Feb/1667. Ackn: 6/Mar/1688/9. Deed delivered in open court by Nicholas Waln, attorney to Samuel Borden unto Arthur Cook, attorney substitute to Samuel Carpenter. Rec: 29/1/1689. Wit: John Whitepaine, Zachariah Whitepaine and Pat. Robinson.

Page 218, 219. Deed. William Hayhurst, Bucks Co., yeoman, eldest son to Cuthbert Hayhurst, dec'd., for £10 from Henry Hudleston, Bucks Co., husbandman, 100 acres lying by the land of James Dilworth ... to land of Richard Hatcher ... north westerly to land of Wm Hayhurst. Ackn: 27/1/1689. Rec: the 29/1/1689. Wit: John Wood, Wm. Beakes and Thos Stackhouse.

P. 219. Deed. Thomas Rowland, Bucks Co., yeoman to Philip Conway, Bucks Co., planter, for £10 a parcel of land containing 100 acres of land granted by warrant dated 13th da, 7th mo, 1686 recorded at Philadelphia in Book A, page 175-176. Ackn: 10/5/1688. Rec: 27/1/1689. Wit: William Smith and Hugh Marsh.

P. 222. Deed. Joseph Growdon, of Bensalem, Bucks Co., gentleman, to Stephen Noel for £33, 202 acres standing by Poquisuik Creek ... to land lying by Stephen Noel. Ackn: 27th da, 1st mo, 1689. Rec: the 30th da, 1st mo, 1689. Wit: Nicholas Hicket and Tho. Fox.

P. 223. Deed. Joseph Growdon, of Bensalem, Bucks Co., Gent., 12th da, 12th mo, 1688 grants to Abel Hiukston 102 acres, beginning at the Poquessuik Creek ... [to the] line of William Reale, northeast to land of Abel Huikston for the yearly rent of two English shillings. Ackn: 27th da, 1st mo, 1689. Rec: 30th da, 1st mo, 1689. Wit: Nicholas Hicket, Tho. Fox and Steven Nowell.

P. 223. Deed. Joseph Growdon, of Bensalem, Bucks Co. 12th da, 12th mo, 1688, to William Reale for £16, 102 acres beginning at Poquessuik Creek ... to land of Abel Huikstons ... . Ackn: 27th da, 1st mo, 1688. Rec: the 1st da, 2nd mo, 1689. Wit: Nicholas Hicket, Tho. Fox and Steven Nowell.

P. 225. Power of Attorney. William Reale, Bucks Co., planter appoints Abell Hinkston, Bucks Co., planter as his lawful attorney to receive from

Joseph Growden the deed bearing the date of 12th da, 12th mo, 1688. Rec: the 1st da, 2nd mo, 1689. Wit: Nicholas Hicket and Tho. Fox.

P. 225. Deed. 20th da, 12th mo, 1688. Joseph Growdon, of Bensalem, Bucks Co., gent., for £16, 102 acres lying on the Postquessuik Creek ... [boundary] to land of William Beal, a mason of aforesaid county. Ackn: 27th da, 1st mo, 1689. Rec: the 1st da, 2nd mo, 1689. Wit: Nicholas Hicket, Tho. Fox and Steven Nowell.

P. 226. Power of Attorney. William Beale, Bucks Co., mason, to Stephen Newell, Bucks Co. mason, to receive a deed for 100 acres. Witnessed 27th da, 1st mo, 1689. Rec: the 1st da, 2nd mo, 1689. Wit: Nicholas Hicket, Tho. Fox and Steven Nowell.

P. 227. Deed. Joseph Growdon, Bucks Co., 10th da, 12th mo, 1688, for £40, 40 acres lying on the River Delaware, beginning near Joseph Growdon's house ... [boundary] to Thomas Fox and Joseph Wilford, shipwrights. Ackn: 10th da, 12th mo, 1688/9. Rec: 1st da, 2nd mo, 1689. Wit: Nicholas Hicket, Peter Hill, William Beale.

P. 227. Power of Attorney. Thomas Fox and Joseph Wilsford, Bucks Co., shipwrights, appoint Abel Hinekston to be their attorney to receive deed of 40 acres. Witnessed 26th da, 12th mo, 1689. Rec: 1st da, 2nd mo, 1689. Wit: Nicholas Hicket and Will Hibbs.

P. 229. Deed. William Dungan, Bucks Co., shoemaker, for £15.10, to Arthur Cook, Bucks Co., 100 acres beginning at a corner marked tree ... to land of William Dungan and John Greene ... . granted by letters patent dated 26th da, 5th mo, 1684. Ackn: 27th da, 1st mo, 1689. Rec: 1st da, 2nd mo, 1689. Wit: Joseph Growdon, William Biles and Nicholas Walln.

P. 231. Lease. On 13 July 1681 between William Penn of Worminghurst, Sussex Co., and Thomas Rowland, of Billingshurst, Sussex, yeoman, for 5 shillings, 2500 acres. Rec: the 2nd da, of 2nd mo, 1689. Wit: William Haig, Harbt Springett, James Swinton, Tho. Cox.

P. 233. Release. 14th da, July, 1681 between William Penn of Worminghurst, Sussex Co, and Thomas Rowland, Sussex Co., yeoman, for £50, 2500 acres. Rec: the 2nd da, 2nd mo, 1689. Wit: William Haig,

Harbt Springett, Js. Swinton.

P. 238. Power of attorney. Thomas Hodson, of Sutton, Chester Co., at present in city of London, appoints William Biles, Pennsylvania, merchant, his attorney to handle his affairs, especially money owed by Jacob Hall, Bucks Co. 10th da, May, 1688. Rec: 2nd da, 2nd mo, 1689. Wit: Philip Ford, Hen. Ingeny, Guit Scovey.

P. 240. Lease. 23 April 1683. William Penn, Worminghurst, Sussex Co., to Thomas Hudson, Sutton, Palatine Co., of Chester, Gent., for 5 shillings, 5000 acres granted by warrant dated 11th da, July, 1681. Rec: 3rd da, 2nd mo, 1689. Wit: Harbt Springett, Tho. Cox, and Sell Craske.

P. 242. Release. 24th da, Apr, 1683. William Penn, Worminghurst, Sussex Co., to Thomas Hudson for £100, land bounded by the River Delaware, twelve miles distant to New Castle town ... Rec: 3rd da, 2nd m, 1689. Wit: Harbt Springett, Tho. Cox, and Sell Craske.

P. 246. Release. William Penn, Worminghurst, Sussex Co., to Thomas Hudson, of Sutton, in the County of Palatine of Chester, gent., for £100, 5,000 acres. Ackn: 24th da, Apr, 1683. Rec: the 3rd da, 2nd mo, 1689. Wit: Harbt Springett, Tho. Cox, and Sell Craske.

P. 247. Release. 25 April 1683 between William Penn of Worminghurst. Sussex Co., and Thomas Hudson, Sutton, County Palatine of Chester, Gent., by his indenture of lease and release bearing the date of 23, Apr, 1683 the said 5,000 acres for £18 granted by a warrant dated 7 July 1681. Rec: the 3rd da, 2nd mo, 1689. Wit: Harbt Springett, Anthony Springett and Sell Crash.

P. 249. Release. William Penn of Worminghurst. Sussex Co., for £18 from Thomas Hudson, Sutton, County Palatine, of Chester. Ackn: 25 April 1683. Rec: the 3rd da, 2nd mo, 1689. Wit: Harbt Springett, Anthony Springett and Sell Crash.

P. 250. Release. William Penn of Worminghurst. Sussex Co., received £9 from Thomas Hudson, of Sutton, County of Palatine, of Chester, gent., being for the purchase of the chief or quit rent of £1.2.6. Ackn: 25th da, Apr, 1683. Rec: the 3rd da, 2nd mo, 1689. Wit: Harbt Springett, Anthony Springett and Sell Crash.

P. 251. Patent. 22nd da, Mar, 1682. To Nicholas Moore, of London, a medical doctor, James Claypoole, a merchant, Philip Ford, William Shorloe of London, both merchants, Edward Peirce of London, a Leather Seller, John Symock and Thomas Brassey of Chesshire, yeoman, Thomas Barker of London, a wire cooper, Edward Brooks, of London, a grocer, are granted a parcel of land containing 20,000 acres for the Free Society of Traders in Pennsylvania. Free Society of Traders shall be incorporated. Ackn: 20th da, 1st mo, 1682. [For more information about the corporation, see original.]

P. 263. Deed. Thomas Holme, Philadelphia, for £28 from Nicholas Waln, 118 acres, beginning at land of John Clawson along side of Neshaminy Creek ... John Spencer's land. Ackn: 18th da, May, 1686. Deed delivered in open court 9th da, 4th mo, 1686. Rec: 9th da, 3rd mo, 1689. Wit: John Cutler, Phineas Pemberton and Robt. Longshore.

P. 264. Deed. Richard Noble, Bucks Co., yeoman, for £120 from Moses Massley, late of Borton Allooph, County of Kent, Kingdom of England, now of Burlington New Jersey, tanner, a parcel of land containing 310 acres standing by the River Delaware adjoining land of Abraham Man ... to land belonging to Ann Clark ... land belonging to Samuel Allen ... land of Jacob Pellison ... land of Henry Bircham. Ackn: 6th da, 7th mo, 1689. Deed delivered 11th da, 7th mo, 1689. Rec: the 12th da, 8th mo, 1689. Wit: Abraham, Sr., John Allen and Tho. Revel.

P. 268. Mortgage. 9th da, 7th mo, 1689, between Moses Masley, late of Borton Allooph, County of Kent, Kingdom of England, and now of Burlington, New Jersey, tanner, and Richard Noble, Bucks Co., yeoman, for £100, 310 acres; 100 acres ... by the lands of Samuel Allen on the north ... Ann Clark on the west and lands of Jacob Pettison ... and land of Henry Birchman. Deed delivered in open court 11th da, 7th mo, 1689. Rec: 12th da, 8th mo, 1689. Wit: Abraham, Sr., John Alton and Tho. Revell.

P. 272. Bond. Moses Masley, late of Borton Allooph, County of Kent, Kingdom of England, and now of Burlington, New Jersey, tanner, bounded unto Richard Noble, Bucks Co., yeoman for £240. Moses Masley has drawn and charged upon himself three bills of exchange, all of the same tenor and date, the consideration of £120 by him payable unto above named Richard Noble on or before the 15th day of May next date above written at or in the dwelling house now or late of John Colson, in Wapping near the Armitage, Middlesex Co., England, teacher of mathematics, for 310 acres in Bucks Co. Rec: the 12th da, 3rd mo, 1689. Wit: Abraham, Sr., John Allen and Tho. Revel.

P. 273. Patent. 12th da, May, 1679, to William Clark, dec'd. a parcel of land containing 309 acres and the court having disposed of 100 acres to Richard Noble for one bushel of winter wheat for every hundred acres. Rec: 12th da, May, 1689. Wit: William Markham and John Goodson.

P. 274. Deed. Henry Paxson, Bucks Co., yeoman, 100 acres adjoining the Neshaminy Creek and land of James Boyden, Bucks Co. (as by a deed from Samuel Allen to Charles Plumley, father of William Plumley, dated of 31 Oct 1682) and also 100 acres lying between land of Joseph Growdon and Nicholas Waln for the yearly rent of 1 English silver shilling. Ackn: 10 da, 12th mo, 1688. Henry Paxson appointed William Paxson, his brother to be his attorney to deliver said deed. Ackn: 27th da, 12th mo, 1688. Rec: 13th da, 8th mo, 1689. Wit: William Paxson, James Paxson and James Plumley.

P. 276. Deed. William Plumley, Bucks Co., yeoman, for 100 acres of land adjoining Neshaminy Creek and the land of Nicholas Waln, being the upper moiety of 90 acres granted to Margery Plumley, now wife of Henry Paxson and mother of William Plumley to Henry Paxson. 100 acres fronting upon Neshaminy Creek and adjoining land of James Boyden which had been conveyed to same by Samuel Allen to Charles Plumley, father of William Plumley, dec'd. 30 Oct 1682. Ackn: 10th da, 12th mo, 1688. Conveyed in open court 11th da, 7th mo, 1689. Rec: 13th da, 8th mo, 1689. Wit: William Paxson, James Paxson and James Plumley.

P. 278. Deed. Thomas Coverdale to Henry Siddall. Daniel Hawkins, Bucks Co., laborer dec'd., by his last will appointed Thomas Coverdale, Bucks Co., laborer and brother-in-law, as his executor of his estate. Daniel Hawkins at the time of his decease possessed 100 acres conveyed to him by Jeffery Hawkins lying on the west side of a run that ran on the land of said Jeffery Hawkins, bounded on the north by land of John Collins and on the east by land of Thomas Dickerson. Thomas Coverdale and his wife, Jane Coverdale to defray the just debts of said Daniel Hawkins for £14.15 from Henry Siddall, Bucks Co. a tailor. Deed for 100 acres conveyed 11th da, 7th mo, 1689. Rec: the 14th da, 7th mo, 1689. Wit: Wm. Beakes and Henry Baker.

P. 279. Deed. Luke Brindley, Bucks Co., mason, for £10 paid by Peter Worrall, Bucks Co., wheelwright, 90 acres lying on the south side of the road ... that leadeth from the Delaware River to Falls. Ackn: 8th da, 4th mo, 1688. Deed conveyed on the 11th da, 7th mo, 1689. Rec: 14th da, 7th mo, 1689. Wit: Wm. Beakes and Joseph Wood.

P. 281. Deed. Nicholas Walln, Bucks Co., yeoman, for £10 paid by William Hayhurst, Bucks Co., yeoman, a parcel of land containing 50 acres alongside the Neshaminy ... [boundary] to land of Richard Thatcher. Ackn: the 11th da, 7th mo, 1689. Rec: the 15th da, 7th mo, 1689. Wit: Wm. Beakes and Joseph Wood.

P. 282. Mortgage. 7 Oct 1689. Between Edward Antill, of the City of New York, merchant, and John Henrick de Brown, City of New York, merchant. Whereas Gilbert Wheeler, of the Falls of Delaware at Crookhorn, on 8 Aug 1682, for £200, sold to Edward Antill, a tract of land lying in what is called Crookhorn ... [boundary running] north to land of Robert Lucas ... south by land of William Biles and west ... containing 230 acres. Whereas Gilbert Wheeler has not paid his debt, Edward Antill for £147.6 sells to John Henrick de Brown the aforementioned tract of land. Rec: 13th da, 10th mo, 1689. Wit: Wm. Colls, Edw. Buckmaster and Cornelius Vander Buriks.

P. 286. Deed. 10 Feb 1689. Henry Flower, Philadelphia, barber, and executor to Enoch Flower, Philadelphia, dec'd. and Thomas Harding, Southampton, yeoman, for £8 to said Enoch Flower in his lifetime and said Mary Flower since his decease, said Henry Flower doth hereby acknowledge and doth acquit and discharge 500 acres of land in Southampton, Bucks Co. beginning at land of Robert Marsh ... south to land of Henry Flower. The said Mary Flower hath granted ... and conveyed to Thomas Harding ... a certain part of the said Henry Flower's five hundred acres ... containing 150 acres. On the 14th da, 1st mo, 1689/90 the within deed was presented in open court by Robert Heaton. Rec: the 17th da, 1st mo, 1689/90. Wit: Jeremiah Elforth, John Donsey and Thomas Harding.

P. 288. Patent. 20 March 1683, to Samuel Allen, 200 acres standing by the Neshaminy Creek ... east northeast by Joseph Growdon's land ... south by Francis Walkers and Company. Ackn: the 28th da, 11th mo, 1688. Rec: the 17th da, 1st mo, 1689/90. Wit: Wm. Markham and John Goodson.

P. 289. Patent. 11th da, 7th mo, 1682, to Samuel Allen for 1 English shilling for each 100 acres on the first day of the first month of every year a parcel of land containing 500 acres lying alongside the Neshaminy Creek adjoining James Boyden's land. Rec: the 28th da, 9th mo, 1688. Rec: the 17th da, 1st mo, 1689/90.

P. 291. Deed. 13th da, Apr, 1682. To John Rowland of Billinghurst, Sussex Co., yeoman, for 5 shillings, 1,250 acres. Rec: the 17th da, 1st mo, 1689/90. Wit: Harbt Springett, Tho. Cox and Ben. Griffith.

P. 292. Deed. 15th da, Apr, 1682, William Penn to John Rowland of Billinghurst, Sussex Co. yeoman for £25, 1250 acres. Rec: the 17th da, 1st mo, 1689/90. Wit: Harbt Springett, Tho. Cox and Ben. Griffith. Release - £25 received from John Rowland for the above mentioned 1,250 acres. Rec: the 17th da, 1st mo, 1689/90. Wit: Harbt Springett, Tho. Cox and Ben. Griffith.

P. 296. Lease. 13th da, Apr, 1682 William Penn, Worminghurst, Sussex Co., to James Dilworth, of Bradley, Lancaster Co., yeoman, 1,000 acres. Rec: the 1st da, 2nd mo, 1690. Wit: James Harrison, Tho. Cox and Ben. Griffith.

P. 297. 14 April 1682. To James Dillworth, of Bradley, Lancaster Co., yeoman, patent for £20 sterling a parcel of land containing of 1,000 acres. Rec: the 1st da, 2nd mo, 1689. Wit: James Harrison, Tho. Cox and Ben. Griffith. Release. William Penn of Worminghurst, Sussex Co. received from James Dilworth the consideration of £20 on 14th da, Apr, 1682. Rec: the 1st da, 2nd mo, 1690. Wit: James Harrison, Tho. Cox and Ben. Griffith.

P. 301. Deed. William Penn of Worminghurst, Sussex Co. to William Darke a certain parcel of land containing 235 acres lying next to land of Charles Biles. Granted by a warrant 13th da, 2nd mo, 1683 patented to William Darke. Rec: the 1st da, 2nd mo, 1690.

P. 302. Deed. 4 July 1682, between William Penn, Worminghurst, Sussex Co., Esquire and John Scarborough, London, blacksmith, for £5 sterling, 250 acres. Rec: 2nd da, 2nd mo, 1690. Wit: Harbt Springett, Tho. Cox and Ben. Griffith.

P. 305. Note. Thomas Glading, Burlington, New Jersey, acknowledges he is indebted to John Carbrow, Neshaminy, for £1.6.9 to be paid on demand. Witnessed 14th da, 12th mo, 1689. Rec: the 2nd da, 2nd mo, 1690. Wit: Benj. Wheath and Francis Stevens.

P. 305. Deed. 24th da, 3rd mo, 1689. Between Samuel Burgess, Bucks Co., and Richard Lundy, Bucks Co., land which John Rowland and Thomas Rowland, his brother, both of Bucks Co., did sell unto Samuel Burgess for £10, a parcel of land containing an estimated 200 acres, bounded on the north by lands of James Hill and east by Timber Swamp, south by lands of Randolph Blackshaw. Wit: Richard Ridgway, Ezra Croasdale and Joseph English. Ackn: 12 March 1689. Rec: 2nd da, 2nd mo, 1690. Memorandum that the within mentioned to except three acres of land to Randolph Blackshaw. On 12th da, 1st mo, 1690 the conveyance was by the within named Samuel Burges and Randolph Blackshaw. Acknowledged and delivered in open court to Richard Lundy. Rec: the 2nd da, 2nd mo, 1690.

P. 306. Deed. Joseph Growdon, Bensalem, Bucks Co., Gent., on 10th da, 12th mo, 1688. grants 100 acres to Claws Johnson, Bucks Co., yeoman for the yearly rent of £19. Ackn: 12th da, 1st mo, 1689/90 conveyance in open court. Rec: the 2nd da, 2nd mo, 1690. Wit: W. Beakes and John Cooke.

P. 308. Deed. John Otter, Philadelphia, yeoman for £10 paid by Francis Rossill, Bucks Co., a certain parcel of land granted to John Otter by Barrent Gerris, Pennsylvania, planter dated 19th Oct, 1682. Ackn: the 20th da, 9th mo, 1689. Rec: the 2nd da, 2nd mo, 1690. John Otter appointed William Beaks, Bucks Co. as his attorney to convey said deed 20th da,9th mo, 1689. Deed delivered 12th da, 1st mo, 1690. Rec: the 2nd da, 2nd mo, 1690. Wit: John Crapp, Jr. and Walter Worrilow.

P. 309. Deed. Israel Taylor, Neshaminy Creek, Bucks Co., chyrurgeon for £24 paid to John Coates, Bucks Co., a parcel of land containing 250 acres abounding land of Joseph Sharp ... land of Thomas Constables ...

to land of Richard Peirce ... containing of 250 acres. Ackn: 13th da, 1st mo, 1689. Deed conveyed in open court 13th da, 1st mo, 1689/90. Rec: the 2nd da, 2nd mo, 1690. Wit: William Biles, Gilbert Wheeler and Henry Margerum.

P. 312. Appointment. John Blackwell, a Receiver General of rents and revenues does grant and transfer all powers and authority to Robert Turner in his absence. 11th da, 1st mo, 1689/90.

P. 312. Deed. Indenture 18th da, 12th mo, 1689 between William Beakes, Bucks Co. and John Worrilow, Chester Co. and Walter Worrilow, of Philadelphia. Witnesseth a marriage between the William Beakes and Elizabeth Worrilow, dau. of Thomas Worrilow, Chester, said William Beakes granted unto said John Worrilow and Walter Worrilow a plantation now in his possession, lying and being near the Falls of the Delaware River containing 300 acres. John Worrilow and Walter Worrilow authorize their trusty friend, Thomas Tunnicliffe, Bucks Co., to receive of William Beakes the above deed. Witnessed 12th da, 2nd mo, 1690. 11th da, 4th mo, 1690 the above conveyance delivered to open court. Rec: the 1st da, 5th mo, 1690. Wit: Joseph Baker and Thomas Tunnicliffe.

P. 315. Deed. Joseph Growdon, Bensalem, Bucks Co., 20th da, 6th mo, 1690 for performing 8 days of work and 1 English shilling, a parcel of land containing 1 acre lying and within the said Joseph Growdon's manor standing by Poquessin Creek. 10th da, 7th da, 1690 above conveyance delivered to open court. Rec: the 1st da, 8th mo, 1690. Wit: Nicholas Hinket, Wm. Reynolds and Grace Growdon.

P. 316. Deed. Samuel Burges, Bucks Co., husbandman for six shillings paid by Thomas Janney, William Biles, Richard Hough, Joseph Hoopes, Bucks Co., yeomen, 6 acres lying in Bucks Co., granted to Samuel Burges by a deed from John Rowland and Thomas Rowland dated 1st da, 10th mo, 1685 in Book Vol. 1, page 10-11. Ackn: 4th da, 4th mo, 1690. Above conveyance delivered to open court by William Yardley, attorney for Samuel Burges. Rec: 1st da, 8th mo, 1690. Wit: Jacob Janney, Enoch Yardley and Joseph Steward.

P. 318. Indenture. 15th da, Nov 16 (1st year of reign of Lord and Lady William and Mary) between John Cups, (or Cuff) axeholder, Somerset

Co., yeoman, and Samuel Beakes, Potishead, axe polisher, Somerset Co., yeoman, for £20 a parcel of land containing 236 acres lying in Bucks Co., held in common by one William Biles and Charles Biles, since divided ... standing at the dividing line and in line of land of William Darke. 11th da, 7th mo, 1690 a conveyance by William Biles, attorney for John Cuft. Acknowledged and delivered in open court to Samuel Beakes. Rec: the 1st da, 8th mo, 1690. Wit: George Bryan, Ben Restoene, William Cox, Notary Public, John Coate, and Will Lane. Bond. John Cuff shall keep and pay the above mentioned parcel of land along with Samuel Beakes Rec: the 1st da, 8th mo, 1690. Wit: George Bryan, Ben Restoene, William Cox, Notary Public, John Coate, and Will Lane.

P. 323. Deed. John Rowland, Bucks Co., yeoman, brother and only heir of Thomas Rowland, for £25 to be paid by Gilbert Wheeler, yeoman Bucks Co. a parcel of land containing 500 acres being part of the land of said Thomas Rowland. 11th da, 7th mo, 1690 the within conveyance was delivered to open court to Gilbert Wheeler. Rec: the 2nd da, 8th mo, 1690. Wit: Thomas Stackhouse, John Smith and Joseph Wood.

P. 325. Deed. Henry Margerum, Bucks Co., yeoman, for £20 paid by John Clark, Bucks Co., 296 acres lying by the land of Jonathan Elridge granted to Henry Margerum by a deed from Edward Luft dated 4th da, 4th mo, 1688 recorded Book A, Vol. 1, page 191-193, 19th da, 10th mo, 1688. 12th da, 7th mo, 1690 conveyance delivered in open court by Henry Margerum to John Clark. Rec: 2nd da, 8th mo, 1690. Wit: James Haywood and Phinehas Pemberton.

P. 327. Deed. Thomas Janney, Bucks Co., yeoman, for two shillings paid him by William Yardley, Richard Hough, Joshua Hoopes and William Beakes, all of Bucks Co., granted a parcel of land containing 72 square rods. 11th da, 7th mo, 1690 the conveyance delivered in open court to above named William Yardley and Joshua Hoopes. Rec: the 2nd da, 8th mo, 1690.

P. 328. Deed. William Clowes, Bucks Co. yeoman, for 250 acres situated on Neshaminy Creek conveyed to him by Joseph Clows, tailor and brother to said William Clowes, grants part of the parcel of land of John Clows, father of said William and Joseph Clowes, dec'd, 29th da, 11th mo, 1686. Land lies between the land of William Yardley and said Clowes' land ... east to land of John Brock. Ackn: 8th da, 7th mo, 1690.

Wit: Jonathan Scaife, Jacob Janney and Ruben Pownall.

P. 331. Power of attorney. Margery Clows, widow of John Clows and mother to Joseph Clows and William Clows, grants her title and interest to all and 250 acres of land to said Joseph Clows. Ackn: 11th da, 7th mo, 1690. Rec: the 3rd da, 8th mo, 1690. Wit: Jacob Janney and John Smith.

P. 332. Deed. Joseph Clows, Bucks Co., for 250 acres situated on the River Delaware aforesaid, conveyed to him by William Clows, Bucks Co., yeoman and his brother, granted unto William Clowes part of 500 acres of land. Ackn: the 11th da, 7th mo, 1690 the within conveyance delivered to open court unto the named William Clows. Rec: the 3rd da, 8th mo, 1690. Wit: Jonathan Scarfe, Jacob Janney and Ruben Pownall.

P. 334. Deed. Phinehas Pemberton, Bucks Co., yeoman, and son and only heir of James Harrison, late of the aforesaid county, in right of his wife Phebe, the dau. of said James Harrison, for £12 paid by James Radcliff, Bucks Co., husbandman, granted a parcel of land containing 200 acres lying in Wrightstown between the land of James Harrison and land of Roger Longworth, Bucks Co. to James Radcliff. Ackn: 11th da, 7th mo, 1690 above conveyance in open court to James Radciff. Rec: the 3rd da, 8th mo, 1690. Wit: Shadrach Walley, Will Yardley and Jonathan Scarfe.

P. 336. Deed. Joseph English, Bucks Co., yeoman, for £45 paid by Samuel Darke, Bucks Co., yeoman, grants a parcel of land containing 200 acres granted to Joseph English by William Biles on 5th da, 5th mo, 1688, recorded in the Book A, Vol 1, page 182, 183. Received of Samuel Dark £45 for the aforementioned, 3rd da, 9th mo, 1690. 10th da, 10th mo, 1690 above conveyance delivered to open court. Rec: 3rd da, 11th mo, 1690. Wit: Phebe Pemberton and Mary Becker.

P. 338. Letter of Attorney. On 26th da, Aug, 1689, Daniel Cox, of London, Doctor of Physick, appeared before notary Nicholas Hayward, dwelling in London, and appoints John Tatham, Esq. and James Bud, merchant, to be his true and lawful attorney, to collect all rents due in East or West Jersey from any owed to Edward Byllyings, late of London, dec'd. June 3rd, 1690 ordered that above letter of attorney be recorded in public records in the Province of West Jersey. June 9, 1690.

Rec: in the public records of West Jersey in folio (260) of Book B. 16th da, 4th mo, 11691 recorded the before letter of attorney the following [to sell any of his lands or lease them in East or West Jersey] being interlined between the 18th and 19th line of said letter of attorney before the recording. Wit: Jere Jenkins and Mark Adler.

P. 341. Deed. James Moore, Bucks Co., laborer, and son James Moore for £5 to him paid by Samuel Dark, Bucks Co., yeoman, grants a parcel of land lying in Bucks Co., containing 5 acres being part of a parcel of land of James Hill of Burlington, granted to said James Moore and son, James Moore by conveyance dated 13th da, 10th mo, 1688 recorded Book A, Vol 1, page 193, 194. Ackn: 16th 7th mo, 1691 the conveyance was delivered in open court. Rec: the 20th da, 8th mo, 1691. Wit: Phinehas Pemberton and Will Yardley.

P. 343. Deed. 24th da, May, 1683 between William Penn, late of Worminghurst, Sussex Co., Esq. and Jacob Hall, of Mawlesfield, County Palatine, of Chester, shoemaker, for five shillings a parcel of land containing 500 acres granted by warrant dated 11 July 1681. Rec: the 21st da, 8th mo, 1691. Wit: Habt. Springett, Anthony Springett and Sell Clarke.

P. 344. Deed. On 25 May 1685 between William Penn, late of Worminghurst, Sussex Co., Esq. and Jacob Hall, of Manlesfield, County Palatine, of Chester, shoemaker, 500 acres for £10. Rec: the 21st da, 8th mo, 1691. Wit: Harbt Springett, Anthony Springett and Sell Clarke.

P. 347. Release. William Penn, late of Worminghurst, Sussex Co., Esq. and Jacob Hall, of Manlesfield, County Palatine, of Chester, shoemaker, releases for £10. Ackn: 25th da, May, 1683. Rec: 2nd da, 8th mo, 1691. Wit: Harbt Springett, Anthony Springett and Sell Clarke.

P. 346. Deed. Joseph English, Bucks Co. yeoman, for £10, paid by Thomas Brock, 27 acres, being part of the 30 acres lying in Bucks Co. conveyed to Joseph English by Samuel Clift, 9th mo, 1682, beginning at a place called Mill Creek ... to join with land of Richard Dungworth. Ackn: 6th da, 2nd mo, 1692. Conveyed in open court the 8th da, 4th mo, 1692. Rec: the 20th da, 4th mo, 1692. Wit: Richard Ridgway, Abigail Stockton.

P. 349. Power of Attorney. Joseph English, Bucks Co., appoints Phinehas Pemberton, Bucks Co. to be his attorney to deliver to Thomas Brock one deed conveying 20 acres. Rec: the 20th da, 4th mo, 1692. Wit: Richard Ridgway, Abigail Stockton.

P. 349. Deed. Samuel Allen, Sr. of Neshaminy Creek, Bucks Co., yeoman, for and in consideration of his affection to his granddaughter, Elizabeth Pegg, dau. of Daniel Pegg, of Philadelphia a certain piece of land lying east of the Neshaminy Creek ... bounded by line of John Baldwin south to land of John Otter ... containing 200 acres. Land being granted to Samuel Allen by a patent dated 28th da, 9th mo, 1688, recorded in rolls of Book A, Vol 1, page 289-290. 8th da, 4th mo, 1692 the above was conveyed in open court unto John Baldwin for the use of Elizabeth Pegg. Rec: the 2nd da, 4th mo, 1692. Wit: Richard Ridgway, Abigail Stockton.

P. 352. Deed. Samuel Allen, Sr. of near Neshaminy Creek, Bucks Co., yeoman for £35 to John Baldwin, Bucks Co., son-in-law of said Samuel Allen, 200 acres. Received of John Baldwin £35 on 4th da, 4th mo, 1692. Rec: the 20th da, 4th mo, 1692. Wit: Tho. Brock, Charles Biles and Samuel Beakes.

P. 354. Deed. John Rowland, Bucks Co., yeoman, and brother and only heir to Thomas Rowland, late of Bucks Co. for £70, to be paid by Henry Baker, Bucks Co., yeoman, 500 acres. Ackn: 8th da, 10th mo, 1691. Deed conveyed in open court 8th da, 4th mo, 1692. Rec: the 10th da, 4th mo, 1692. Wit: John Cooke, John White and William Croasdale.

P. 357. Deed. Jacob Hall, Bucks Co., shoemaker, formerly of Mattlesfold, Chester Co., Old England, for £15 paid by Thomas Hudson, of Sutton, Chester Co., Old England, Gent., 500 acres. Ackn: 8th da, 4th mo, 1692 conveyance delivered in open court unto William Biles, attorney for Thomas Hudson. Rec: the 1st da, 4th mo, 1692. Wit: Arthur Cooke, Joseph Growdon and Wm. Yardley. Power of Attorney. Jacob Hall, Philadelphia Co., shoemaker, appoints Joseph Charley, Bucks Co., husbandman, to appear in open court and acknowledge and deliver said deed of 500 acres unto Thomas Hudson. Rec: 10th da, 4th mo, 1692. Wit: Wm. Yardley, Joseph Milnor.

P. 359. Deed. Samuel Allen, of near Neshaminy Creek, Bucks Co.,

37

yeoman, for the natural love and affection, gives to his son Samuel Allen, Jr. a parcel of land standing alongside of Neshaminy Creek ... [boundary] south to land of Francis Walker and Company containing 200 acres. Ackn: 8th da, 4th mo, 1692. Rec: the 15th da, 4th mo, 1692. Wit: Richard Ridgway, John Baldwin and Samuel Beakes.

P. 361. Deed. Richard Ridgway, Bucks Co., yeoman for £101 paid to him by Samuel Beakes, Bucks Co., yeoman, 120 acres bounding land of William Biles ... land of John Ackerman ... Ackn: 8th da, 4th mo, 1692. Rec: the 16th da, 4th mo, 1692. Wit: Joshua Ely, Christopher Snoden and Charles Biles.

P. 363. Bond. Henry Baker, Bucks Co., yeoman and Job Bunting, Bucks Co., carpenter, owe and are indebted unto John Rowland, Bucks Co., yeoman, for £10 to be delivered at the Ferry House in Burlington on and before the 25th da, 1st mo, 1692. Ackn: 7th da, 4th mo, 1692. Rec: 15th da, 7th mo, 1692. Wit: Richard Hough, Phinehas Pemberton.

P. 363. Bond. Samuel Beakes, Bucks Co., yeoman, firmly bound unto Richard Ridway, Bucks Co., tailor, for £100, to be paid before 26th da, 2nd mo, 1694. Wit: Joshua Ely, Christopher Snowdon.

P. 364. Bond. [Same as page 363 above - except to be delivered 25th da, 1st mo, 1694.] Ackn: 7th da, 4th mo, 1692. Rec: 15th da, 7th mo, 1692. Wit: Richard Hough, Phinehas Pemberton.

P. 364. Bond. [Same as page 363 above - except to be delivered 25th da, 1st mo, 1695.] Ackn: 7th da, 4th mo, 1692. Rec: 15th da, 7th mo, 1692. Wit: Miles Foster, John Barclay, Jnieolls Rich. Jones.

P. 365. Power of Attorney. Edward Antill, now of New York, Gent., appoints William Nicholls, of the city of New York, Gent., his attorney to act in his stead concerning his lands in the provinces of New York, New Jersey and Pennsylvania. Rec: the 25th da, 7th mo, 1692.

P. 366. Bond. [Same as page 363 above - except to be delivered 25th da, 1st mo, 1696.]

P. 366. Bond. [Same as page 363 above - except to be delivered 25th da, 1st mo, 1697.]

P. 366. Bond. [Same as page 363 above - except to be delivered 25th da, 1st mo, 1698.]

P. 367. Patent. To Peter Groome, land bounded by Thomas Hold's land ... to Jos. Jones ... containing 320 acres, warrant dated 26th da, 8th mo, 1683. Ackn: 25th da, 4th mo, 1690. Rec: 20th da, 7th mo, 1692. Wit: Samuel Carpenter and William Markham.

P. 368. Deed. This indenture made the 20 Nov 1690 between Anthony Morgan, Peter Groome and Hugh Marsh of the one part and Josias Hill all of Bucks Co., a parcel of land beginning at corner of Thomas Hold's land ... southwest to Jos. Jones land ... containing 200 acres granted to Peter Groome by a patent dated 25th da, 4th mo, 1690 recorded in Book A, page, said land Peter Groome sold unto Hugh Marsh who sold same parcel of land to Anthony Marsh, but no deed passed between parties. This indenture that the said Anthony Morgan for £16 to be paid by Josias Hill with the consent of Hugh Marsh and Peter Groom. 14th da, 7th mo, 1692 the above deed conveyed in open court. Rec: 20th da, 7th mo, 1692. Wit: Israel Taylor, John Meredith and John Webster.

P. 370. Power of Attorney. Peter Groom, West Jersey, Burlington Co., husbandman appoints his brother Thomas Groom of Byberry, Philadelphia Co., carpenter, to be his lawful attorney. Rec: the 20th da, 7th mo, 1692. Wit: Josiah Hill, Hugh Marsh.

P. 370. Deed. Henry Baker, Bucks Co., for £35, to be paid by Job Bunting, Bucks Co., carpenter, son in law of Henry Baker a parcel of land lying near the land of William Buckman ... Thomas Constable's land ... containing a total of 248 acres. Ackn: 15th da, 7th mo, 1692 a deed conveyed in open court to Job Bunting. Rec: the 21st da, 7th mo, 1692. Wit: Samuel Beakes, Abraham Cox and Edmond Lovett.

Volume 2

P. 1. Deed. John Austin, of Philadelphia Co., ship carpenter, for £23, to Nicholas Waln, Bucks Co., a parcel of land standing by the Neshaminy Creek containing 60 acres. Ackn: 7th da, 4th mo, 1692. Rec: the 1st da, 8th mo, 1692.

P. 2. Deed. Elizabeth Bennet, sole executrix of the late Edmund Bennet, her husband, for £36, to Nicholas Waln, a piece of land lying along side the Neshaminy Creek containing 340 acres. Ackn: 2/9/1692. Rec: 17/10/1692.

P. 4. Patent to Edmund Bennet, 16/10/1689, a parcel of land containing 500 acres adjoining southerly by Richard Skatiger's land. Rec: the 17/10/1692.

P. 4. Deed. Richard Lundy, of Bucks Co., for £27.10, to Francis Rosill of the same county a certain parcel of land containing ... northwest adjoining land of Francis Rossill thence north northwest to land of William Say and Robert Wheeler... containing 500 acres. Ackn: 12/7/1692. Rec: 16/10/1692.

P. 6. Patent to Thomas Janney, a parcel of land standing by the Delaware River west southwest to land of Richard Hough, containing 550 acres. Ackn: 16th da, 10th mo, 1689. Rec: the 16/10/1692.

P. 7. Deed. Thomas Green and his wife, Rachel, of Cold Spring, Bucks Co., for £10, to Thomas Brock of Burlington Ferry, Bucks Co. a parcel of land containing 5 ½ acres. Ackn: 8th da, 1st mo, 1692. Rec: 10th da, 1st mo, 1692.

P. 8. Deed. Thomas Green, a yeoman and his wife, Rachel of Cold Spring, Bucks Co. for £10, to Anthony Burton of Buckingham, Bucks Co. a parcel of land, 5 ½ acres. Ackn: 8 March 1692. Rec: 10th da, 1st mo, 1692.

P. 9. Power of Attorney. Joseph Holden of Southampton Co., appoints Hugh Marsh, Southampton Co. his attorney to collect all monies due him in the sale of stock upon Horba Park Farm. Wife, Margaret Holden also gives her consent. Rec: 10th da, 1st mo, 1692.

P. 10. Indenture. 3 July 1682. William Penn of Worminghurst Co. of Sussex to John Scarborrow of London, blacksmith, for 5 shillings, 250 acres. Rec: 10th da, 1st mo, 1692.

P. 11. Patent. To Israel Taylor, son of Christopher Taylor, 250 acres lying along Neshaminay Creek for 1 shilling the first month of each year.

Ackn: 18th da, Feb, 1692/3. Rec: the 16th da, 2nd mo, 1693.

P. 12. Deed. Israel Taylor, Bucks Co., chyrurgeon, for £15.10 to James Yates, of said county, 250 acres in Newtown, Bucks Co. Ackn: 14th da, 2nd mo, 1693. Rec: 16th da, 2nd mo, 1693.

P. 13. Patent. To Robert Marsh a parcel of land in Philadelphia Co. adjoining land of Enoch Flowers ... [near] land of John Gilberts containing 500 acres for 1 shilling. Ackn: 16th da, 5th mo, 1684. Rec: the 16th da, 2nd mo, 1693.

P. 14. Deed. Hugh Marsh and Sarah Marsh, widow of Robert Marsh and mother of Hugh, of Bucks Co., he a husbandman to John Eastbourn, for £40, to John Eastbourn 300 acres in Southampton Township. Ackn: 14th da, 2nd mo, 1693. Rec: the 16th da, 2nd mo, 1693.

P. 16. Deed. Samuel Beakes, sheriff of Bucks Co., to Joseph Growdon. John Dueplovie of the city of Philadelphia on the 10th da, 7th mo, 1690, recovered a judgment against Joseph Holden, Bucks Co. in the amount of £13.18.7 and £1.9.7. Also Philip Richards of Philadelphia recovered against Joseph Holden £10.2.3 and £1.8. Cornelius Empson of Castel Co. recovered against Joseph Holden £8.15.4. Joseph Holden's land was taken in execution the 28th da, 11th mo, 1691. Joseph Growden for £70 bought the land of Joseph Holden containing 450 acres lying in Southampton adjoining the land of Hugh Marsh. Ackn: 18th da, 2nd mo, 1693. Rec: the 19th da, 2nd mo, 1693.

P. 17. Patent. To Francis Done a parcel of land containing 8 acres for 1 shilling. Ackn: 16th da, 12th mo, 1689. Rec: the 19th da, 2nd mo, 1693.

P. 18. Patent. William Penn of Worminghurst Co. of Sussex to William Wiggans, 8 acres, beginning at land of Francis Done ... south by John Moores ... south southeast by Edward Samway's land, for 1 shilling. Ackn: 8th da, 4th mo, 1691. Rec: 19th da, 2nd mo, 1693.

P. 19. Patent. To Edward Samway, 8 acres adjoining land of William Wiggans ... south by John Moore's land for 1 shilling. Ackn: 3rd da, 4th mo, 1691. Rec: the 19th da, 2nd mo, 1693.

P. 20. Patent. To Thomas Bond, 16 acres in the liberties of Philadelphia adjoining Francis Done's land ... north to John Moones, for 1 shilling. Ackn: 19th da, Oct, 1691. Rec: 19th da, 2nd mo, 1693.

P. 21. Patent. To Thomas Bond a parcel of land bearing the breadth of 26 feet and 300 feet in length in the high street of Philadelphia ... adjoining Thomas Rowland's land ... for 1 English silver shilling. Ackn: 20th da, Oct, 1691. Rec: the 19th da, 2nd mo, 1693.

P. 22. Patent. To Thomas Hudson 100 acres lying by the river Delaware near unto John Hough's land ... for 1 shilling. Ackn: 15th da, Mar, 1692/3. Rec: no. date.

P. 23. Richard Wheeler of Falley, Southtowne County, married, gives his power of attorney to John Budd, Bucks Co., a merchant to collect all monies bequeathed to him by his uncle, Benjamin Roberts. Ackn: 1st da, Dec, 1692. Rec: 19th da, 2nd mo,1693.

P. 24. Thomas Bennet, executor, Richard Wheeler, executor, and Hannah Roberts to John Budd. Thomas Bennett and Mary, wife, of the Town of Weymouth, Dorcet County and Richard Wheeler and Sarah, his wife of Heith, Southton County and Hannah Roberts of Weymouth, Dorcet County, a spinster, sisters of the deceased Benjamin Roberts, late of Bucks Co. appoint John Budd, Bucks Co. as their attorney to collect and bargain for the property of Benjamin Roberts, dec'd. Ackn: 12th da, Dec, 1692. Rec: 19th da, 2nd mo, 1693.

P. 25. Patent. To Thomas Hudson a parcel of land containing 100 acres adjoining land of John Hough, standing along the River Delaware for 1 shilling. Ackn: 15th da, Mar, 1692/3. Rec: 19th da, 2nd mo, 1693.

P. 25. Patent. To Thomas Wolfe, 200 acres adjoining land of Christopher Bennet ... to land of John Rowland ..., for 1 shilling. Ackn: 27th da, 11th mo,m 1693. Rec: 19th da, 2nd mo, 1693.

P. 26. Abraham Cox and wife to Edward Pearson. Abraham Cox, Bucks Co., a yeoman and Sarah, his wife and sister to Thomas Wolfe, dec'd. for £40 to Edward Pearson, Mason, Bucks Co., 120 acres standing by the swamp adjoining land of Christopher Bennett thence north west ... land of Anthony Burton ... to land of Arthur Cooke. Ackn: 15th da, 1st mo,

1693. Rec: 19th da, 2nd mo, 1693.

P. 28. Patent. To Phineas Pemberton 172 acres in Wrightstown, Bucks Co. standing by the Neshaminah Creek for 1 shilling. Ackn: 1st da, Dec, 1693.

P. 29. Patent. To John Acruman 213 acres by the River Delaware for 1 shilling. Ackn: 31st da, 5th mo, 1694. Rec: 19th da, 1st mo, 1694.

P. 29. Thomas Brock, Sheriff, Bucks Co. for Mary Beakes, Bucks Co., administratrix of her late husband, William Beakes recovered in a judgement against Joseph Chorley and his wife, Mary the consideration of £54 and £3.6 by levying said consideration against land of the said John Acreman, 200 odd acres. Ackn: 13th da, 1st mo, 1694. Rec: 13th da, Mar, 1694.

P. 31. Deed. Mary Beaks to Joseph Chorley. Whereas John Ackerman, late of Bucks Co., husbandman, dec'd. by his indenture bearing the date of 25th da, 10th mo, 1684 for £40 did sell to William Beakes a parcel of land lying between the land of Richard Ridgway and Daniel Brinson. Said land conveyed to Joseph Chorley and his wife. Ackn: 13th da, 1st mo,1694. Rec: 19th da, 1st mo, 1694.

P. 33. Commission to Phineas Pemberton to be clerk for Bucks Co. Ackn: 10 Sep 1695. Rec: 1st da, 2nd mo, 1696.

P. 33. By the death of Thomas Lloyd, the office of Master Rolls is vacant and Phineas Pemberton is appointed to be clerk for Bucks Co. Ackn: 15th da, Feb, 1695/6. Rec: the 1st da, 2nd mo, 1696.

P. 34. Power of Attorney. John Nicholls and Elias Nicholls, brother of John, both of Bucks Co., give to Mahlon Stacy, of the province of West Jersey, yeoman, and Henry Baker, Bucks Co., yeoman, the power of attorney to demand and receive all monies due them. Ackn: 17th da, 5th mo, 1688. Wit: James Crosley and John Sawthy. Rec: in open court 9th da, 8th mo, 1697.

P. 35. Indenture. 20 March 1694. William Beaks of Bucks Co., yeoman, and his wife, Elizabeth, on the one part and John Snowden, of White Hill, Burlington Co., yeoman. A grant was made on 26 July 1681 to

William Beakes, yeoman (father of above named William Beaks) of Blackwell, Sumerset County, England, for a parcel of land containing 1000 acres. Mary Beakes, Bucks Co., widow of and administratrix of aforesaid William Beakes of Blackwell, dec'd. and Stephen Beakes, Samuel Beakes and Abraham Beakes, sons of the aforesaid Mary Beakes and heir to aforesaid William Beaks did grant to the first named William Beaks a parcel of land lying between the land of William Venables and land of John Persons containing 300 acres. William Beaks and wife, Elizabeth for £160 convey same to John Snowden. Ackn: 20th Mar, 1694. Wit: Thomas Lambert, William Emley and Samuel Beakes. Power of Attorney. Samuel Beakes appointed power of attorney to deliver the deed. Ackn: 12th da, 4th mo, 1695. Rec: 10th da, 2nd mo, 1696.

P. 38. Deed of jointure dated the 18th da, 12th mo, 1689 and recorded in the Rolls office for Bucks Co., Book A, Vol 1-page 312-314 made by William Beaks aforesaid of the above mentioned 300 acres to John Worrlew and Wallie Worrlew in trust for Elizabeth Worrilew, their sister and now wife of the said William Beakes was surrendered in open court in the Bucks Co. the 12th da, 4th mo, 1694 by Samuel Beakes.

P. 38. Power of attorney. John Worrilew of Chester Co. surviving trustee to William Beakes and Elizabeth, his wife appoints and authorizes Samuel Beaks of Bucks Co. to deliver the deed. Wit: William Warell and William Emley, Jr. Rec: the 10th da, 2nd mo, 1696.

P. 39. Bond. William Beakes, Bucks Co., yeoman, is bound unto John Snowden, of White Hill, Burlington Co., for £120 for 300 acres. Ackn: 20 March 1694. Wit: Thomas Lambert, William Emley and Samuel Beakes. Rec: the 10th da, 2nd mo, 1696.

P. 40. Patent granted to heirs of William Beakes, 300 acres for 1 shilling. Ackn: 17th da, 9th mo, 1688. Rec: 10th da, 2nd mo, 1696.

P. 41. Deed. Elinor Allen, widow and relict of Nathaniel Allen, late of Philadelphia, cooper, dec'd. Nehemiah Allen, son and heir of said Nathaniel, Lydia Smart, widow, and dau. of said Nathaniel, Thomas Bradford and Thomas Paschel, co-executors, for £100 from Joseph Kirke of Philadelphia, a mariner, convey 400 acres lying on the Delaware River. Ackn: 30th da, 8th mo, 1694. Wit: John Paine, Mary Heath,

Elizabeth F. Cook, William Galt. Ackn: at Philadelphia, 30 Oct 1694. Rec: 10th da, 2nd mo, 1696.

P. 42. Indenture. Abraham Beakes, Crook-horn, Bucks Co., yeoman, and Joseph Stewart, of same town and county, husbandman, for £7, 90 acres lying by the land of John Palmer. Ackn: 21st da, Nov, 1693. Wit: Jacob Janney, Daniel Hoopes and James Yates. Rec: 11th da, 2nd mo, 1696.

P. 43. Deed. Joseph Steward, Bucks Co. to Richard Hough, of aforesaid county, for £8, 90 acres lying next to land of William Beakes and Veneables orphans ... land of Henry Marjoram ... land of Andrew Ellet. Ackn: 20th da, 7th mo, 1694. Wit: Jacob Janney, Ruben Parnall, William Biles, Jr. Rec: 9th da, 8th mo, 1695.

P. 44. Deed. John Budd, town and county of Philadelphia, merchant and attorney to Thomas Bennett and Mary, his wife of Wymouth, Dorcet County, mariner, and to Richard Wheeler and Sarah his wife of Heith, Parish Fawley, South Town County, mariner, and to Hannah Roberts of Wymouth Dorcet County, which Mary Bennett, Sarah Wheeler and Hannah Roberts were sisters and co-heirs to Benjamin Roberts, late of the Bucks Co., dec'd., for £25 paid to John Budd from Thomas Rogers, of Bucks Co., husbandman, a parcel of land lying next to land of Abraham Wharley ... land of Shadrack Walley's land ... containing 225 acres and also 25 acres. Ackn: the 12th da, 10th mo, 1694. Wit: Thomas Brock, William Paxson, Thomas Terry. Rec: the 12th da, 10th mo, 1694.

P. 45. Power of Attorney. Daniel Beaks, Bucks Co. appointed attorney for John Budd. Wit: Thomas Brock, William Paxson and Thomas Terry. Rec: 11th da, 2nd mo, 1696.

P. 46. Indenture. 11 Sep 1695. Thomas Rogers, Bucks Co., husbandman, to Shadrach Walley, of said county, husbandman, for £31.10 225 acres lying next to land of Abraham Wharley ... together with 25 acres lying in New Town. Ackn: 11 Sep 1695. Wit: Daniel Rudley and James Hick. Rec: the 11th da, 2nd mo, 1696.

P. 47. Deed. John Smith, Bucks Co., blacksmith, for £25 from John Burling, Burlington Co., 50 acres lying by the land of Widow Langhorne

... to line of Henry Paxson ... to line of Henry Pawlin. Ackn: 3rd da, 10th mo, 1692. Wit: Mary Scaife and Jonathan Scaife. Rec: 11th da, 2nd mo, 1696.

P. 48. Deed. John Burling, Bucks Co., wheelwright, for £29 from William Paxson, Bucks Co., yeoman, 50 acres lying along land of Widow Langhorn ... to land of William Paxson ... to line of Henry Paxson ... line of Henry Pawlin. Ackn: 9th da, 8th mo, 1695. Rec: the 9th da, 8th mo, 1695.

P. 49. Deed. Charles Biles, Maidenhead, yeoman, for £18 from Abel Janney, Bucks Co., blacksmith, 236 acres lying next to land of William Darks. Ackn: 12th da, 7th mo, 1694. Wit: Phineas Pemberton, Phebe Pemberton. Rec: 12th da, 7th mo, 1694.

P. 50. Deed. John Horner, Burlington Co., husbandman, granted to James Harrison, Bucks Co., dec'd, (father-in-law of Phineas Pemberton, Bucks Co., yeoman) by Edward Billing, Westminster, Middlesex County, gentlemen by deed of lease and release dated 11th da, 2nd mo, 1682. John Horner granted to Phineas Pemberton and his wife, Phebe, the only dau. of James Harrison a parcel of land containing 480 acres. Ackn: 20th da, 12th mo, 1693. Wit: Israel Taylor and Robert Heaton. Rec: 11th da, 10th mo, 1695.

P. 51. Bond. John Horner, province of New Jersey, husbandman, bound and obligated to Phineas Pemberton, Bucks Co., yeoman, for a sum of £50. 20th da, 12th mo, 1693. The condition of this obligation is that John Horner, his brothers, Joshua Horner and Isaac Horner and his sister, Mary Horner when they attain the ages of 21 years, to quit claim a parcel of land containing 480 acres which John Horner, their father, late of Burlington Co., dec'd. had purchased from James Dilworth 5th da, 4th mo, 1686. Wit: Richard Mathis, Henry Siddal and Joseph Kirkbride. Rec: the 13th da, 2nd mo, 1696.

P. 51. Deed. Job Bunting, New Town, Bucks Co. for £160 paid by Stephen Twining of said town and county, husbandman, 200 acres in New Town ... and one piece of meadow land lying by land of Thomas Constable. Ackn: 10th da, 10th mo, 1695. Wit: Jonathan Scaife, William Crosdel and Enoch Yardley. Rec: 13th da, 2nd mo, 1696.

P. 52. Bond. Stephen Twining, New Town, Bucks Co., husbandman, is bound to Job Bunting for the sum of £60. The condition of this obligation is that Stephen Furning to pay £30 of the money received from wheat taken to the mill of Samuel Carpenter before the 25th da, 1st mo, 1697. Wit: Enoch Yardley and Jonathan Scaife. Rec: the 13th da, 2nd mo, 1696.

P. 52. Bond. Stephen Twining, New Town, Bucks Co., husbandman, is bound to Job Bunting for the sum of £60. The condition of this obligation is that Stephen Twining to pay £30 of the money received from wheat taken to the mill of Samuel Carpenter before the 25th da, 1st mo, 1698. Wit: Enoch Yardley, Jonathan Scaife and William Crosdell. Rec: the 13th da, 2nd mo, 1696.

P. 53. Deed. Thomas Williams, Burlington Co., carpenter and Rebecca, his wife (formerly the wife of William Bennett, late of Bucks Co., dec'd.) for £90 paid by Abraham Cox, Bucks Co., yeoman, 200 acres standing along the Delaware River ... to land of Widow Daugan ... to land of Joseph Large containing. Being a tract of land formerly owned by Mordecai Bowden and by him sold to Charles Pickering 21st da, 6th mo, 1683. Ackn: 2nd da, 9th mo, 1695. Wit: Joseph Growden, Phineas Pemberton, Joseph Kirkbride, Benjamin Swett, Jeremiah Dungan. Rec: 12th da, 2nd mo, 1695.

P. 54. Deed. Rebecca Bennet, Ann Bennet, Sarah Bennet, daus. of William Bennet late of Bucks Co., dec'd., for £60 from Abraham Cox, Bucks Co., yeoman, 200 acres. Ackn: 4th da, 9th mo, 1695. Wit: Joseph Growdon, Phineas Pemberton, Joseph Kirkbride. Rec: the 14th da, 2nd mo, 1696.

P. 55. Deed. Nicholas Waln, Middletown, Bucks Co. for — from John Stakehouse a parcel of land lying in Middletown containing 200 acres. Ackn: 10th da, 1st mo, 1695. Wit: John Cowgill and Jonathan Scaife. Rec: 14th da, 2nd mo, 1696.

P. 56. Deed. Prudence Betridge, widow and sole executrix of Marke Betridge, late of Southampton, Bucks Co., yeoman, dec'd., for £30 from George Willard, Chester Co., yeoman, 100 acres lying next to land of Samuel Allen north ... land of William Buckman ... land granted by a patent to Thomas Rowland dated 13th da, 7th mo, 1686 recorded in

Book A, Vol 1, page 219. Ackn: 4th da, 3rd mo, 1695/6. Wit: Obadiah Holt? and David Lloyd. Rec: 11th da, 1st mo, 1695/6.

P. 57. Deed. Joseph English, Burlington Co., yeoman, and son-in-law of Samuel Clift, late of Bucks Co., dec'd., for £20 from Thomas Brock and Anthony Burton, both of Bucks Co., 22 acres beginning at the line of John White ... along the River Delaware ..., lying in Buckingham, Bucks Co. Ackn: 20th da, 12th mo, 1695. Wit: Michael Newbould and Peter White. Rec: the 16th da, 2nd mo, 1696.

P. 58. Deed. Joseph English, Burlington Co., yeoman, and son-in-law of Samuel Clift, late of Bucks Co., dec'd. for 5 shillings from Peter White, yeoman, and son-in-law of Joseph English and for natural affection, 22 acres beginning at land of John White ... lying in Buckingham, granted to Samuel Clift and descended to Joseph English as heir of said Samuel Clift. Ackn: 20th da, 12th mo, 1695. Wit: Michael Newbould and Peter White. Rec: the 16th da, 2nd mo, 1696.

P. 59. Power of Attorney. Joseph English, Burlington Co., West Jersey appoints Phineas Pemberton, Bucks Co. as his attorney to deliver a deed to open court for 11 acres to his son-in-law, Peter White, yeoman, being part of 22 acres of land lying ... in Bucks Co.. and a like deed for 11 acres to Thomas Brock and Anthony Burton of the aforesaid county. Ackn: 20th da, 12th mo, 1695. Witnessed: Michael Newbould and Hannah English. Rec: 16th da, 2nd mo, 1696.

P. 59. Deed. Thomas Fairman of the town and county of Philadelphia, yeoman, for £10, 200 acres lying in town of Southampton ... Peter Groom. Land which was purchased from William Stanley, dec'd., granted to said William Stanley by a warrant dated 4th da, May, 1682.

P. 60. Deed. 29th da, May, 1695. Israel Taylor, Chester, to John Swift, chyrugeon of Bucks Co., yeoman, for £20, 60 acres, a part of 500 acres situated ... confirmed by a patent to Christopher Taylor 17th da, 2nd mo, 1684 beginning by Mill Creek. Ackn: 29th da, May, 1695. Wit: Robert Stacy and Thomas Fairman. Rec: the 11th da, 1st mo, 1696. Joseph Wood named as attorney for Israel Taylor.

P. 60. Patent. To William Biles, a parcel of land in Bucks Co. lying alongside of Delaware river ... [near] land of Joshua Board ... to land of

Richard Ridgway ... 173 acres granted by a warrant 9th da, 3rd mo, 1684 to William Biles. Rec: 16th da, 2nd mo, 1696.

P. 61. Deed. William Biles of Bucks Co., yeoman, for £80, to Samuel Beaks, aforesaid county, yeoman, 173 acres lying by Delaware river ... land of Joshua Board ... to land of Richard Ridgway, granted by a patent dated 31st da, 5th mo, 1684. Ackn: 14th da, 2nd mo, 1693. Rec: 11th da, 1st mo, 1695/6.

P. 62. Deed. William Croasdell and John Crosdell, sons and heirs of Thomas Crosdell, late of the Bucks Co., dec'd., for £14, paid by Jonathan Scaife, 100 acres lying by land of Robert Heaton, Jr., ... land of Jonathan Scaife, which is part of a tract of land granted by a patent dated 28 June 1692. Ackn: 10th da, 6th mo, 1695. Wit: Ezra Croasdell and Robert Heaton. Rec: 11th da, 1st mo, 1695/6.

P. 63. Deed. William Croasdell and John Crosdell, sons and heirs of Thomas Crosdell, late of Bucks Co., dec'd. for £24 paid by Robert Heaton, Jr. aforesaid county, husbandman, 170 acres lying at line of Robert Heaton, Sr. ... to land of said Croasdells ... land of Walter Bridgman, granted by a warrant dated 8th da, 1st mo, 1692. Ackn: 12th da, 10th mo, 1694. Witness Jonathan Scaife, William Darbe, William Hayhurst and John Cowgill. Rec: 11th da, 1st mo, 1695/6.

P. 64. Deed. John Green and his son, Thomas Green Bucks Co., yeomen, and Katherine Green, wife of John Green, and mother to said Thomas, for £100 paid by Joseph Large of aforesaid county, 200 acres lying in Buckingham in the aforesaid county, granted by patent dated 7th da, 4th mo, 1687. Ackn: 20th da, 3rd mo, 1693. Wit: William Dungan, Thomas Dungan, Edward Doyle, Jeremiah Dungan, Edward Doyle, Jeremiah Dungan, Jr. Rec: 17th da, 2nd mo, 1696. Power of Attorney. John Green, Thomas Green, and Katherine Green appoint John Cook as attorney to appear in open court to deliver to Joseph Large the above deed. Ackn: 12th da, 9th mo, 1694. Wit: Joseph Knight and Thomas Fairman. Rec: 17th da, 2nd mo, 1696.

P. 66. Indenture. 2nd da, 9th mo, 1694. Joseph Large, Bucks Co., husbandman and Samuel Carpenter of Philadelphia Co., for £50, 200 acres along the Delaware river [boundary] to land formerly of Mordecai Bowden but now the land of Thomas Williams ... land of William Dungan

... granted by a patent dated 20th da, 9th mo, 1693. Ackn: 2nd da, 9th mo, 1694. Wit: John McComb, Thomas Green, Thomas Fairman. Rec: 17th da, 2nd mo, 1696. Samuel Carpenter, of Philadelphia, merchant, appoints John Cook, Bucks Co., yeoman, to appear in open court for above mentioned conveyance. Ackn: 9th da, 9th mo, 1694. Wit: Joseph Knight, Thomas Fairman. Rec: 17th da, 2nd mo, 1696.

P. 68. Bond. Joseph Large, Bucks Co., husbandman, bound to Samuel Carpenter, Philadelphia, for the sum of 140 pounds. Wit: John McComb, Thomas Green, Thomas Fairman. 2nd da, 9th mo, 1694. Rec: 17th da, 2nd mo, 1696.

P. 68. Deed. Clement Dungan, Bucks Co., yeoman, for £7, to Joseph Large, aforesaid county, yeoman, 50 acres lying by the Delaware river ... [boundary near] land of Edward Doyal ..., part of land warranted dated 7th da, 1st mo, 1692. Ackn: 12th da, 1st mo, 1695/6. Wit: William Paxon, Job Bunting. Rec: 17th da, 2nd mo, 1696.

P. 69. Deed. Randle Blackshaw, Bucks Co., yeoman for £6 paid by Ralph Cowgill, of aforesaid county, husbandman, and son-in-law to said Randal, 112 acres standing on south side of Randle's land ... to land of John Smith. Land is part of a land granted to James Harrison late of Bucks Co., dec'd., released 30th da, 6th mo, 1682. Ackn: 1st da, 1st mo, 1694. Wit: William Biles, Richard Hough, Phineas Pemberton. Rec: 18th da, 2nd mo, 1696.

P. 70. Power of Attorney. Randel Blackshaw appointed Phineas Pemberton to acknowledge and deliver a deed in open court to Joseph Kirkbride and one to Ralph Cowgill, his son-in-law. Ackn: 11th da, 1st mo, 1695/6. Rec: 18th da, 2nd mo, 1696.

P. 70. Deed. Peter White and Elizabeth, his wife, Bucks Co., yeoman, for £15.10 paid by Samuel Carpenter, of town and county of Philadelphia, merchant, a parcel of land lying in Buckingham, Bucks Co. lying by Delaware river ... land of Peter White ... land of Phineas Pemberton ... land of John White ... land of Brock and Burton ..., part of land granted to Joseph English 20th da, 12th mo, 1695. Ackn: 16th da, 4th mo, 1696. Wit: Thomas Brock, Anthony Burton, William Croasdell, John Town. Rec: 1st da, 5th mo, 1696.

P. 71. Deed. 16th da, 1st mo, 1695. Peter White, his wife Elizabeth, granddaughter to Samuel Clift, late of Bucks Co., yeoman, of the one part and Thomas Brock and Anthony Burton, both of the aforesaid county, yeomen, for an unknown consideration a parcel of land lying in Buckingham ... corner of John White's land containing 22 acres ..., which descended to Joseph English, son-in-law to said Clift. Ackn: 13th da, 1st mo, 1695. Wit: Thomas Musgraves, John Smith, John Town, Phineas Pemberton. Rec: 1st da, 5th mo, 1696.

P. 73. Indenture. 8th da, 4th mo, 1696. Thomas Brock, Bucks Co., yeoman, of one part for an unknown consideration to Anthony Burton, yeoman of aforesaid county, two parcels of land lying in Buckingham containing 11 acres of a tract of land granted to Thomas Brock, Anthony Burton and Peter White, by Joseph English dated 20th da, 12th mo, 1695 and since divided. Ackn: 8th da, 4th mo, 1696. Wit: William Emley, Joseph Crop, Thomas P. Kirk. Rec: 1st da, 5th mo, 1696.

P. 75. Deed. Matts Keen, Dance Loyke, Elizabeth Jonson and Katherine Johnson, joint tenants by the last will of John Clawson, dec'd. for £9 paid by Britain Johnson, Neshaminy Creek, Bucks Co., 50 acres. Ackn: 30th da, Dec, 1695. Wit: Thomas Fairman, James Boyden, John Erickson. Rec: 1st da, 5th mo, 1696.

P. 76. Deed. Thomas Fairman for £11 paid him by Dunken Williams, near Neshaminay Creek, 100 acres ... standing by land of Nehemiah Allen ... to land of said Dunken ... to land of Nathaniel Harden and is part of 4000 acres granted by a warrant 29th da, Oct, 1684 to Stanley and Peter Burton. Ackn: 4 Sep 1695. Witness. James Boyden, James Boyden, Jr. Edward Land. Rec: 10th da, Jun, 1696.

P. 77. Deed. 17th da, 3rd mo, 1694. Ralph Ward of town and county of Philadelphia, cordwainer, and Thomas Jenner of said place, carpenter, to Thomas Stakehouse, Jr., Middle Township, Bucks Co., for £30, 240 acres lying on east side of Neshaminy Creek granted by warrant to Philip Alford dated 7th da, 6th mo, 1682. Ackn: 17th da, 3rd mo, 1694. Wit: John Furniss, John Town, Ezra Croasdell. Rec: 1st da, 5th mo, 1696.

P. 79. Deed. Joseph Growden, Bucks Co., Gent., for £86 paid by John Naylor, of said county, 450 acres which was formerly in possession of

Joseph Holden and sold unto Joseph Growden 10/2/1693 by Samuel Beakes the sheriff. Ackn: 13/1/1694. Wit: William Biles, Richard Hough. Rec: 2/5/1696.

P. 80. Deed. Samuel Beakes, Bucks Co., yeoman for £23, paid by John Neild of said county, laborer, 236 acres lying by line of William Dark ... to land of said Samuel Beakes, purchased from John Cuff of Ashhole, Somerset Co., yeoman. Ackn: 10th da, 4th mo, 1696. Rec: 2/5/1696.

P. 81. Deed. William Biles, Bucks Co. and Jane, his wife, formerly the wife of Thomas Adkison, late of aforesaid county, dec'd. for the better education of children of aforesaid Thomas Adkison and for £90 paid by George Biles, 300 acres lying along line of John Rowland ... lands of William Duncan ... lands of Randle Blackshaw ... lands of Charles Brigham. Ackn: 10th da, 4th mo, 1696. Wit: Joseph Growdon, Henry Baker, Samuel Beakes. Rec: 10th da, 4th mo, 1696.

P. 82. Bond. William Biles of Bucks Co., yeoman is bound unto Phineas Pemberton and Richard Hough, both of aforesaid county, yeomen, for £180. William Biles shall pay to Isaac Adkison, eldest son of Thomas Adkison, late of aforesaid county, dec'd. (and son-in-law of William Biles), William Adkison, and Samuel Adkison each the sum of £30 when they become 21 years of age, and they shall release all title to 300 acres which was taken up and sealed by his father Thomas Adkison, lying by the land of John Rowland. Ackn: 10th da, 4th mo, 1696. Wit: Joseph Growdon, Henry Beakes and Samuel Beakes. Rec: 2nd da, 5th mo, 1696.

P. 83. Deed. Henry Marjoram for £80 to Henry Baker, of aforesaid county, 250 acres standing by Delaware River ... [boundary] to land of Henry Margoram lately purchased from Richard Hough. Ackn: 8th da, 4th mo, 1696. Wit: Jonathan Scaife, Joshua Cooper, William Biles. Rec: 2nd da, 6th mo, 1696.

P. 84. Deed. Anthony Burton, Bucks Co., yeoman, to William Croasdale for £4.10 a lot of land, lying in Buckingham, Bucks Co. ... a corner of Samuel Bown's land ..., part of 11 acres granted to Burton and Thomas Brock by a deed from Joseph English dated 20th da, 12th mo, 1695 since partitioned between Brock and Burton dated 8th da, 4th mo, 1696. Ackn: 22nd da, 4th mo, 1696. Wit: Joseph Wood, Joseph Kirkbride and

Daniel Gardner. Rec: 2nd da, 5th mo, 1696.

P. 85. Deed. Anthony Burton, Bucks Co., yeoman, for £3.15 paid by Henry Baker of the aforesaid county, yeoman, 11 acres lying in Buckingham beginning at land of Thomas Brock, which Joseph English granted to Burton by deed dated 8th da, 4th mo, 1696. Ackn: 27th da, 4th mo, 1696. Wit: Joseph Wood, Joseph Kirkbride, Daniel Garner. Rec: 2nd da, 5th mo, 1696.

P. 86. Deed. Thomas Brocket, Anthony Burton, Peter White and Elizabeth, his wife all of Bucks Co., for £7, paid by Phineas Pemberton for a parcel of land containing 1 ½ acres lying in Buckingham ... [boundary] at line of John White's land ... to Mill dam ... to Cedar Street. William Crosdale appointed power of attorney to deliver deed. Ackn: 16th da, 4th mo, 1696. Wit: Henry Baker, Samuel Carpenter, John Towne, William Crosdell. Rec: 3rd da, 5th mo, 1696.

P. 89. Deed. John Otter, of Philadelphia Co., merchant, for £12 paid by Henry Baker, Bucks Co., yeoman, 225 acres ... [boundary near] land of Jonathan Eldridge ... containing in the whole 250 acres granted by a patent to said John Otter dated 23rd da, 1st mo, 1687/8. Ackn: 4th da, 4th mo, 1694. Wit: John Jones, Richard Woodworth. Rec: the 1st da, 8th mo, 1696.

P. 90. Patent. To John Otter, 225 acres lying by land of Jonathan Eldridge, dated 3rd da, 11th mo, 1683. Ackn: 3rd da, Mar, 1687/8. Rec: 1st da, 8th mo, 1696.

P. 91. Deed. Randel Blackshaw, Bucks Co., yeoman, for £6.8, paid by Joseph Kirkbride of aforesaid county, yeoman, a parcel of land containing 3 and 4 acres lying by land of Joseph Kirkbride ...land of Randel Blackshaw granted by deed from James Harrison, late of aforesaid county, dec'd. 30th da, 6th mo, 1682. Ackn: 14th da, 12th mo, 1693. Wit: Richard Hough, Jane Duncan and Phineas Pemberton. Rec: 9th da, 7th mo, 1696.

P. 92. Deed. Joseph Kirkbride, Bucks Co., carpenter, for £50, to Gideon Freeborn, Rhode Island, yeoman, 500 acres, granted by warrant dated 25th da, 6th mo, 1684 to Thomas Adkinson. Land lying next to Joseph Howell's land ... land of Arthur Cokes. Thomas Adkinson affirmed sale dated 12th da, 8th mo, 1687 to Joseph Kirkbride by deed recorded Book A, Folio 132, Vol 1. Ackn: 23 July 1696. Wit: Samuel Beaks and William Crosdell. Rec: 1st da, 8th mo, 1696.

P. 94. Deed. William Dark, Bucks Co., for a certain amount of money by son, John Dark and natural affection which William Dark has for son, 500 acres beginning at corner of land of Charles Biles, granted by warrant dated 13th da, 2nd mo, 1683 to William Dark, glover. Ackn: 1st da, 10th mo, 1696. Wit: Thomas Brock and Steven Newell. Rec: 11th da, 10th da, 1696.

P. 95. Deed. Samuel Bowne, son and heir of John Bowne, late of Long Island, New York, dec'd.. for 6 shillings paid by Hannah Willets and for the natural love and affection which he bears towards the said Hannah, the only child of his sister, Abigail, and Richard Willets of Jericoe, Oyster Bay, Queens Co., 500 acres lying next to land of Robert Turner along Neshaminy Creek, granted by a patent dated 10th da, 2nd mo, 1680. Ackn: 7th da, 4th mo, called June, 1696. Wit: John Rodman, John Dole and Samuel Haight. Rec: 11th da, 10th mo, 1696. Richard Willits, of Jerico, New York, guardian unto his dau., Hannah Willets appoints Samuel Beaks, Bucks Co., as his attorney to receive the deed for above property.

P. 96. Deed. James Harrison, late of Bucks Co., dec'd. did grant, for a certain amount of money paid by William Kenerly, 250 acres of land, being part of the 5000 acres purchased by said James Harrison from William Penn bearing the date of 20th da, 2nd mo, 1682 but the said 250 acres not being confirmed to said William Kenerley (formerly of the county of Chester, Kingdom of England) to be conveyed to said William Kennerly by deed executed by Phineas Pemberton. Ackn: 5th mo, 1st mo, 1696. Wit: Richard Hough, William Biles and Henry Baker. Rec: 12th da, 1st mo, 1696/7.

P. 97. Deed. Peter White, Bucks Co., yeoman, and his wife Elizabeth, for £12 paid by Joseph Growden, of Trevose, Bensalem, Bucks Co., Gent., 1/2 acre being part of a moiety [one-half] of 22 acres, deed from his father-in-law, Joseph English, bearing the date of 20/12/1695. Thomas Brock and Anthony Burton being the purchasers of the other half of the 22 acres on 16/1/1695. Ackn: 8th da, 10th mo, 1696. Wit: Stephen Beakes, Samuel Beakes and Anthony Burton. Rec: 12th da, 1st mo, 1696/7.

P. 99. Deed. Clement Dungan, Bucks Co., yeoman, for £5 paid by Edward Doyle of aforesaid county, 50 acres lying beside the Delaware River ... [boundary] to land of widow Dungan ... to land of Clement Dungan ... to land of Joseph Large, which is part of a tract granted to Clement Dungan by a patent dated 7th da, 11th mo, 1692. Ackn: 9th da, 4th mo, 1696. Wit: John Cutler and John Webster. Rec: 12th da, 1st mo, 1696/7.

P. 100. Patent. 16th da, 10th mo, 1689. 100 acres formerly rented by John Webster and which said John Webster now purchases together with 55 acres ... land of William Duncan ... Gilbert Wheeler ... said land granted by a warrant dated 11 Feb 1692/3 for 1 shilling for each hundred acres. Ackn: 24 March 1692/3. Wit: William Markham and Robert Turner. Rec: 12th da, 1st mo, 1696/7.

P. 101. Deed. John Webster to Samuel Burgess, Jr., for £22, 150 acres lying in Bucks Co. ... [boundary adjoining] land of William Duncan ... to land of Gilbert Wheelers, granted by a warrant dated 11 Feb 1692/3 to John Webster. Ackn: 1st da, 10th mo, 1696. Wit: Richard Hough, Daniel Gardner and Samuel Burgess. Rec: 12th da, 1st mo, 1696/7.

P. 102. Deed. Thomas Dure, Bucks Co., laborer, for £30, paid by William Darby, of aforesaid county, 54 acres beginning at land of Samuel Darke ... said land granted to Thomas Dickerson, late husband to Alice Dickerson by dec'd. from Philip Conway dated 6th da, 4th mo, 1687 and by her to Thomas Dure. Ackn: 1st da, 10th mo, 1696. Wit: Richard Hough, Daniel Gardner, Samuel Burgess. Rec: 12th da, 1st mo, 1696/7.

P. 103. Deed. William Sandford, of Mill Creek near Peter Aldrich's Island, planter, for £2, 106 acres, to Henry Bircham, late of Molberton, Norfolk County, Kingdom of England, a linen weaver, now of Mill Creek, land granted to Richard Noble ... [boundary adjoining] land of William Sandford ... to Peter Aldrich's island ... Ackn: 23rd da, ?/1696/7. Rec: 12th da, 1st mo, 1696/7.

P. 104. Deed. 4th da, Sep 1694. Henry Bircham, of Burlington, West Jersey, weaver and Margaret his wife on one part and William Hinges, of late Bermudas, 206 acres granted by a warrant dated 23rd da, 8th mo, 1682 for £23. Ackn: 4th da, Sep, 1694. Wit: Samuel Harriott, Miriam Harriott and George Hutchinson. Rec: 10th da, 1st mo, 1696/7. Page 104, 105. Phineas Pemberton appointed attorney to receive the above deed. Wit: Thomas Billis, Thomas Bibb. Rec: 12th da, 1st mo, 1696/7.

P. 105. Deed. 9 Sep 1696. William Henges and Ann, his wife, of Barmudoes, Burlington Co., West New Jersey, a sailor, to Thomas Bills of Burlington, linen weaver, on the other part. Whereas by the appointment of Edmund Andrews formerly governor of New York and by order of the court, William Sanford was seized of 206 acres of land granted by a warrant dated 23 Oct 1682 containing 106 acres did convey to Henry Burchen(?) and Margaret, his wife, of Burlington, by deed date 4 Sep 1694. William Henges and wife, Ann did grant for a consideration of £20 a parcel of land containing 106 to Thomas Bills. Ackn: 9th da, Sep, 1696. Wit: Obadiah Horton, Thomas Richards and Thomas Bibb. Rec: 23rd da, 7th mo, 1696.

P. 107. Deed. Arthur Cook, and Margaret, John Cook and his wife Mary, Philadelphia Co. for £245 paid by John Circuit, Bucks Co., 400 acres granted by a warrant dated 9th da, 5th mo, 1684 lying at corner of land of William Dungan ... by Delaware River. Ackn: 20th da, 8th mo, 1696. Wit: Joseph Burkett, Phineas Pemberton. Rec: 12th da, 1st mo, 1696/7.

P. 108. Bond. Arthur Cook and John Cook, of Philadelphia, yeoman are bound unto John Circuit, Bucks Co. for £490, for a parcel of land containing 400 acres. Ackn: 20th da, 8th mo, 1696. Wit: Joseph Walter and Phineas Pemberton. Rec: 12th da, 1st mo, 1697/7.

P. 109. Deed. William Biles, Bucks Co. yeoman, and attorney to William Lawrence of Sutton, Chester Co., Kingdom of England for £250, to him paid and secured by John Talman, Joseph Shinn, Samuel Shinn, and Benjamin Field, yeomen, all of Flushing, Queens, Long Island, New York. The receipt where of said William Biles does hereby acknowledge and doth acquit and forever discharge to William Lawrence, attorney for John Talman, Joseph Shim, Samuel Shim and Benjamin Field a tract of land lying in Bucksburg ... [near] land of Denis Rockford containing 5000 acres granted to Thomas Hudson dated 23 rd da, Apr, 1683 recorded in Book A, Vol 1, 240, 249. Ackn: 9th da, 1st mo, 1696/7. Wit: Richard

Hough, Joseph Milinor, Enoch Yardley, Phineas Pemberton. Rec: 10th da, 1st mo, 1696/7. Stephen Beakes appointed attorney to appear in open court to receive the above deed. Wit: Joseph Mathis, Abigail Pemberton, Phineas Pemberton. Rec: 12th da, 1st mo, 1696/7.

P. 110. Deed. Joshua Hooks, of Makefield, Bucks Co., yeoman, for £50, a parcel of land granted to Daniel Hooks and his begotten, Jane Worrellow, his intended wife, granted to Joshua Hooks by warrant dated 13th da, 8th mo, 1683. Ackn: 8th da, 10th mo, 1696. Wit: Ruben Pownall, Jacob Janney, Abel Janney. Rec: 12th da, 1st mo, 1696/7.

P. 112. Deed. William Biles, Bucks Co. yeoman, and attorney to Thomas Hudson of Sultoy(?), Chester Co., Kingdom of England, Gent., for £25 from Mathias Harvey, 100 acres lying between land of George Stone and Joseph Milner, part of a warrant to Thomas Hudson dated 24th da, May, 1683 ... near land of Richard Hough. Ackn: Henry Baker, Jamey Howeyte, Phineas Pemberton, Abigail Pemberton. Rec: 12th da, 1st mo, 1696/7.

Page 111. Power of Attorney. Mathias Howie, of Flushing on Long Island, New York do appoint Peter Worrall to appear in open court to receive the deed. Ackn: 21st da, 11th mo, 1696/7. Wit: Phineas Pemberton and Abigail Pemberton. Rec: 12th da, 1st mo, 1696/7.

P. 113. Deed. John Clark, late of Bucks Co. and now of West Jersey, Burlington Co., husbandman, for £15 paid by Joseph Milnor of aforesaid Bucks Co., a parcel of land lying next to land of Jonathan Eldridge ... being part of a tract granted to Edward Cuff by patent dated 14th da, 4th mo, 1688 and sold to Henry Marjorum by deed dated 12th da, 1st mo, 1689 recorded in Book A, Vol 1, page 325, 326 containing 206 acres. Ackn: 1st da, 10th mo, 1696. Wit: Seth Hill, James Howertz, John Nield. Rec: 1st da, 11th mo, 1696.

P. 114. Deed. Robert Heaton, Jr. Bucks Co., for £75 paid by Jonathan Scaife, of said county, 107 acres lying by land of Robert Heaton, Sr. ... to land of Walter Bridgman ... to lands of Thomas Crosdale, part of land granted by patent dated 8th da, 4th mo, 1692 to Thomas Crosdell and John Crosdell, heir of Thomas Crosdell by deed dated 11th da, 1st mo, 1695/6 recorded in Volume A, Vol 1, page 63, 64. Ackn: 10th da, 1st mo, 1696/7. Wit: John Croasdell, Ralph Cowgill, Joseph Milner. Rec: 26th da,

1st mo, 1697.

P. 115. Deed. Abel Janney, Bucks Co., blacksmith for £45 paid by Richard Hough, of aforesaid county, 236 acres granted by a patent dated 13/2/1683 to Charles Biles and William Biles and since divided into two equal parts and sold to said Abel Janney. Ackn: 6/1/1696. Wit: Jonathan Scaife, Daniel Hooks and Stephen Beakes. Rec: 26/1/1697.

P. 116. Deed. Enoch Yardley, Bucks Co., yeoman, for a certain deal made by Reuben Pownall of aforesaid county, 2 acres lying along Delaware River ... [boundary] to said Reuben Pownall, part of land patented dated 3 Jan 1687/88 to William Yardley, dec'd. father of said Enoch Yardley. Ackn: 9th da, 4th mo, 1696. Wit: James Willis, Jacob Janney. Rec: 27th da, 1st mo, 1697.

P. 117. Deed. Elizabeth Bennett, of city and county of Philadelphia and Edmund Bennett, late of aforesaid county, dec'd., for £54 from Thomas Yardley, Burlington Co., West Jersey, a parcel of land lying ... [near] land of Richard Dungworth, granted to said Dungworth by warrant dated 20th da, 3rd mo, 1683 ... and after laid out to said Edmond Bennett by warrant bearing date 5 Sep 1692. Ackn: 10th da, 1st mo, 1696. Wit: John Griffin, John Otter and Enoch Yardley. Rec: 2nd da, 1st mo, 1697.

P. 118. Deed. Samuel Clift, of Bucks Co., husbandman, sold to Richard Dungworth, of said county, joyner, for £5, 50 acres lying alongside Mill Creek. If it is convenient to build a mill upon said creek, both parties are jointly concurred to do so. Said Richard is to have three years to pay said amount. Rec: 27th da, 1st mo, 1697.

P. 119. Deed. Richard Dungworth, of near Tawron, joyner, sendeth greeting whereas Samuel Clift, late of Bucks Co., husbandman, dec'd. by writing dated 23rd da, 9th mo, 1682 conveyed a parcel of land containing 50 acres beginning at land of Richard Dungworth for £7 paid by Edmund Bennett of Mill Creek, Bucks Co. yeoman. Ackn: 13 Oct 1683. Wit: Edward Land and Robert Roe. Rec: 27th da, 1st mo, 1697.

P. 119. Deed. John White, Buckingham, Bucks Co., yeoman, for £4 paid by John Smith, 37 acres lying in the town of Buckingham, standing by land of Richard Burgess ... to land of John White, patented on 10th da,

12th mo, 1690. Ackn: 6th da, 1st mo, 1696/7. Wit: Samuel Darke, Abraham A. Cox and John Town. Rec: 30th da, 1st mo, 1697.

P. 120. Deed. John Smith, Bucks Co., blacksmith, for £15 paid by John Town, Buckingham, aforesaid county, a parcel of land lying in Buckingham ... by land of Francis Rossell ... to land of John Smith ... to land of Thomas Brooks. Ackn: 8th da, 1st mo, 1696/7. Wit: Joseph Kirkbride, Stephen Beakes, John Town. Rec: 30th da, 1st mo, 1697.

P. 121. Deed. John Smith, Bucks Co., blacksmith for £9 paid by Thomas Musgrove, York County, Kingdom of England, clothier, 18 ½ acres lying in Buckingham ... land of John Town, which is part of land John Smith purchased from John White by deed dated 6th da, 12th mo, 1696/7 ... land of Thomas Brock ... Ackn: 8th da, 1st mo, 1696/7. Wit: Stephen Beakes, Joseph Kirkbride, John Town. Rec: 30th da, 1st mo, 1697.

P. 123. Deed. John Town, Bucks Co., weaver, for £7 paid by Samuel Carpenter, of city and county of Philadelphia, merchant, a parcel of land lying near the old house formerly Francis Rossell's ... to land that John Town bought from John Smith. Ackn: 9th da, 1st mo, 1696/7. Wit: Stephen Beakes, Daniel Hookes, Joseph Kirkbride. Rec: 30th da, 1st mo, 1697.

P. 123. Deed. Henry Pawlin, Bucks Co. husbandman for £16 paid him by Richard Burgess of aforesaid county, 480 acres lying by land of Arthur Cooks ... land of Henry Paxson. Ackn: 14 Dec 1689. Wit: James Paxson, William Plumly and Israel Taylor. Rec: 26th da, 1st mo, 1697.

P. 123. Deed. John Smith, Bucks Co., blacksmith, for £11 paid by Richard Burgess, of said county, a parcel of land. Ackn: 25 Oct 1695. Wit: Joseph Town, Anthony Burton, Andrew Heath and William Emley. Rec: 6th da, 2nd mo, 1697.

P. 125. Patent. To Robert Carter, 250 acres, standing by land of William Carter, granted by a warrant dated 23rd da, 3rd mo, 1683 for 1 shilling. Ackn: 28th da, 10th mo, 1684. Rec: 6th da, 2nd mo, 1697.

P. 126. Deed. John Carter, Bucks Co., husbandman, for £50 paid to him by John Smith of aforesaid county, 250 acres, granted by a patent dated 28th da, 10th mo, 1684 to Robert Carter, father of John Carter, said acreage allotted and set out after death of said Robert Carter, dated 1st da, 8th mo, 1689. Ackn: 12th da, 1st mo, 1696. Wit: James Heywood, William Dark, Phineas Pemberton, Abigail Pemberton. Rec: 6th da, 2nd mo, 1697.

P. 127. Deed. Randal Blackshaw, Bucks Co., yeoman, for £400 paid by Joseph Kirkbride, of aforesaid county, yeoman, 500 acres bound by land formerly of Thomas Smith ... land formerly of Leills and Rowlands ... part of lands said Randal Blackshaw purchased from James Harrison, late of aforesaid county, dec'd., dated 13th da, 6th mo, 1682. Ackn: 1st mo, 1st mo, 1696/7. Wit: Jacob Janney, Enoch Yardley and Joseph Milnor. Rec: 6th da, 2nd mo, 1697.

P. 128. Deed. Randal Blackshaw, Bucks Co. to Nehemiah Blackshaw, son of Randal Blackshaw, for a certain sum of money, 800 acres adjoining land of John Clows, laborer of aforesaid county, laid out to Randal Blackshaw, land purchased from James Harrison, dec'd. of aforesaid county last day, 6th mo, 1682. Ackn: 1st da, 1st mo, 1696. Wit: Jacob Janney, Enoch Yardley, Joseph Milnor. Rec: 6th da, 2nd mo, 1697.

P. 129. Deed. Randal Blackshaw, Bucks Co., for the natural affection he has towards his grandsons, to Abraham Cowgill and Nehemiah Cowgill, sons of Ralph Cowgill and for consideration of 6 shillings, a certain lot of land lying in Wrightstown, containing 200 acres lying next to land of James Harrison ... purchased from said James Harrison, deed dated 13th da, 6th mo, 1682. Ackn: 1st da, 1st mo, 1696/7. Wit: Jacob Janney, Enoch Yardly, Joseph Kirkbride. Rec: 6th da, 2nd mo, 1697.

P. 130. Deed. Ralph Cowgill, Bucks Co., husbandman, for £35 paid by Joseph Kirkbride, of aforesaid county, 112 acres lying next to land of formerly Randal Blackshaw, granted to Randal Blackshaw by deed dated 5th da, 1st mo, 1694, recorded in Bucks Book B, page 69, 70. Ackn: 11th da, 1st mo, 1696/7. Wit: Joseph Milnor, Enoch Yardley, Jacob Janney. Rec: 8th da, 2nd mo, 1697.

P. 131. Deed. Israel Taylor, late of Bucks Co. and now of Tenecum Island, Oyster Co., chyrugeon, son and heir of Christopher Taylor, late of Tenecum, Gent., dec'd., land granted by a warrant dated 15th da, 5th mo, 1684 containing 500 acres granted by a patent at Philadelphia in Patent Book A, page 191. To Christopher Taylor by deed dated 7th da,

2nd mo, 1685, recorded in Philadelphia, Book C2, Vol 3, page 63. Said Israel Taylor did sell 150 acres out of said 500 acres to Christopher Wetherill and 60 acres to John Swift for £100 to be paid by John Griffith, Bucks Co., cordwainer. Ackn: 22nd da, Mar, 1697. Wit: John Brock, James Heaton and Da. Lloyd. Rec: 8th da, 2nd mo, 1697.

P. 132. Indenture. 10th da, 3rd mo, 1685. Edward Smith, Burlington, West Jersey, yeoman, to Joseph Kirkbride of Bucks Co., linen weaver, for £13.10, 150 acres beginning at land of Robert Lucas, granted by warrant dated 28th da, 4th mo, 1683 and laid out by warrant to Edward Smith dated 6th da, Apr, 1689. Ackn: 1st da, 2nd mo, 1697. Wit: Richard Guy, Thomas Coleman and James Hill. Rec: 8th da, 2nd mo, 1697.

P. 133. Deed. Grace Langhorne, Bucks Co., relict of Thomas Langhorne, late of said county, dec'd., and Jeremiah Langhorne, her son and William Biles, said county, her son-in-law and Sarah Biles, her dau., wife of said William, for £18 paid by William Paxson of aforesaid county, 90 acres ... [boundary adjoining] land of James Paxon, part of a tract of land granted by warrant dated to Thomas Langhorne 5 Sep 1687. Ackn: 9th da, 4th mo, 1697. Wit: Thomas Stackhouse, Jr. and John Boerdaill. Rec: 9th da, 6th mo, 1697.

P. 134. Deed. Joseph Growdon, Bucks Co. for £70, paid by William Duncan of aforesaid county, 600 acres, [boundary adjoining] land of Thomas Knight. Ackn: 1st da, 2nd mo, 1697. Wit: Stephen Newel and Francis Searle. Rec: 9th da, 6th mo, 1697.

P. 136. Deed. Samuel Carpenter, of Philadelphia, merchant, and Phineas Pemberton, Bucks Co., attorneys for Thomas Musgrove, of Halifax, Yorkshire Co., England, clothier, 600 acres ... [boundary adjoining] land of James Claypool, being part of 1200 acres granted to Henry Bayley late of Yorkshire, dec'd., and whose son and heir, by the name of Henry Bayley conveyed on 15 Dec 1696 for £50 secured to be paid by Valentine Hudleston of Dartmouth, Briston Co., Massachusetts. Ackn: 3rd da, 6th mo, 1697. Wit: David Lloyd, Isaac Waterman, James Hawirth and Abigail Pemberton. Rec: 8th da, 7th mo, 1697.

P. 138. Deed. Charles Read, Philadelphia, taylor, and husband to Annie, the late wife of Edward Stanton, late of Bucks Co., joiner, dec'd., for £40 paid by Thomas Rogers of aforesaid county, husbandman, 100 acres lying in Bucks Co. ... [boundary adjoining] land of Robert Hall, granted by a patent dated 2nd da, 6th mo, 1684 to Ralph Smith and said Ralph Smith by his will dated 9th da, 2nd mo, 1685 appointed James Harrison, to sell said 110 acres to Edward Stanton dated 1st da, 4th mo, 1686. Ackn: 13th da, 6th mo, 1694. Wit: John Rowland, Edmund Lovett and Edward Mayot. Rec: 24th da, 1st mo, 1697. [See Book a, page 42.]

P. 139. Deed. Thomas Rogers, Bucks Co., husbandman, for £60 paid by Edmund Lovett, 103 acres granted by Charles Read and Annie, his wife to Thomas Rogers on 13th da, 6th mo, 1694. Ackn: 12th da, 10th mo, 1694. Wit: Samuel Beakes and Joseph Steward. Rec: 24th da, 7th mo, 1697.

P. 140. Deed. Edmund Lovett, Bucks Co. yeoman, for £25 paid by John Rowland of aforesaid county, 100 acres adjoining said Lovett's land ... fronting the Delaware River, granted to Thomas Rogers by deed from Charles Read and Annie, his wife, dated 13th da, 6th mo, 1694. Ackn: 7th da, 7th mo, 1697. Wit: Abraham Cox and John Shaw. Rec: 24th da, 7th mo, 1697.

P. 141. Deed. Joseph Paul, Oxford Township, Philadelphia Co., a parcel of land by Southampton, Bucks Co. ... land of John Parsins ... to land of Arthur Cook, Job Howell and Philip Conway ... containing 206 acres confirmed to Joseph Paule by deed from Edward Bremman, parish of Shepton, Summersset, Kingdom of England, clothier dated 10th da, 7th mo, 1685, said 256 acres granted as part of 100 acres granted by warrant dated 10th da, Mar, 1682 for £24 paid by George Willard of township of Marple, Chester Co., yeoman. Ackn: 21st da, Aug, 1697. Wit: William Gabitas, John Shaw and Francis Cook. Rec: 11th da, 8th mo, 1697.

P. 142. Deed. William Buckman, Newton, Bucks Co., yeoman, for £24 paid by John Shaw, of said county, yeoman, 300 acres lying next to land of Jacob Howell ... to land of Thomas Rowland ..., granted to William Buckman by warrant dated 13th da, 7th mo, 1686. Ackn: 7th da, 9th mo, 1697. Wit: James Paxon, William Croasdell, John Rowland. Rec: 11th da, 8th mo, 1697.

P. 143. Patent. Granted for 1 shilling for each 100 acres, 300 acres lying next to land of Thomas Rowland ... land by Neshaminah Creek ... land of Thomas Revells. To Elizabeth Barber, relict of John Barber, dec'd. and Robert Webb, new husband of Elizabeth Barber dated 7th da, 6th mo, 1684. Ackn: 5th da, Oct, 1692. Wit: Samuel Carpenter, and William Markham. Rec: 11th da, 8th mo, 1697.

P. 143. Indenture. 17 March 1695 between Robert Webb, of town and county of Philadelphia and Elizabeth his wife to William Buckman, Bucks Co., husbandman, for £30, 300 acres standing by Neshaminah Creek ... land of Thomas Revells. Ackn: 17 March 1695. Wit: Jacob Hall and John Beckman. Rec: 11th da, 8th mo, 1697.

P. 145. Deed. Joseph Growden, Bucks Co., Gent., for £60 paid by Francis Searle, Bensalem, Bucks Co., 450 acres lying next to land of William Duncan ... to land of Joseph Growden ... land of Francis Searle. Ackn: 1st da, 6th mo, 1697. Wit: William Biles and Richard Heough. Rec: 11th da, 8th mo, 1697.

P. 146. Deed. Joseph Growdon, Bensalem, Bucks Co., Gent., paid by Thomas Knight of Bensalem of aforesaid county, yeoman, 80 acres lying in Bensalem ... [boundary] Francis Searle's land ... by Thomas Scott's land. Ackn: 1st da, 6th mo, 1697. Wit: William Biles and Richard Heough. Rec: 12th da, 8/1697.

P. 146. Deed. Thomas Stackhouse of Middletown, Bucks Co., joiner, for £7.10 paid by Ezra Croasdale, Middletown, weaver, 240 acres, purchased from Ralph Ward and Thomas Jenner both of Philadelphia, granted to Philip Alford and conveyed to Thomas Jenner and Ralph Ward 10th da, 3rd mo, 1694 recorded in Book B, Vol 1, page 77, 78 on 1/5/1696. Ackn: 5/8/1697. Wit: David Powell, Thomas Jenner and Henry Marjorun. Rec: 12th da, 8/1697.

P. 148. Deed. 28 June 1692. William Penn, Worminghurst, Sussex Co. granted to Thomas Crosdall, dec'd., and William Crosdell and John Crosdell, sons of Thomas Crosdall of Bucks Co., sold 270 acres leaving 400 acres in the possession of William Crosdell and John Crosdell. William Crosdell for 197 acres lying next to creek already granted by John Crosdell or warranted to be granted, he will at any time join with the said William Crosdell in sale of 197 acres lying near land of Robert Heaton ... [boundary adjoining] land of Jonathan Scaife ... land of Walter Bridgman. Ackn: 1/8/1697. Wit: Ralph Cowgill and Edmund Cowgill. Rec:

12th da, 8/1697.

P. 149. Deed. John Rowland, Bucks Co., and Priscilla, his wife, for £20 paid by Arthur Cook of the town and county of Philadelphia, merchant, a parcel of land lying next to land of Anthony Burton and Edward Pearson and land of Abraham Cox and Edmund Lovett, being part of land granted by warrant dated 2/6th mo, 1684 to Ralph Smith, dec'd. and by said Ralph Smith's last will dated 9th da, 2/1685 to Priscilla, wife of John Rowland. 10th da, 1st mo, 1694. Wit: Mahlon Stacy, Nicholas Waln, Edward Mayes and Phineas Pemberton. Rec: 12th da, 8/1697.

P. 150. Indenture. 7th da, Dec/1697. Joseph Growdon, Bensalem, Bucks Co. to Claus Johnson, of aforesaid place, yeoman, for £77, 200 acres near Neshaminah Creek adjoining land of Nathaniel Harding ... land of Samuel Allens, conveyed to Joseph Growdon by Thomas Fairman attorney of Robert Fairman dated 4th da, 10th mo, 1696. Ackn: 7 Dec 1697. Wit: Jacob Grosbeck, Johannis Vandegrift, Nicholas Vandegrift. Rec: 10th da, 10th mo, 1697.

P. 151. Deed. Joseph Growdon, Bucks Co., Gent., for £73 paid by Nicholas Vandergrift, Bensalem, Bucks Co., yeoman, a parcel of land lying in Bensalem along Delaware River adjoining land of Frederick Vandergrift. Ackn: 1st da, 5th mo, 1697. Wit: Jacob Grosbeck, Frederick Vandergrift, Leondert Vandergrift. Rec: 8/10th mo, 1697.

P. 153. Deed. Joseph Growdon, Bucks Co., gent., for £97, paid him by Leonard Vandegift, Bensalem, aforesaid county, yeoman, two pieces of land lying in Bensaleum near Delaware River adjoining land of Barndt Virkirks land ... land of Frederick Vandegrift ... to land of Nicholas Vandegrift, containing 106 acres. Ackn: 1st da, 5th mo, 1697. Wit: Nicholas Vandegrift, Jacob Grosbeck, Johannes Vandegrift. Rec: 10th da, 10th mo, 1697.

P. 154. Deed. Joseph Growdon, Bucks Co., for £106, paid by Johannes Vandegrift of Bensalem, two parcels of land in Bensalem lying on Delaware River, adjoining land of Barndt Virkirks land ... containing 106 acres for one lot and to land of Joseph Kirk ... containing 135 acres. Ackn: 1st da, 5th mo, 1697. Wit: Leonard Vandegrift, Nicholas Vandegift and Jacob Grosbeck. Rec: 11th da, 10th mo, 1697.

P. 155. Deed. Joseph Growdon, of Bensalum, Bucks Co., gent., for £50, paid by Frederick Vandegrift, Bensalem, aforesaid county, 106 acres lying in Bensalem by the land of his brother Nicholas Vandegrift ... land of Leonard Vandegrift. Ackn: 1st da, 5th mo, 1697. Wit: Johannes Vandegrfit, Nicholas Vandegrift, Jacob Grosbeck. Rec: 11th da, 10th mo, 1697.

P. 156. Deed. Joseph Growdon, Bensalum, Bucks Co., gent., for £50, paid by Barndt Virkirk of Bensalem, aforesaid county, yeoman, 106 acres lying in Bensaleum ... by land of Johannes Vandegrfit ... land of Leonard Vandegrift. Ackn: 1st da, 5th mo, 1697. Wit: Leonard Vandegrift, Nicholas Vandegrift and Jacob Grosbeck. Rec: 11th da, 10th mo, 1697.

P. 157, 158. Deed. Joseph Growdon, Bensalem, Bucks Co., gent., for £50 paid by Jacob Groisbeck, Bensalem, aforesaid county, yeoman, 106 acres lying in Bensalem beginning at line of Delaware River ... to land of formerly Walter Forrest ... land of John Gilbert ... to land of Johannes Vandegrift. Ackn: 1st da, 5th mo, 1697. Wit: Nicholas Vandegrift, Johannes Vandegrift and Leonard Vandegrift. Rec: 11th da, 10/1697.

P. 158. Bond. John Rowland, Bucks Co., yeoman, is bound to Arthur Cook, town and county of Philadelphia, merchant, for £50, dated 10th da, 1st mo, 1694. John Rowland to fulfill all covenants and grants of 193 acres purchased from Arthur Cook. Wit: Mahlon Stacy and Nicholas Waln. Rec: 11th da, 10th mo, 1697.

P. 159. Deed. John Smith, Bucks Co. for £40 paid by Henry Baker 100 acres lying by land of Richard Lurdys ... by land of Randal Blackshaw. Ackn: 15th da, 1st mo, 1696/7. Wit: John Harrison and Phineas Pemberton. Rec: 11th da, 10th mo, 1697.

P. 160. Indenture on 4th da, 10th mo, 1696. Thomas Fairman of Philadelphia Co., yeoman and attorney of Robert Fairman of the parish of St. Savious Southwark, Surrey, Kingdom of England, brewer, to Joseph Growdon, Bucks Co., for £95, 500 acres lying by Neshaminah Creek bounded by land of Samuel Allen ... Thomas Fairman, now in the possession of John Bowen by a sham sale of Anna Salter's ... land of Nathaniel Harding ... land of Joseph Growdon. Ackn: 4th da, 10th mo, 1696. Wit: Joshua Hastings and William Crossdell and Isaac Few. Rec:

11th da, 10th mo, 1697.

P. 161. Deed. Edward Evans, Philadelphia Co., husbandman, for £12 paid by Joseph Growdon, Bucks Co., 100 acres lying near Richard Davis, acquired by warrant 25 Apr 1682 by Francis Andrews and after his decease to his wife Elizabeth Andrews, and by her last will devised to Edward Evans, her kinsman and sole heir. 18/5th mo, 1698. Ackn: 6th da, 1st mo, 1696. Wit: David Lloyd, William Taylor. Rec: 11th da, 10th mo, 1697.

P. 162. Deed. Mathias Harvie of Makefield, Bucks Co., yeoman, for £20 paid by Joseph Milnor, of Makefield, yeoman, 10 acres lying in Makefield adjoining the line of Joseph Milnor. Ackn: 1st da, 7th mo, 1697. Wit: Thomas Brock, Anthony Burton. Rec: 11th da, 10th mo, 1697.

P. 163. Deed. William Biles, Bucks Co., yeoman, a parcel of Savanna or meadow land lying near land of Richard Heough ... being part of 100 acres of Savanna granted to Thomas Hudson, Sutton, Chester Co., Kingdom of England, dated 15 March 1692/3, to Richard Heough for £25 containing 25 acres. Ackn: 1st da, 8/1697. Wit: Thomas Growdon and Thomas Jenner. Rec: 11th da, 10th mo, 1697.

P. 164. Deed. Joseph Kirkbride, Bucks Co. yeoman, for £13.10 paid by Peter Webster of aforesaid county, husbandman, 50 acres lying next to widow Lucas's land ... to land of Samuel Dark ... being part of land granted by warrant dated 10th da, 3rd mo, 1689. Ackn: 8/10th mo, 1696. Wit: Samuel Dark and James Moore. Rec: 11th da, 10th mo, 1697.

P. 165. Deed. James Wood, son and heir of Richard Wood, late of city of Bristol, wire cooper, sends greetings. Whereas William Penn by lease and released dated 26 Sep 1681 and Richard Collins of Bath, Sumerset, clothier, for for the consideration therein mentioned granted 1200 acres to said Richard Collins, recorded in Philadelphia roll office. Richard Collins sold to Richard Wood on 20 May 1683, 1250 acres, recorded in Book A, page 244. After Richard Wood's decease it descended to his son James Wood. A parcel of land to Joseph Kirk, Philadelphia containing 50 acres for £16. Ackn: 4 Aug 1696. Wit: Abraham Carpenter and Thomas Cooke. Rec: 11th da, 10th mo, 1697.

P. 166. Deed. Samuel Carpenter, city and county of Philadelphia, merchant and sole executor of last will of Frances Rossill, late of Bucks Co., dec'd., dated 5th da, 8/1694, did give unto William Smith, Bucks Co., 100 acres out of his 500 acres which said Frances Rossill had purchased from Richard Lundy and did give unto Ralph Boone, Bucks Co. 200 acres of the 500 acres. Ackn: 1st da, 6th mo, 1697. Wit: Joseph Growdon, David Lloyd and Phineas Pemberton. Rec: 14th da, 10th mo, 1697.

P. 167. Deed. Thomas Brock, Buckingham, Bucks Co. yeoman, for £10 paid by Samuel Oldale, a lot of land lying in Buckingham next to land of William Crosdell, part of 11 acres conveyed by deed from Joseph English dated 20/12th mo, 1695 to Thomas and Anthony Brock. Ackn: 1st da, 7th mo, 1697. Wit: Joseph Milnor, Will Taylor and Edward Mayes. Rec: 14th da, 10th mo, 1697.

P. 168. Deed. Thomas Brock, Buckingham, Bucks Co. yeoman, for £8 paid by Edward Mayes of said county, weaver, a lot of land lying in Buckingham lying next to land of Phineas Pemberton adjoining land of Anthony Brock. Ackn: 1st da, 7th mo, 1697. Wit: Joseph Milnor, Will Taylor, Samuel Oldal. Rec: 14th da, 10th mo, 1697.

P. 169. Deed. John Rowland, Bucks Co., for £18 paid by Daniel Burgess of aforesaid county, wheelwright, 300 acres adjoining lands of Gilbert Wheeler, part of land granted to John Rowland and his brother, Thomas Rowland, by patent dated 30th da, 7th mo, 1685. Ackn: 3rd mo, 10th mo, 1697. Wit: Samuel Darke, Henry Marjorum and Phineas Pemberton. Rec: 16th da, 10th mo, 1697.

P. 170. Deed. John Towne, Bucks Co., yeoman, for £4 paid by Rebecca Wileford of said county, widow, a parcel of land lying in Buckingham adjoining land of Thomas Musgrove, part of land purchased by said John Towne from John Smith by deed dated 8/1st mo, 1697. Ackn: 7th da, 10th mo, 1697. Wit: Stephen Beakes and Enoch Yardley.

P. 171. Deed. Henry Baker, Bucks Co., yeoman, for £50 paid by Stephen Wilson of said county, yeoman, 250 acres, granted to Thomas Rowland by patent dated 15th da, 4th mo, 1685 and after decease of Thomas Rowland granted to Henry Baker by deed dated 8/10th mo, 1691. Ackn: 1st da, 8/1697. Wit: Samuel Beakes, Samuel Darke and Richard Heough. Rec: 8/10th mo, 1697.

P. 172. Deed. Robert Lucas, Bucks Co., yeoman, for £60 paid by his brother, Edward Lucas of aforesaid county land which was granted to said Robert Lucas from his father, Robert Lucas, dec'd., original patent dated 1st da, 5th da, 1684 containing 170 acres. Ackn: 4/10/1697. Wit: Samuel Beakes, John Town and Joseph Milnor. Rec: 8/10th mo, 1677.

P. 173. Patent. To Robert Lucas, 170 acres land of Gilbert Wheeler dated 9/3/1684. Ackn: 31st da, 5th mo, 1684. Rec: 16th da, 10th mo, 1697.

P. 173. Deed. A certain parcel of land in Bucks Co., bounded westward with vacant land and land of William Dark and land of Peter Webster and land formerly Jeffery Hawkins vacant containing 244 acres which said land Robert Lucas late of aforesaid county dec'd. in his life purchased from William Penn on 6/12/1687 and did give to his wife, Elizabeth. Elizabeth Lucas, relict of Robert Lucas and sole executrix of will and Giles Lucas and Edward Lucas, sons of the said Robert Lucas and Elizabeth Lucas, for £60 paid by Robert Lucas. Ackn: 6/10/1697. Wit: Samuel Dark, Stephen Wilson and Samuel Beakes. Rec: 16/10/1697.

P. 174. Deed. John Scarborough, Middlesex, Bucks Co. husbandman, for £24 paid him by Thomas Bayes, of Middletown, Bucks Co., 60 acres beginning at Thatcher's line, part of 250 acres granted by patent dated 14 July 1682. Ackn: 9th da, 1st mo, 1698. Wit: Joseph Kirkbride, Joshua Hoopes and Thomas Stackhouse. Rec: 10th da, 4th mo, 1698.

P. 174. Deed. James Dilworth, Philadelphia Co., yeoman, for £24 paid by Martin Wilderlaw, Bucks Co., 60 acres beginning at Neshaminah adjoining land of Widow Hearst, part of 500 acres granted by patent dated 10/8/1682. Ackn: 9/8/1697. Wit: Robert Heaton, Richard Waln. Rec: 10/4/1698.

P. 176. Deed. Daniel Jones, of Philadelphia, cordwainer, assigns to Daniel Smith, Burlington, West Jersey, butcher, 500 acres received from Andrew Robinson, for £60. Ackn: 11 Oct 1696. Wit: Edward Cole, Peter Reoudy(?). Rec: 10th da, 4th mo, 1698. Samuel Beakes appointed attorney to receive the deed for above conveyance.

P. 178. Deed. Samuel Robinson, gent., heir of Andrew Robinson, of the town of Philadelphia, merchant, for £100 from Daniel Jones, Philadelphia, 500 acres. Rec: 1st da, 4th mo, 1698.

P. 178. Deed. James Dilworth, of Philadelphia Co., yeoman, for £270 paid by Robert Heaton of Bucks Co., yeoman, 400 acres by the river Neshamiah, part of a patent dated 14th da, 2/1682 and the residue of 500 acres granted by warrant dated 10th da, 9th da, 1682. Ackn: 12th da, 8/1697. Wit: Nicholas Waller, Richard Waller. Rec: 11th da, 4th mo, 1698.

P. 178. Deed. Nicholas Waln, Philadelphia Co., yeoman, for £60 paid by Robert Heaton, Bucks Co., yeoman, 340 acres, granted by patent to Edmund Bennett dated 18/9th mo, 1690 and descended to Elizabeth Bennett, relict of said Edmund by his last will dated 2/9th mo, 1692. Ackn: 1st da, 10th mo, 1797. Wit: David Lloyd, John Cadder, Phineas Pemberton.

P. 180. Deed. Richard Burgess, brazier, and Elizabeth, his wife, Buckingham, Bucks Co., for £33 paid by Edmund Cowgill and Israel Morris, of said county, laborers, 40 acres lying in Newtown beginning at post of Arthur Cooks adjoining land of Henry Paxson, part of a patent granted to Henry Paullin dated 28 Nov 1680 and part to Richard Burgess and recorded 26th da, 1st mo, 1696 in Book B, page 123, 124. Ackn: 11th da, 10th mo, 1697. Wit: Henry Paxson, William Paxson and Jonathan Scaife. Rec: 11th da, 4th mo, 1698.

P. 181. Deed. James Paxson, Bucks Co. yeoman, for £100 paid by William Paxson, Jr., son of the said James Paxson, husbandman, 286 acres lying next to William Paxson ... to widow Langhorne's land, part of a patent dated 28/11th mo, 1692/3. Ackn: 8/4th mo, 1698. Wit: John Addington, William Darbe, Jonathan Scaife. Rec: 11th da, 4th mo, 1698.

P. 182. Thomas Hodson, of Mandesfield, Chester Co., Kingdom of England, two parcels of land, one containing 1000 acres late in the possession of Jacob Hall, and the other containing 5000 acres belonging to Thomas Hodson. William Biles appointed attorney to conduct business particular to these parcels of land. Ackn: Edward Cherry, John Hough, James Barber and John Houghton. Rec: 1st da, 5th mo, 1698.

P. 184. Job Bunting of Nottingham, Burlington Co., West New Jersey, yeoman, has quit claim to Stephen Twining of Newtown, Bucks Co. yeoman, all obligating debts. Ackn: 16th da, 3rd mo, 1698. Wit: Jeremiah Scaife and Jonathan Scaife. Rec: 1st da, 5th mo, 1698.

P. 185. Deed. Ralph Boone, Bucks Co., carpenter, and William Smith, of aforesaid county, laborer, for £20 paid by Thomas Brock of aforesaid county, yeoman, 300 acres, given to said Ralph Boone and William Smith by Francis Rossill, late of Bucks Co., dec'd. by will dated 5th da, 8/1696. Ackn: 1st da, 5th mo, 1698. Wit: Walter Pumphary, Daniel Beakes, William Biles, Jr., John White and John Dungan, Mary Huff. Rec: 16th da, 7th mo, 1698.

P. 186. Deed. Henry Flower, of town and county of Philadelphia, barber, for £29 paid by Thomas Hardin of Southampton, husbandman, 350 acres adjoining land of said Hardin ... land of Robert England ... land of George Jackman, originally granted to Enoch Flower, dec'd., by patent dated 2/8/1689 and conveyed to said Henry Flower by deed. Ackn: 25 April 1698. Wit: Thomas Gardiner, Phil Paulk, James Wood. Rec: 16th da, 7th mo, 1689.

P. 187. Deed. Thomas Brock, Bucks Co., yeoman, for £42 paid by Samuell Carpenter, Philadelphia, a parcel of land lying in Buckingham ... in the line that divides land of Thomas Brock ... line of formerly Francis Rossell's land ... 8 acres, part of land which Samuel Clift, dec'd., by last will dated 23rd da, 9th mo, 1682 devised to his son Joseph English and Joseph English by deed dated 10th da, 9th mo, 1683 conveyed three acres to Francis Rossell and to said Thomas Brock 27 acres by deed dated 6th da, 2/1692. Ackn: 1st da, 6th mo, 1698. Wit: John White, Francis White, Phineas Pemberton. Rec: 17th da, 7th mo, 1698.

P. 188. Deed. Clement Dungan, Thomas Dungan, Jeremiah Dungan and John Dungan, sons of Thomas Dungan, late of Bucks Co., yeoman, dec'd., for £250 paid by Walter Pumphary, 200 acres lying at corner of land of Joseph Large ... land formerly Mordecai Bowden, part of 400 acres patented to Thomas Dungan, Sr. on 1 Oct 1692. Ackn: 2/2/1698. Wit: William Biles, John Scarbrough and Phineas Pemberton. Rec: 20/7th mo, 1698.

P. 189. Deed. Clement Dungan, Jeremiah Dungan and John Dungan, sons of Thomas Dungan, for £60 paid by their brother, Thomas Dungan, 100 acres lying in Bucks Co. along river Delaware adjoining land formerly William Bennett ... to corner of Edward Doyle's land, part of land granted to Thomas Dungan dated 1 Oct 1692. Ackn: 22/5th mo, 1698. Wit: William Biles, Jr., John Scarborough and Phineas Pemberton. Rec: 20/7th mo, 1698.

P. 190. Indenture. 7th da, 11th mo, 1698. Thomas Fairman, Philadelphia Co. to James Plumly of Bucks Co., yeoman, for £60, 582 acres in Southampton, granted to Thomas Fairman by deed from Allen Foster and Mary, his wife, dated 14th da, 3rd mo, 1684 and is part of 1100 acres patented to Allen Foster on 3 May 1682. Land adjoining land of Joseph Pail and land of John Rush for use of John Jones of London. Ackn: 7th da, 11th mo, 1698. Wit: John Readman, William Hearn, John Condon. Rec: 20/11th mo, 1698.

P. 192. Deed. James Jacob of Philadelphia, cordwainer, a parcel of land in Southampton to Nicholas Randall, originally granted by patent 5th da, 2/1689 to John Luff of Philadelphia containing 225 acres adjoining land of Richard Wood. Whereas Philip Howell of Philadelphia, taylor and Mary Pearl late wife of Richard Hilliard, carpenter and Thomas Pearl, her new husband, by their indentures dated 30 July 1696 granted to James Jacob for £18.10, 250 acres. Ackn: 28/3rd mo, 1698. Wit: Mary Cooke, Francis Cooke, John Walker. Rec: 21st da, 7th mo, 1698.

P. 193. Deed. Anthony Burton, Bucks Co., yeoman, for £8 paid by Jeremiah Dungan, of aforesaid county, laborer, a parcel of land lying on the bank in Buckingham adjoining Walter Pumphary's land and land of Thomas Brock conveyed by deed from Joseph English dated 20/12th mo, 1695 and partitioned between Thomas and Anthony Brock by deed date 8/4th mo, 1696. Ackn: 5th da, 5th mo, 1698. Wit: Samuel Darke and Stephen Beakes. Rec: 21st da, 7th mo, 1698.

P. 194. Deed. Bartholomew Thatcher and Joseph Thatcher to Robert Heaton for £61.12, a parcel of land formerly owned by Cuthbert Hearst along Paxson's land ... land of John Scarborough and land formerly Nicholas Walln's ... containing 250 acres, conveyed to Richard Thatcher, dec'd., by deed dated 13th da, 8/1690 and by him devised by his last will dated 13/8/1690 to sons, Bartholomew Thatcher, Joseph Thatcher and Amos Thatcher. Ackn: 25th da, 4th mo, 1698. Wit: Henry Grubb, John

P. 196 Indenture. 10th da, 10th mo, 1698. Henry Paxson of Bucks Co., yeoman, and Margery Paxson his wife and Elizabeth Burgess, dau. of said Henry Paxson and relict of Richard Burgess late of Buckingham, dec'd., to James Plumly and John Plumly, sons in law to said Henry Paxson, husbandman, a parcel of land ... east of Henry Paxson's land ... land formerly of William Carter ... for £500, 500 acres. Ackn: 10th da, 10th mo, 1698. Wit: Jonathan Scaife, Joshua Hooks and William Paxson, Jr. Rec: 17th da, 10th mo, 1698.

P. 197. Patent. To Henry Paxson, 500 acres alongside Neshaminah Creek adjoining Henry Pawlings land ... to land of William Carter. Ackn: 17th da, 3rd mo, 1698. Rec: 17th da, 10th mo, 1698.

P. 199. Indenture. 3rd da, 7th mo, 1698. Samuel Carpenter, Philadelphia merchant, to Henry Baker, Bucks Co., yeoman, for £450, 25 acres in Buckingham adjoining land of Thomas Brock and Thomas Yardley ... land of Francis Rossill, late of Buckingham which said Frances Rossill was granted land by patent dated 30th da, 9th mo, 1689 ... Ackn: 3rd da, 7th mo, 1698. Wit: Abraham Hardman, Henry Mallows, Sarah Gow. Rec: 17th da, 10th mo, 1698.

P. 203. Deed. Charles Read and Amey, his wife, town and county of Philadelphia, merchant, 500 acres, granted by patent on 24 Jan 1681 to Amey Child late wife of Edward Stanton late of Bucks Co., dec'd., and now wife of Charles Read, for £25 paid by John Scarborough, Bucks Co., yeoman. Ackn: 10th da, 10th mo, 1698. Wit: Thomas Masters, Charles Plumby, and Daniel Camble. Rec: 20/10th mo, 1698.

P. 205. Deed. Henry Baker, Bucks Co., yeoman, for £140 paid by William Biles of aforesaid county, two parcels of land adjoining land of Richard Lundy containing 290 acres. Ackn: 1st da, 7th mo, 1698. Wit: Samuel Beakes, Richard Hough, Joseph Kirkbride. Rec: 20/10th mo, 1698. [Original deed gave previous purchasers of land].

P. 207. Indenture. 25 Apr 1683. William Penn, Worminghurst, Sussex Co. to Thomas Hudson, Sutton, Palatine Co., gent., for £9.1, for every 100 acres of 5000 acres, the first of March forever. Ackn: 25 April 1683. Wit: Haibs Springett, Thomas Coxe, Sell Craske. Rec: 29/10/1698.

P. 207. Deed. Peter White, Bucks Co., yeoman, to John Headley, Bucks

Co., carpenter, for £50, a parcel of land lying next to land of Robert Hall [boundary on the] line of Edmund Lovett, containing about 250 acres, part of land granted to George White and devised to Peter White by will dated 9th da, 7th mo, 1687 Ackn: 29th da, 10th mo, 1698. Wit: Joseph Large, Wallen Pumphary. Rec: 13th da, 1st mo, 1698/9.

P. 208. Deed. John White, Francis White, William White, Joseph White and Benjamin White, sons of George White, late of Bucks Co., dec'd., a parcel of land granted to George White by patent and by his will 9th da, 7th mo, 1687 devised to Peter White, another of his sons 500 acres of said land. If sd. Peter White should die, land to go to brothers. Adjoining lands of Robert Hall ... land of John White, Elizabeth White and Francis White. Francis White, William White, Joseph White, and Benjamin White have already quit claimed to John White the remaining part of 500 acres for six shillings ... adjoining land of Edmund Lovett for six shillings paid by Peter White. Ackn: 8/10th mo, 1698. Wit: Joseph Large, William Codery, John White, Francis White, Joseph White, Benjamin White, Ann White, Abigail Curtis, John Town, Francis White. Rec: 13th da, 1st mo, 1698.

P. 210. Deed. John White, Buckingham, Bucks Co., yeoman, for money paid him by Elizabeth White, Bucks Co., widow, and mother of said John, 250 acres adjoining land of Robert Carter ... line of Peter White. Ackn: 11 Mar 1695. Wit: Phineas Pemberton, Francis White, Elizabeth White, Jr. and Peter White. Rec: 14th da, 11th mo, 1698/9.

P. 212. Deed. Elizabeth White, relict of George White, Bucks Co., dec'd., yeoman, and executrix of his last will, Peter White, Francis White, William White, Joseph White and Benjamin White, sons of said George and Elizabeth White a parcel of land containing 200 acres, part of the land devised by will dated 9 Sep 1687 - for £92 paid by John White, son of said George and Elizabeth White and brother to Peter, Francis, William, Joseph and Benjamin White. Ackn: 29th da, 4th mo, 1698. Wit: Henry Grubb, Phineas Pemberton. Rec: 14th da, 1st mo, 1698/9.

P. 214. Deed. William Biles, Bucks Co., yeoman, and attorney for Thomas Hodson, Mandesfield, Chester Co, Kingdom of England, 100 acres, patent dated 15 Mar 1692, for £12.10 paid by Henry Baker. Land lying by land of Richard Heough ... land of Mathias Harvies ... Ackn: 7th da, 12th mo, 1698. Wit: Joseph Growdon, John Swift and Mahlon Stacy. Rec: 14th da, 1st mo, 1698/9.

P. 215. Deed. John White, Buckingham, Bucks Co., cooper, and Joan, his wife and dau. of Robert Carter, late of aforesaid county, dec'd., for £36 paid by Francis White, brother of sd. John White, a parcel of land lying next to line of John White and land of Elizabeth White and John White - 100 acres, part of land granted by patent dated 9th da, 5th mo, 1686 to William Carter and his heirs, and by William Carter assigned to afsd Robert Carter on back of sd patent on 23/5/1686. Which sd 100 acres of land was set out after the decease of Robert Carter by order of the orphans court to dau, Joan Carter as her portion dated 1st da, 8/1689 ... land of Peter White ... land of John White. Ackn: 29th da, 4th mo, 1698. Wit: Henry Grubb, Phineas Pemberton, Richard Ratcliff, Samuel Beakes. Rec: 14th da, 1st mo, 1698/9.

P. 218. Deed. Israel Taylor, of Tenecum Island, Chester, son and heir of Christopher Taylor, dec'd. and Joseph Taylor, Philadelphia, the other heir and John Buzby, of Philadelphia, a weaver and Mary his wife, the only dau. of Christopher Taylor for £200 paid by Robert Healy, Bucks Co., yeoman, 500 acres granted to Christopher Taylor on 6/2/1686. Ackn: 18 Nov 1697. Wit: Anthony Morris, David Lloyd, Jonathan Dickinson. Rec: 24/1/1698/9.

P. 219. Deed. James Plumly, Bucks Co., yeoman 2 May 1682 to Thomas Fairman, of Shackampton for £80 a parcel of land containing 500 acres part of 1100 acres granted by William Penn to Alen Foster, and Mary his wife. Thomas Fairman to James Plumly to John Morris a parcel of land containing 500 acres for £80. Ackn: 6/11/1698/9. Wit: John Swift, David Powell, Francis Cooke. Rec: 14/1/1698/9.

P. 221. Deed. Frederick Vandegrift, Bucks Co., yeoman, for £55 paid by Barndt Virkirk of aforesaid county, 32 acres lying in Bensalem; said land confirmed to Frederick Vandegrift by heirs of Joseph Growdon on 1/5/1698. Ackn: 12/10/1698. Wit: John Gilbert, Nicholas Vandegrift and Peter Worrall. Rec: 24/1/1698/9.

P. 222. Deed. Barndt Vankirk, Bensalem, yeoman, for £5 paid by Leonard Vandegrift of aforesaid county, 3 acres. Ackn: 12/10/1698. Wit: John Gilbert, Peter Worral, Nicholas Vandegrift. Rec: 24/1/1698/9.

P. 223. Deed. Isabel Cutler, widow and admr. of Edmund Cutler, Bucks Co., dec'd., 200 acres, adjoining land of widow Plumly and land of Elizabeth Walmsley, patented 29/11/1685 to Nicholas Waln and granted to said Isabel Cutler 6/4/1686. Sale of land is for the payments of husband's debts who died intestate and for the care of her children - £45 paid by William Paxson, Sr. Ackn: 10/8/1698. Wit: Elizabeth Kingston, Thomas Walmsley, John Cutler. Rec: 8/1/1698/9.

P. 225. Deed. William Biles of Bucks Co., yeoman, atty for Thomas Hodson, of Mandesfield, Chester Co., England, 1000 acres lying between lands of George Stout and Joseph Milnor, for £275 paid by Mathias Harvie. Ackn: Joseph Growdon, John Swift and Mahlon Stacy. Rec: 25/1/1699.

P. 227. Power of Attorney. John Nichols and Elias Nichols, brothers, Bucks Co., appoint Mahlon Stacy, West Jersey and Henry Baker of Bucks Co., yeoman, to be their personal representatives. Ackn: 17/4/1688. Wit: James Crosley, John Saxby. Rec: 25/1/1698.

P. 228. Deed. Sarah Clows, relict of William Clowes, for 22 shillings granted to Richard Hough, Bucks, yeoman and brother-in-law to Sarah, 250 acres. Ackn: 5/3/1697. Wit: Francis Little, Abigail Pemberton, Phineas Pemberton. Rec: 27/11/699.

P. 229. Deed. Nicholas Waln, Philadelphia, yeoman, for £20 paid by John Town, Bucks Co., yeoman, 118 acres, part of the land granted to Nicholas Waln from Thomas Holme dated 18 May 1686. Ackn: 6/10/1698. Wit: Richard Townsend, William Hayhurst. Rec: 27/1/1699.

P. 230. Indenture. 12/7/1692 between Thomas Fairman, of Shackamaxon, Philadelphia attorney for Robert Fairman, of London, merchant to Samuel Allen, Jr. and Jane, his wife of Neshaminah Bucks for £15, 100 acres, part of land granted to Robert Fairman on 25/5/1687 adjoining land of Joseph Growdon ... Samuel Allen ... Ackn: 12/7/1692. Wit: Joseph Willcox and Zechariah Whitpaine. Rec: 27/1/1699.

P. 231. Deed. William Biles, attorney for Thomas Hodson of Mandesfield, Chester Co., Kingdom of England, 100 acres, granted on 15 March 1692/3 to Thomas Hodson, adjoining land of Henry Baker ... conveyed to Richard Hough dated 1/8/1697 for £12.10. Ackn:

8/12/1698/9. Wit: Joseph Growdon, John Swift and Mahlon Stacy. Rec: 27/1/1699.

P. 233. Deed. Griffith Owen, John Humphreys, Rowland Ellis, David Lloyd, all of Philadelphia, attorneys for Richard Davids, Welsh Pool, Montgomery Co., dominion of Wales, for £100 paid for said Richard Davids by Joseph Growdon of Treose Bucks Co., a parcel of land to Joseph Growdon, adjoining land of Francis Andrews, containing 500 acres. Ackn: 6/1/1698/9.

P. 234. Deed. William Crosdell and John Crosdell, heirs of Thomas Crosdell, for £140 a tract of land lying by corner of Walter Bridgman adjoining land of Thomas Crossdell - to John Cowgill. Ackn: 20/12/1698/9. Wit: Joseph Kirkbride, William Hayhurst, Robert Heaton. Rec: 28/1/1699.

P. 235. Deed. Richard Thatcher, dec'd., for £12 paid by John Scarborough, 100 acres, part of the land formerly owned by Edmund Bennett ... land of John Pennington ... formerly owned by Richard Thatcher, Sr., said land Richard Thatcher, Sr. by last will devised to son Richard Thatcher. Ackn: 6/12/1698. Wit: Phineas Pemberton, Abigail Pemberton and Israel Pemberton. Rec: 28/1/1699.

P. 236. Deed. A tract of land lying in Bensalem, Bucks Co., ... land Abel Hinkston ... containing 202 acres ... part of land of Joseph Growdon ... dated 24/Oct 1681 for £31 paid by William Beal of aforesaid county. Ackn: 16/12/1698/9. Wit: Stephen Beakes and Jeremiah Langhorne. Rec: 28/1/1699.

P. 237. Deed. Anne Clark and Martha Dawson, now wife of John Dawson, bricklayer, Chester Co., PA, both daus. of William Clark for £30 a parcel of land containing 209 acres paid by Henry Bowin, Bucks Co., husbandman. Ackn: 10/12/1698/9. Wit: Samuel Lewis, Elizabeth Lewis. Rec: 28/1/1699.

P. 238. Deed. Joseph Kirkbride, Bucks Co., to Randal Blackshaw, for ..., 150 acres confirmed to Edward Smith by deed on 10/3/1689 and another parcel formerly of Randal Blackshaw 112 acres confirmed to Joseph Kirkbride dated 1/1/1696. Ackn: 1/1/1698/9. Wit: Samuel Dark, Joseph Wood and John Scarborough. Rec: 28/1/1699.

P. 240. Indenture. 2/1/1698. Randal Blackshaw, Bucks Co., yeoman, to Nehemiah Blackshaw, son of said Randal, for natural love and affection and £20, 112 acres lying by land of Peter Webster ... Joseph Kirkbride. Ackn: 2/1/1698. Wit: Samuel Dark, Joseph Wood and John Scarborough. Rec: 28/1/1699.

P. 242. Deed. Job Howell, Philadelphia, yeoman, to Heugh Ellis, of Philadelphia, husbandman, for £3.10, 200 acres. Ackn: 16/98/1698. Wit: Michell Bircher and John Webster. Rec: 28/1/1699.

P. 243. Deed. John Shaw, Bucks Co., yeoman, for £9 paid by George Willard, of aforesaid county, 100 acres. Ackn: 17/12/1698/9. Wit: John Swift, Samuel Beakes, Phineas Pemberton. Rec: 28/1/1699.

P. 244. Deed. Joseph Chorley, Bucks Co., yeoman, and Mary his wife, formerly wife of John Acerman, late of aforesaid county, dec'd. and James Acerman, son of said John, and James Heyworth, of aforesaid county, husbandman and Mary his wife, dau. of said Acerman two parcels of land - 213 acres which was granted to John Acerman 3/1/1684 taken by sheriff and sold 13/1/1694 for debts of John Acerman to Joseph Chorley 13/1/1694 and the other tract adjoining being the half part of 205 acres granted to Daniel Brinson on 31/5/1684, then by said Brinson confirmed to John Nichols and Elias Nicholas on 1/3/1686 ... and conveyed to Joseph Chorley - sd Joseph Chorley and his wife, Mary, James Acreman and James Heywarth, and his wife for £320 paid by John Harrison. Ackn: 22/3/1699. Wit: William Biles, William Emley, Thomas Butte and Daniel Beakes. Rec: 13/5/1699.

P. 246. Deed. William Paxson, Jr., Bucks Co., for £50 paid by John Scarbrough of aforesaid county, yeoman, 40 acres. Ackn: 14/4/1699. Wit: John Carter, Joseph Ball and Abigail Paxson. Rec: 15/7/1699.

P. 247. Deed. John Scarbrough, Bucks Co., 80 acres near the land of Thomas Bayns, for £90 to Henry Hudleston, of aforesaid county, yeoman. Ackn: 4/7/1699. Wit: George Biles, Enoch Yardley, Jonathan Scaife. Rec: 15/7/1699.

P. 249. Deed. Joseph Growdon, Bensalem Bucks Co., Gent., for £18 paid by William Crosadell of aforesaid county, yeoman, a parcel of land lying in Buckingham ... a tract of land purchased from Peter White and wife, Elizabeth dated 8/10/1696. Ackn: 11/7/1699. Wit: Samuel Beakes and Jeremiah Langhorne. Rec: 16/7/!699.

P. 250. Deed. William Herst, Bucks Co., yeoman, and eldest son of Cuthbert Herst, late of aforesaid county, for £4 paid by Henry Hudleston, aforesaid county, yeoman, 12 acres, part of land patented to Cuthbert Herst on 29/10/1685. Ackn: 4/7/1699. Wit: George Biles, William Darby. Rec: 16/7/1699.

P. 251. Power of Attorney. John Scarborough, of Parish of St. Sepulcher, London, blacksmith, appoints John Scarborough, Jr. his son, living in Bucks Co., PA, to be his attorney, to receive all moneys due him. 15 Oct 1696. Wit: William Penn, Jr., Thomas Barnard, Samuel Harrison, Robert Hutchinson. Rec: 18/7/1699.

P. 252. Deed. Joseph Growdon, of Bensalem, Bucks Co., 90 acres adjoining land of Jeremiah Langhorne, for £36 paid by Thomas Stackhouse, Jr, of aforesaid county, yeoman. Ackn: 17/8/1699. Wit: John Swift, William Croasdell. Rec: 18/8/1699.

P. 254. Patent. To Joseph Jones on 16/10/1689 - 500 acres granted by warrant dated 7/9/1683 adjoining land of Thomas Fairman ... land of Joal Jelson. Ackn: 20 Dec 1690. Wit: Wm. Markham, Robert Turner and John Goodson. Rec: 20/8/1699.

P. 254. Power of Attorney: John Swift, of Southampton, Bucks Co., by virtue of attorneyship, granted by Joseph Jones, the elder, Southampton Co., England to convey 500 acres of land to Peter Chamberlin and Lucy Chamberlin, Bucks Co.. Ackn: 4/6/1699. Wit: William Croasdall, James Plumby, Samuel Beakes. Rec: 18/8/1699.

P. 255. Indenture. Richard Ridway, Burlington Co., West Jersey, yeoman, to Daniel Garner, Bucks Co., cordwainer, for £10, 108 acres. Ackn: 22 April 1699. Wit: Joshua Smith, Abigail Ridgway, Richard Ridgway, Jr. Rec: 20/8/1699.

P. 256. Deed. Daniel Garner, Bucks Co., cordwainer, a certain parcel of land adjoining land of Stephen Beaks ... Richard Wilson ... John Luffs, containing 229 acres (except 2 acres which have been sold to Richard Wilson), for £72.10 paid by Joseph Jenney, carpenter of aforesaid county. Ackn: 2/7/1699. Wit: Jonathan Scaife, Thomas Jenney and Enoch Yardley. Rec: 20/8/1699.

P. 258. Deed. Phineas Pemberton, Bucks Co., yeoman, 500 acres adjoining land of Thomas Bond ... Thomas Hodson, part of 5000 acres granted to James Harrison on 20 April 1682, for £25 paid to James Harrison in his lifetime by George Stone, and wife Phebe, dau. of James Harrison of aforesaid county and said Phineas Pemberton affirms. Ackn: 18/8/1699. Wit: Joseph Growdon, Samuel Beakes. Rec: 20/8/1699.

P. 259. Deed. Grace Langhorne, relict and administratrix of Thomas Langhorne, and Jeremiah Langhorne her son and Sarah Biles her dau. and wife of William Biles, Jr., 100 acres adjoining land of Thomas Stackhouse, to Thomas Stackhouse for the yearly rents due the proprietary. Ackn: 18/8/1699. Wit: Robert Heaton, Jr. and John Croasdale. Rec: 20/8/1699.

P. 261. Deed. Thomas Brock, Bucks Co., yeoman, for £25 paid by Joseph Kirkbride, 11 acres adjoining land of Jeremiah Dungan ... to land of Anthony Burton. Ackn: 18/8/1699. Wit: Walter Humphray, George Biles and Christopher Snowdon. Ackn: 19/8/1699. Rec: 20/8/1699.

P. 262. Deed. Thomas Brock, Bucks Co., yeoman, for £10 paid by Richard Peirce of said county, carpenter, 11 acres adjoining land of Anthony Burton ... land granted to Joseph English 10/12/1695. Ackn: 5/7/1699. Wit: Walter Humphary and Christopher Snowdon. Rec: 20/8/1699.

P. 263. Deed. Stephen Wilson, Burlington Co., West New Jersey, carpenter, for £80 from Stephen Twining, Bucks Co., yeoman, 250 acres, part of 500 acres granted to Thomas Rowland and by deed to John Rowland, said brother said Thomas. Ackn: 17/7/1698. Wit: John Smith and William Hayhurst. Rec: 19/8/1699.

P. 264. Deed. Joseph Growdon, for £9 paid by Abel Hinckstone of aforesaid county, 204 acres lying in Bensalem, beginning at a corner of land of William Beal. Ackn: 16/12/1699. Wit: John Swift, Henry Baker, Richard Hough. Rec: 20/89/1699.

P. 265. Deed. Joseph Growdon, for £28.15 paid by Garrett Nausand, of aforesaid county, husbandman, 150 acres. Ackn: 10/12/1698. Wit: Thomas Stackhouse, Thomas Yardley and Francis Searle. Rec: 20/8/1699.

P. 266. Deed. Joseph Growdon, Bucks Co., for £28.15 paid by Cornelius Vansand of aforesaid county, husbandman, 150 acres lying in Bensalum, adjoining land of John Talthurs, granted to Joseph Growdon on 25 Oct 1681. Ackn: 10/12/1698/9. Wit: Thomas Stackhouse, Thomas Yardley and Francis Searle. Rec: 20/8/1699.

P. 267. Deed. Jane Chapman, relict of John Chapman, late of Bucks Co., dec'd., for £10 paid by William Smith, of said county, yeoman, 100 acres in Wrightstown and another parcel containing 14 acres confirmed to said John Chapman on 7 Oct 1684. Ackn: 1/10/1697. Wit: William Biles, Samuel Beakes, Jonathan Scaife. Rec: 20/8/1699.

P. 268. Deed. Henry Paxson, Bucks Co. and wife, Margery Paxson, and Abel Hinchkston, of said county and Elizabeth his wife, formerly wife of William Plumly and dau.-in-law to said Margery Paxson and James Plumly, Bucks Co. and son to said Margery Paxson 100 acres adjoining land of Nicholas Waln, for £30, for the use of the children of aforesaid William Plumly by Thomas Walmsly, of aforesaid county, husbandman. Ackn: 8/7/1699. Wit: Edward Carter, John Plumly and Peter Wood. Rec: 20/10/1699.

P. 270. Indenture. Samuel Carpenter, for £70 paid by Joseph Large 100 acres. Ackn: 1/9/1699. Wit: John J..., Robert Hodson. Rec: 20/10/1699.

P. 271. Deed. Samuel Carpenter, Philadelphia City and County, carpenter, has received £70 from Joseph Large, Bucks Co., for redemption of 100 acres adjoining land of Mordecai Bowdon. Ackn: 1/9/1699. Wit: David Lloyd, Aurelius Hoskins, Robert Hodgson. Rec: 20/10/1699.

P. 272. Deed. William Dungan, Bucks Co., cordwainer, land granted on 1/4/1688, rolls office Book A, Vol. 1, page 229, 230, granted to Arthur Cook, late of aforesaid county, dec'd., 100 acres adjoining land of Edmund Lovett, for £6, 8/11/1699. Now William Dungan quit claims land to Margaret, relict of Arthur Cook and son John Cook. Ackn: 16/9/1699. Wit: Robert Hodgson, Joseph Large, John Surkel. Rec: 20/10/1699.

P. 273. Deed. 21 May 1695 between Susannah Tunniclif, widow of Thomas Tunniclif, Bucks Co. yeoman dec'd. and sole executrix of last will of Thomas Worrilaw, of Chester Co., yeoman, conveyed 1000 acres for £50 to Francis Tunneclif. Ackn: 1/1/1695. Wit: John Brock, Henry Margerom, Ruben Pownal. Rec: 21/10/1699.

P. 275. Deed. Francis Tunneclif, Bucks Co., cordwainer, 21 March 1681 to John Alsop 1000 acres of land, for £1.10 ... said land granted by deed 19 June 1684 to Thomas Tunnecift, who devised same to wife, Susanna Tunnicleff by will 20/3/1695, extx of sd will and by her was granted to her kinsman, Francis Tunneclif. Ackn: 1/6/1698. Wit: Mary Hodgson, Abigail Pemberton, Phineas Pemberton. Rec: 21/10/1699.

P. 276. Deed. Francis Tunniclif, Bucks Co., a tract of land containing 280 acres, part of a tract confirmed to John Alsop dated 2 March 1681, for £40 to Abel Janney. Ackn: 1/6/1698. Wit: Mary Hodgson, Abigail Pemberton, Phineas Pemberton. Rec: 22/10/1699.

P. 277. Deed. Abel Janney, Bucks Co. yeoman for £21.1 paid by his brother Thomas Janney, of aforesaid county, yeoman, 7 1/4 acres. Ackn: 10/6/1698. Wit: Samuel Dark, George Biles, Joseph Clowes. Rec: 22/10/1699.

P. 278. Deed. Joseph Growdon, Bensalem, Bucks Co., 21 acres adjoining land of Abel Hinchkstone, for £11.11 to William Baker. 1/1/1699. Wit: Peter Worral, William Biles, Jr. Rec: 16/1/1699.

P. 279. Deed. Thomas Fairman, Philadelphia Co., gent., for £20 paid by Michael Frederick, Philadelphia Co., husbandman, 86 acres adjoining land of Nathaniel Hardin ... John Bown ..., part of the land granted by deed dated 18/3/1688. Ackn: 24 Jan 1698/9. Wit: Michael Lvyken, Elner Lvyken, George Gary. Rec: 16/2/1700.

P. 280. Deed. Joseph Growdon, of Bensalem, Bucks Co., for £40 paid by Samuel Olddel, a parcel of land adjoining land of William Croasdale ... to River Delaware. Ackn: 10/2/1700. Wit: William Biles, Richard Hough, Samuel Beakes. Rec: 16/2/1700.

P. 282. Deed. John Bowne, Bucks Co. for £9, paid by Joseph Growdon, same county, 250 acres. References to Thomas Fairman and Joseph

Growdon. Ackn: 26 March 1697. Wit: Edward Bolton, Margaret Matthews. Rec: 16/2/1700.

P. 283. Deed. Jonathan Scaife, 140 acres adjoining land of John Hough to land of Widow Musgrand ... to land of Jonathan Scaife ... which 500 acres is part of 1000 acres granted to John Shire by release dated 10 April 1682 and by him 6/7/1682 conveyed to Richard Colbourn and by sd Colbourn released on 24 April 1683 to Joseph Drake and by him on 29 April 1684 granted to Jonathan Scaife - for £7 paid by John Rumford. Ackn: 19/12/1699. Wit: William Paxson, Sr. John Hough, Sr. and John Shaw. Rec: 16/2/1700.

P. 284. Deed. Thomas Dungan, Bucks Co., husbandman, 100 acres lying near the land of William Bennett ... to land of Edward Doyls, part of 200 acres granted to Thomas Dungan dated 1 Oct 1692 and by Clement Dungan, Jeremiah Dungan and John Dungan, sons of Thomas Dungan confirmed to their brother, Thomas Dungan, first above named by deed 22/5/1698 - for £100 paid by John Scott of aforesaid county. Ackn: 12/10/1699. Wit: George Biles, Edward Carter, Clement Dungan. Rec: 16/2/1700.

P. 286. Deed. William Biles, Bucks Co., attorney to Thomas Hodson, Macclesfield, Chester Co., kingdom of England, a certain tact of land standing by the division line of Philadelphia and Bucks Co. ... containing 5000 acres of land confirmed to Thomas Hodson dated 26/12/1684, to William Lawrence, gent., John Tallman, Joseph Thorn, Samuel Thorn and Benjamin Field, all of Flushing, Queens Co., Rhode Island for five shillings per annum. Ackn: 5/3/1698. Wit: Edward Penington, William Stevenson. Rec: 17/2/1700.

P. 287. Deed. Joseph Growdon, 100 acres, part of 5000 acres, for £30 paid by Stephen Sands of Bensalem, husbandman. Ackn: 3/1/1698. Wit: Stephen Beaks, Jeremiah Langhorne. Rec: 17/2/1700.

P. 289. Deed. Josias Hill, for £112 paid by John Elett of Carcus Hook, Philadelphia Co., taylor, 200 acres. Ackn: 13/1/1699. Wit: Anthony Morgan, Elizabeth Morgan, Francis Cooke. Rec: 17/2/1700.

Volume 3

P. 1. Deed. Samuel Richardson, Philadelphia Co., yeoman, to Phineas Pemberton for £35, 300 acres adjoining land of Thomas Rudyard, granted by patent on 29/11/1684 and recorded in Book A, Folio 160, Philadelphia. Wit: Anthony Morris, William Hudson. Ackn: 20/9/1699. Rec: 20/1/1 699.

P. 2. Deed. Richard Hough, Bucks Co., yeoman, to John Watson, Bucks Co., yeoman, for £70, 235 acres adjoining land of William Dark, granted by warrant dated 13/2/1683 to Charles Biles and William Biles and by them divided and Charles Biles confirmed his portion to Abel Janney by deed on 12/7/1694 and by him confirmed to said Richard Hough on 6/1/1696. Ackn: 5/1/1699. Wit: William Biles, Jr., Thomas Yardley, Phineas Pemberton. Rec: 20/1/1699.

P. 3. Mortgage. John Watson, Bucks Co., yeoman, to Richard Hough for £70, 236 acres. 11/9/1699. Wit: Thomas Yardley, William Biles, Phineas Pemberton. Rec: 21/1/1699.

P. 5. Deed. Margaret Cook, relict and sole executrix of Arthur Cook, and John Cook, son and heir of said Arthur Cook of Frankford, Philadelphia Co., for £69 paid by Phineas Pemberton, 203 acres adjoining land of Joseph Large ... formerly land of Edmund Lovets ... of Parson and Burton's land, part of land granted to Ralph Smith by patent dated 2/6/1684 which said Ralph Smith devised by will to Priscilla Rowland, wife of John Rowland who conveyed same to said Arthur Cook. Ackn: 20/9/1699. Wit: Joseph Large, William Dungan, Robert Hodgson. Rec: 21/1/1699.

P. 7. Deed. Joseph Large, Bucks Co., weaver, for £72.5, to Phineas Pemberton, 100 acres, part of land granted on 25/5/1693 to John Green, recorded in Book A, Vol 1, page 116, 117 and conveyed by him to Joseph Large by deed 20/9/1693. Ackn: 6/9/1699. Wit: John Scaiff, John Surket, Jr., William Surket. Rec: 22/1/1699.

P. 8. Release. Joseph Large, Jr. and Richard Large, sons of Joseph Large, Bucks Co., both husbandman, for divers good causes and consideration they quit claim to Phineas Pemberton, Bucks Co., yeoman, 100 acres adjoining land of Edmund Lovets ... land of Mordecai Borden.

Ackn: 6/9/1699. Wit: John Surket, Thomas Phillips, Robert Sanders. Rec: 22/1/1699.

P. 9. Deed. Edmund Lovett and Joseph Kirkbride, Bucks Co., yeomen, and trustees to the children of Abraham Cox, late of aforesaid county, dec'd. to Penticost Teage of the town and county of Philadelphia, woolcomer, and surviving executor of Sarah Cox, relict of Abraham Cox, two tracts of land containing 200 acres which Rebecca Williams confirmed to Abraham Cox by deed dated 2/9/1695. Adjoining the land of Thomas Pemberton. Land sold to Pentecoast Teage for £255 for use of children of said Abraham and Sarah Cox. Ackn: 24/11/1699. Wit: Anthony Morris, Phineas Pemberton, Joseph Wood, Edmund Lovett, Richard Hough. Rec: 23/1/1699.

P. 12. Patent. Granted by warrant dated 14/4/1690. To Robert Turner, 1000 acres on Neshaminah Creek adjoining Anthony Tomekin's land ... to John Bounds land. Wit: Samuel Carpenter, William Markham. Rec: 3/6/1699.

P. 13. Deed. Robert Turner, for £60 paid by Charles Brooks, Chester Co., yeoman, 1000 acres. Ackn: 13/5/1700. Rec: Philadelphia 14/1/1699/1700. Witness: Robert Turner. Rec: 1/4/1700.

P. 13. Deed. Charles Brooks to John Bleeker of Philadelphia Co., 1000 acres, granted to Robert Turner and by him confirmed to Charles Brooks. [See above entries.] 15/1/1700. Wit: Francis Cook, Mary Cook, Caspar Hood.

P. 15. Deed. Humphrey Morrey, of Philadelphia, merchant, and John Goodson of town and county of Philadelphia, chirurgeon, attorneys for Mary Crow of the Parish of St. Buttolph without Aldersgate, London, Kingdom of England, 225 acres, patented on 5 April 1688 to Benjamin Roberts Sr, adjoining land of Abraham Whealeys ... land of Shadrack Walleys... together with 25 acres in Newtown, warrant dated 18/10/1683 and said Benjamin Roberts, died without issue and the land descended to his sister, said Mary Crow who now conveys same for £25 to Shadrack Walley, Bucks Co., yeoman. Ackn: 3 May 1700. Wit: Samuel Giddon and Francis Cook. Rec: 29/4/1700.

P. 15. Deed. Charles Brooks, Chester Co., yeoman, 23 Aug 1699 granted to Robert Turner for £80, 1000 acres adjoining land of Anthony Tomkins ... land of John Brown ... Neshaminy Creek, assigned to Robert Turner by a patent bearing date of 13th of this instant. Ackn: 15/1/1700. Wit: Francis Cook, Mary Cook, Caspar Hood and Jacob Clark Parbelbert. Rec: 20/4/1700.

P. 16. Deed. Phineas Pemberton to Robert Hodgson for £80, 200 acres adjoining land formerly of Thomas Rudyard, granted by warrant dated 29/11/1684, recorded in the Rolls office, Philadelphia, book A, folio 160, to Thomas Bowman which he granted to Samuel Richardson 3/4/1686 which he granted to Phineas Pemberton 20/9/1699 and now granted to Robert Hodgson, yeoman, Philadelphia. Ackn: 23/3/1700. Wit: Samuel Beakes, Samuel Dark. Rec: 20/4/1700.

P. 18. Deputation. Thomas Story appointed Phineas Pemberton deputy for Office of the Registry for Bucks Co. 26/4/1700. Rec: 18/5/1700.

P. 19. Deed. Margaret Cook, sole executrix of Arthur Cook late of Frankford, Philadelphia Co., dec'd. and John Cook, only son and heir of said Arthur Cook, for £140 to Clement Dungan and Thomas Dungan, 1000 acres. Ackn: 11/1/1699/1700. Wit: Joseph Growdon and William Biles and Richard Hough. Rec: 26/5/1700.

P. 20. Release. Isaac Atkinson, Bucks Co., cordwainer, for £39.12 paid by Wm. Biles, father-in-law to said Isaac being full sum of obligation dated 10/4/1696 granted to George Biles, son of sd Wm. Biles a tract of land adjoining John Rowland ... Wm. Dungan and ... Randle Blackshaw ... lands of Charles Brigham ... 300 acres. Ackn: 11/4/1700. Wit: Wm. Atkinson, Jane Biles, Phineas Pemberton. Rec: 27/5/1700.

P. 21. Deed. John Smith, Bucks Co., blacksmith, 250 acres adjoining land of William Carter, part of land granted by patent to Robert Carter and confirmed to John Carter, son of Robert Carter by order of the orphans court 1/8/1689 and by John Carter conveyed to said John Smith in 1696 - for £280, to Daniel Jackson of aforesaid county. Ackn: 10/8/1700. Wit: John Hough, Thomas Brock, John Gay. Rec: 22/8/1700.

P. 22. Deed. Thomas Brock, Bucks Co., yeoman, 300 acres by name of Shadrick Hill, adjoining land of Ralph Boone, land which William Smith granted to Thomas Brock by deed dated 1/5/1698 for £30. Ackn:

10/8/1700. Wit: Daniel Atkinson, John Gay, John Hioff. Rec: 22/8/1700.

P. 23. Deed. Anthony Burton, Bucks Co., carpenter, two lots lying in Buckingham Bucks Co. ... near land of Richard Pierce, part of land granted to said Burton and Thomas Brock, dated 20/12/1695 containing 11 acres for £10 paid by Peter Webster of aforesaid county, husbandman. Ackn: 20/1/1699/1700. Wit: Phineas Pemberton and Alice Pemberton. Rec: 23/8/1700.

P. 25. Deed. Samuel Smith and Elizabeth, his wife, dau. of Edmund Lovett of Bucks Co., yeoman, 250 acres. Said land granted to Edmund Lovett by warrant dated 27/5/1684, for £40 released from Elizabeth Lovett to Edmund Lovett. Ackn: 6/9/1700. Wit: Alice Pemberton and Phineas Pemberton. Rec: 22/8/1700.

P. 26. Deed. Peter White and Elizabeth his wife, Burlington Co., West Jersey, yeoman, for £40, 11 acres adjoining land of Samuel Carpenter. Ackn: 11/2/1700. Wit: John White, James Moon. Rec: 24/8/1700.

P. 27. Deed. John Rowland, Bucks Co., yeoman, and Priscilla Rowland his wife, 300 acres adjoining land formerly of Thomas Atkinson and now George Biles, warranted by patent dated 22/3/1686, for £350 paid by John Hiett. Ackn: 11/4/1700. Wit: William Croasdell, Peter Wood and Edward Hureley. Rec: 24/8/1700.

P. 29. Deed. Robert Heaton, senior of Middleton, Bucks Co., yeoman, for £150 paid by Robert Heaton, Jr. of aforesaid county, 440 acres, part of the land granted to James Dilworth 14/2/1682. Ackn: 14/11/1700. Wit: Thomas Heough, John Cutler. Rec: 22/11/1700.

P. 31. Deed. Peter White, Burlington Co., West Jersey, yeoman, and Elizabeth his wife, for £7 paid by Anthony Burton, Bucks Co., yeoman, 3 acres and allowance for a road, part of 11 acres which Joseph English, father of said Elizabeth by deed dated 20/12/1695 granted to Peter White . Ackn: 24/10/1700. Wit: John Town, Steward Magoo, Jeremiah Dungan. Rec: 22/11/1700.

P. 32. Deed. John Guy, son of Edward Guy late of Bucks Co., yeoman dec'd., 200 acres adjoining land of William Biles, granted by patent dated 21/5/1685 to Samuel Dark and by said Samuel Dark to John Radley by deed dated 18/6/1693 which he granted to Edward Guy and said land descended by law to said John Guy, brother of Edward Guy and Esther Guy, dau. of said Edward Guy. Now granted to Isaac Atkinson, Bucks Co., yeoman for £32. Ackn: 9/10/1700. Wit: Abraham Senior, John Atkinson and William Biles. Rec: 23/11/1700.

P. 34. Deed. William Paxson for £5 paid by his son-in-law Thomas Walmsley, Bucks Co., 200 acres. Ackn: 10/1/1700. Wit: Joseph Kirkbride, Jacque Verrier, William Darke, Edward Carter. Rec: 19/1/1700.

P. 35. Deed. Samuel Baker, son and heir of Henry Baker, late of Bucks Co., yeoman, dec'd., to Thomas Hilborne, a parcel of land adjoining land of Jonathan Eldridge and land of Arthur Cook, 225 acres together with 25 acres in village of Town Stead of Newtown, granted to John Otter who conveyed same to Henry Baker on 4/4/1694 who by his will devised same to his son Nathan Baker but before he died he sold the same to Thoms Hilborne of Shrewsberry of East Jersey and died without making an alteration in his will. Now Samuel Baker, at the request of Nathan Baker, being a minor, between the age of 16 and 17 years, confirms the land to Thomas Hilborne for £60. Ackn: 20/11/1700. Wit: Daniel Radley, Nathan Baker, David Lloyd. Rec: 11/1/1700.

P. 36. Deed. 8 March 1701 between Hugh Alash, Abington Township, Philadelphia, husbandman, to Philip Pecker, township of Doblin and aforesaid county for £30 a certain parcel of land.

P. 36. Deed. Richard Lundy to Thomas Dure, 103 acres, for £90, near land formerly sold by Samuel Burgess to Randle Blackshaw and land sold by Richard Lundy to Ralph Sutton. Ackn: 9/4/1700. Wit: William Biles, Jr., James Moon. Rec: 20/4/1700.

P. 38. Deed. William Biles, Bucks Co., yeoman, 100 acres adjoining land of William Biles and Charles Biles ... to land of Josiah Hoopes and John Pulmer, confirmed to Philip Conway by patent dated 15/5/1684, for £20 paid by William White, aforesaid county, husbandman. Ackn: 16/3/1701. Wit: John Routledge, John Heough. Rec: 20/7/1700.

P. 39. Deed. Francis White, Bucks Co., for £50 paid by his brother Benjamin White, Kent Co., PA, yeoman, 200 acres. Ackn: 10/4/1701. Wit: John Pidecock, James Heaton, Jonathan Gresoe. Rec: 21/4/1701.

P. 41. Deed. A tract of land above the Falls of Delaware, part of 500 acres which John Rowland by deed dated 9/7/1690 granted to Gilbert Wheeler, aforesaid county, yeoman, for £20 paid by John Pedecock. Ackn: 21/3/1701. Wit: Richard Bull, Sarah Bull, Wm. Biles. Rec: 21/1/1701.

P. 43. Deed. John Scarborough, Bucks Co., yeoman, and son of John Scarbrough of London, Kingdom of England, blacksmith, 100 acres, warranted to said John Scarborough dated 20/3/1682, land running by Richard Thatcher ... land of James Paxson. Ackn: 61/1/1700. Witness: Joseph Kirkbride, Edward ---, William Nutt. Rec: 21/4/1701.

P. 44. Deed. James Moon, Jr., son of James Moon, Bucks Co., yeoman, 120 acres adjoining land of Samuel Darke ... land of Randle Blackshaw ... land of James Hill, for £50 paid by his said father, James Moon. Ackn: 6/4/1701. Wit: John Snowden, Henry Margerum, William Biles, Jr. Rec: 23/4/1701.

P. 45. Deed. Thomas Dure, Bucks Co., weaver, 400 acres on the Delaware River between lands formerly laid out to Thomas Bond and the land laid out to Thomas Hodson containing 500 acres which said land George Stone late of aforesaid county, weaver, dec'd., purchased from James Harrison and since the death of James Harrison, Phineas Pemberton who married Phebe the only child of James Harrison, since her decease confirmed the same to George Stone by deed 18/8/1699. George Stone has since died intestate and said Thomas Dure being nephew to said George Stone did on 10 Ober 1700 adminster his estate and now conveys for £58 by James Moone, Junr., 200 acres of the above described 500 acres. Ackn: 4th mo, 1701. Wit: Henry Margerum, John Snowdon, William Biles, Jr. Rec: 21/4/1701.

P. 47. Deed. Henry Paxson, Bucks Co., yeoman, and Margery Paxson his wife, and James Plumly of said county, son of Margery, 125 acres adjoining Thomas Walmsley's land and the land of Joseph Growdon, granted by patent to Margery Plumly, widow, dated 1/3/1685 and now conveyed to Joseph Snowden for £20. Ackn: 11/1/1700. Wit: William Biles, Jr., Jeremiah Langhorne, Daniel Doane. Rec: 20/4/1701.

P. 49. Deed. Stephen Howell, Kent, PA, yeoman, a tract of land beginning at the corner of the land of Joan, late wife of John White and adjoining land of John Headley, 100 acres, part of 500 acres granted by patent 9/5/1686 to William Carter and by him confirmed to Robert Carter on the back of the patent dated 23/5/1686 and after the death of Robert Carter by order of orphans court on 23/5/1686, a portion was confirmed to Margaret Carter, dau. of Robert Carter which is now confirmed for £35 paid to John Carter. Ackn: 14/11/1700. Wit: John Brinclae, Benjamin White. Rec: 25/1/1701.

P. 51. Deed. Jane Scot, relict and executrix of John Scot, late of Bucks Co., yeoman, whose will dated 17/8/1700 directed that land be sold to pay debts and toward assistance and education of his children - for £115 paid by Tobias Dymock and his wife, Sarah, Philadelphia, merchant, a parcel of land containing 100 acres. Ackn: 27/6/1701. Wit: Thomas Stone, John Wilkens, Maurice Lisle. Rec: 18/8/1701.

P. 53. Deed. Edward Mayos of Bristol, formerly called Buckingham, Bucks Co., yeoman, a lot in Bristol which is the moiety of the lot which Thomas Brock by deed dated 1/7/1697 confirmed to Edward Mayos and is part of the 11 acres which Joseph English, son-in-law and heir to Samuel Clift, dec'd. took up - for £5 paid by Anthony Burton of Bristol Township, carpenter. Ackn: 6/6/1701. Wit: Joseph Kirkbride, Thomas Brock. Rec: 15/8/1701.

P. 55. Deed. Jeremiah Dungan, Bucks Co., yeoman, two lots of land lying in Bristol, Bucks Co., adjoining land of Anthony Burton, for £60 paid by Joseph Kirkbride. Ackn: 29/6/1701. Wit: William Beakes, William Hayhurst, Abell Janney. Rec: 5/8/1701.

P. 56. Deed. John Scarbrough, Bucks Co., yeoman, for £50 paid by Mary Baker, widow, a parcel of land. Ackn: 12/12/1700/01. Wit: William Atkinson, Jane Biles and William Biles. Rec: 16/8/1701.

P. 57. Deed. Edward Mayos of Bristol, Bucks Co., yeoman, a lot which is the moiety of the lot that said Edward purchased from Thomas Brock and is part of the 11 acres lying in Bristol which Joseph English, son in law and heir to Samuel Cliffe dec'd., who in his lifetime took and settled the same with other lands, on 20/12/1795 confirmed to Thomas Brock and Anthony Burton and since laid to said Brock as his share - for £5 paid by Phineas Pemberton. Ackn: 1/7/1701. Wit: Joseph Kirkbride, Thomas Brock. Rec: 17/8/1701.

P. 58. Deed. Thomas Brock, Bucks Co., yeoman, a parcel of land adjoining land of Samuel Baker ... land of Anthony Burton and Joseph Kirkbride, part of land granted to Samuel Clift in his lifetime then by will to Joseph English, his son in law - for £17 paid by Edward Mayos of Bristol, aforesaid county, yeoman. Ackn: 29/6/1701. Wit: Samuel Baker, Adam Harker. Rec: 18/8/1701.

P. 59. Deed. Anthony Burton, Bristol Township, Bucks Co., a certain lot of land adjoining land of Edward Mayos purchased from Thomas Brock ... and part of tract of land which Samuel Cliff ... for £6 paid by Edward Mayos. Ackn: 13/6/1701. Wit: Joseph Kirkbride, Thomas Brock. Rec: 18/8.1701.

P. 61. Indenture. 7 Nov 1701 between John Cook, son of Arthur Cook, of county of Philadelphia and Margarget Cook, City of Philadelphia, widow of Arthur Cook to Thomas Hillborne, of Shrousbury, East Jersey, yeoman for £110 a parcel of land containing 528 acres. Ackn: 7 Nov 1701. Wit: Thomas Storry, Thomas Masters. Rec: 20/10/1701.

P. 63. Deed. Joseph Growdon, Bensalem, Bucks Co., gentlemen, for £20 paid by Margaret Cook, of Philadelphia, widow, 400 acres, part of land granted to said Joseph Growdon on 24 Oct 1681. Ackn: 13/9/1700. Wit: Elizabeth Growdon, Sarah Growdon, Phineas Pemberton. Rec: 20/10/1701.

P. 64. Deed. Stephen Beakes of Bucks Co., yeoman, to Samuel Beakes and Phineas Pemberton of said county 203 acres for the divers good causes and considerations. Ackn: 5 May 1699. Wit: Edward Lucas, Isaac Atkinson, James Acreman. Rec: 23/10/1701.

P. 65. Deed. Thomas Curtis, of Philadelphia, barber chururgeon, a parcel of land lying in Bucks Co. adjoining land of Joan, wife of John White, 100 acres, part of 500 acres granted by patent to William Carter dated 9/5/1686 and by him confirmed to Robert Carter on 23/5/1686 on the back of the patent on 23/5/1686, which 100 acres was set out after the death of Robert Carter by the Orphans Court as part of the estate granted to Margaret, dau. of Robert Carter, wife of Thomas Curtis -for £18 paid by Stephen Nowell, Kent Co., PA, a mason. Ackn: 11/4/1701. Rec: 23/10/1701.

P. 67. Deed. Andrew Heath and his wife, Elizabeth, John Hutchinson and wife Joyce by her maiden name Venables and Francis Venables, young woman, all of Hopewell Township, Burlington Co., New Jersey for £50 paid by Peter Worrall, Bucks Co., yeoman, 220 acres lying in Makefield Township, part of land formerly of William Venables, dec'd., and his relict Elizabeth now Elizabeth Heath. Ackn: 2nd mo, 1701. Wit: John Bainbridge, John Knowles, William Emley, Joseph Clows and James Hargroves. Rec: 9/8/1702.

P. 69. Deed. Indenture 16 March 1702, Thomas Revell of Burlington town and county, West Jersey, gent., executor of last will of Mrs. Elizabeth Tatham, late of Burlington, widow dec'd., to William Stevenson, Burlington, gent. and Thomas Stevenson, Bucks Co., gent., 2500 acres devised to said Elizabeth Tatham by her dec'd. husband, John Gray alias Tatham late of Burlington, by dated 15 Oct 1700 - for £300 paid by William Stevenson and Thomas Stevenson. Ackn: 16 March 1702. Wit: George Deacon, Christopher Snowden, Robert Hickman, Emanuel Smith. Rec: 22/8/1702.

P. 72. Deed. Indenture 20 Jan 1701. Thomas Revell, Burlington, West Jersey, gent., surviving trustee and supervisor for selling and disposing land of the late Elizabeth Tatham, Burlington, to Thomas Stevenson, Jr. of Long Island, New York, yeoman - 2000 acres for £50. Ackn: 20 Jan 1701. Wit: Henry Grubb, Nathan Allen, William Stevenson. Rec: 24/8/1702.

P. 75. Released Deed. Thomas Knight assigns his interest to Thomas Scott 1/4/1702. Wit: Abraham Griffith, Jeremiah Bartholemew. Rec: 4/8/1702.

P. 75. Deed. Samuel Carpenter, city and county of Philadelphia, merchant, and sole executor of the last will dated 5/8/1694 of Frances Rossill, late of Bucks Co., dec'd. did give unto the sons of Samuel Burgess of said county 200 acres out of the tract of 500 acres which said Rossill had purchased from Richard Lundy and at the request of the rest of the children of Samuel Burgess, the said Samuel Carpenter quit claims to John Burgess. Ackn: 17/12/1701/02. Wit: George Clough, Enoch Pearson, Israel Pemberton. Rec: 25/8/1702.

P. 76. Deed. Joseph Growdon, of Bensalem, Bucks Co., gent., a parcel of land lying in Bensalem ... to William Duncan for 1 shilling each year. Ackn: 16/8/1701. Wit: David Lloyd, Thomas Stevenson. Rec: 27/8/1702.

P. 78. Deed. Israel Taylor, son and heir of Christopher Taylor, dec'd., Joseph Taylor son of said Christopher, and Isaac Norris, Philadelphia, merchant and David Lloyd, of same place gent., executors of last will of Thomas Lloyd, dec'd., a tract of land adjoining land of William Hough ... land of Francis Richardson's children, 562 acres, part of the land granted by warrant dated 26 Feb 1682 to said Christopher Taylor, for £120 paid by Thomas Yardley. Ackn: 2/12 Feb 1701/2. Wit: John Macklier, Edward Evans, Israel Taylor. Rec: 28/8/1702.

P. 79. Deed. Phineas Pemberton for £20 paid by John Penquite of Wrightstown, Bucks Co., 200 acres. Ackn: 15/7/1701/1702. Wit: William Hayhurst, John Cowgill. Rec: 29/8/1702.

P. 81. Deed. John Jones of Philadelphia, merchant and the surviving executor of Henry Jones, late of Philadelphia, merchant, 125 acres adjoining land of John Town - to Joseph Growdon, for £39. Ackn: 20/2/1698. Wit: Anthony Morris, Clement Plumstead, David Lloyd. Rec: 1/9/1702.

P. 82. Deed. Margaret Atkinson, of Bellmount, Bensalem, Bucks Co., widow and executor of Christopher Atkinson, late of Scotforth, Gloucester Co., England, for £80 paid by Joseph Biltert, of Weskichetts, Bensalem, carpenter, 500 acres lying in Buckingham, adjoining land of William Say and Robert Wheeler ... line of James Straiton ... and Thomas Paxson. Ackn: 8/4/1702. Wit: Joseph Growdon, George Dungan, John Cutler. Rec: 9/9/1702.

P. 83. Deed. Henry Boyen, Bucks Co. yeoman and Jane Boyen [Bowen] his wife, dau. of Robert Carter, late of aforesaid county, yeoman, dec'd., 400 acres granted by patent on 9/5/1686 to William Carter which William Carter granted to Robert Carter on 23/4/1686. 100 acres of said parcel granted to Jane Boyer - to John White for £62 . Ackn: 10/11/1702. Wit: Charles Lavaller, William Forderoy.

P. 86. Deed. 12 June 1702. George Biles, Bucks Co., yeoman and Solomon Warder of same county, yeoman, 300 acres adjoining land of John Rowland ... Anthony Burton ... William Biles ... Randall Blackshaw

- which land was sometime in the possession of Thomas Atkinson, laid out to him for 300 acres, but said Thomas Atkinson not having paid for it, it was purchased from the proprietary by William Biles, and later by William Biles and his wife Jane (widow of Thomas Atkinson), sold to said George Biles - to Solomon Warder, yeoman, for £350. Ackn: 12 June 1702. Wit: Thomas Watson, Cornelius Van Sands, William Beakes. Rec: 23/9/1702.

P. 87. Deed. John Hiett, Bucks Co., yeoman, 300 acres adjoining land of Thomas Atkinson but now George Biles, granted to John Rowling by patent 22/3/1686 300 acres and John Rowling and his wife, Priscilla granted same to John Hiett by deed dated 11/4/1700 for £400 paid by Thomas Watson, tanner of said county. Ackn: 2/4/1702. Wit: Joseph Kirkbride, Edward Kempe, Jacob Urher. Rec: 25/9/1702.

P. 88. Deed. John Stackhouse, of Middletown, Bucks Co., yeoman, land lying in Newtown, Bucks Co. adjoining land of Thomas Revells ... land of William Bennetts... containing 300 acres bought from Samuel Hough by deed 4/4/1702, part of land granted by Israel Taylor, son and heir of Christopher Taylor, dec'd. and Joseph Taylor other son, for £120. Ackn: 10/4/1702. Wit:; Matthew Wildman, John Cutler, Thomas Baynes. Rec: 25/9/1702.

P. 90. Deed. Elizabeth Levalley and Charles, her husband, dau. of Robert Hall, late of Bucks Co., dec'd., 275 acres adjoining land of John Headley, confirmed to Robert Hall by patent on 8/12/1685. Land deeded to John Hall and Elizabeth Hall, children of Robert Hall in orphans court dated 18/11/1700 - for £60 paid by John Rowland of aforesaid county, yeoman. Ackn: 29/11/1702. Wit: John White, William Corderey. Rec: 27/9/1702.

P. 91. Deed. John Parsons, Philadelphia Co., carpenter, 290 acres near falls of Delaware River adjoining land of William Beaks, confirmed to John Parsons and wife by patent on 16 Sep 1701 - for £40 paid by Joseph Kirkbride of Bucks Co., yeoman. 1/10/1701. Wit: John Falked, Nicholas Fairlamb, Samuel Powell. Rec: 5/10/1702.

P. 93. Deed. Edward Cowgill and Israel Morris both of Newtown, Bucks Co., husbandmen for £50 paid by Thomas Hilborn of aforesaid place, 130 acres in Newtown adjoining land of Thomas Hillborn, part of a tract sold to said Edward Cowgill and Israel Morris by Richard Burgess and Elizabeth his wife by deed on 11/4/1697. Ackn: 13/6/1702. Wit: Adam Harker, John Cutler, John Chapman, Rec: 7/11/1702.

P. 94. Deed. William Duncan, Bensalem, Bucks Co., yeoman, for £150 paid by Gabriel Baynes, of Falls Township, Bucks Co., yeoman, 145 acres, granted to William Duncan by patent on 24 March 1692/3. Ackn: 21/7/1702. Wit: Peter Worrall, John Cutler. Rec: 7/11/1702.

P. 95. Deed. Thomas Yardley and William Yardley, sons of William Yardley, late of Bucks Co., yeoman, dec'd., who by last will 14/9/1694 bequeathed to Enoch Yardley a tract of land laid out for 500 acres and to sons Thomas and William the moiety of the said tract. For £40 pounds paid by said Enoch Yardley. Ackn: 10/4/1702. Wit: Jacob Janney, Joseph Pemberton, Wm. Beakes. Rec: 8/11/1702.

P. 97. Deed. Jonas Keen, Bucks Co., yeoman, and wife Francis, sole dau. of Francis Walker, dec'd., and John Williams son of Dunk Williams and William Williams of said county, yeoman, other son of Dunk Williams, a parcel of land in Bucks Co., adjoining land of Jonas Keen, 135 1/4 acres, part of a tract called Point Pleasant containing 450 acres which by patent dated 25 March 1696 was granted to said Francis Walker and said Dunk Williams - for £7 to Claus Johnson. Ackn: 5 Sep 1702. Wit: Thomas Brock, Edward Mayos. Rec: 14/11/1702.

P. 98. Deed. 16/5/1702. Walter Pumphrey of Bucks Co., carpenter, to Job Bunting of sd county, yeoman. Clement Dungan, Thomas Dungan, Jeremiah Dungan and John Dungan, sons and heirs of Thomas Dungan of sd county, dec'd. by deed 2/2/1698 granted to Walter Pumphrey a certain tract of land adjoining land of Joseph Large and land of Mordecai Bowden - 200 acres for £240 paid by Job Bunting. Ackn: 16/5/1702. Wit: Samuel Smith, John Kinlow, William Beakes. Rec: 15/11/1702.

P. 99. Deed. Israel Taylor of Tenecum Island, PA, chirurgeon, son of Christopher Taylor, late of Philadelphia, gent. and Joseph Taylor of Philadelphia, cordwainer the other said son of Christopher a tract of land in Newtown, Bucks Co. adjoining Thomas Revell's land, 564 acres, granted to said Christopher Taylor on 20 Oct 1681 - Now sold for £75, paid by Samuel Hough of Newtown, carpenter. Ackn: 2 June 1702. Wit: Robert Heaton, David Lloyd, John Stackhouse. Rec: 15/11/1702.

P. 101. Deed. William Crosdell, Buckingham, Bucks Co., yeoman, son of Thomas Crosdell, late of New Key (Hey?), York Co., England, yeoman, dec'd., and John Crosdell, Bucks Co., yeoman, the other son of Thomas Crosdall, a parcel of land leased and released on 21 April 1682, granted to said Thomas Crosdale, 1000 acres. Whereas 250 acres were purchased by Thomas Stackhouse and sold but not conveyed by the said Stackhouse to Nicholas Walne, who sold his interest to Robert Heaton, Bucks Co. for the sum of £20. Ackn: 28/2/1702. Wit: Samuel Hough, John Stackhouse. Rec: 18/11/1702.

P. 102. Deed. William Atkinson, Bucks Co., for £63 paid by William Biles, Bucks Co., father in law to said William Atkinson a parcel of land. Ackn: 9/10/1702. Wit: Samuel Burgess, Solomon Warder, William Beakes. Rec: 20/11/1702.

P. 103. Deed. Thomas Williams of Burlington of West Jersey and his wife Rebecca Williams, sole extx. and widow of William Bennett formerly of Long Ford in the Parish Harmondsworth of Middlesex Co. but late of Bucks Co., PA, Robert Edwards of Burlington afsd., cooper, and his wife Sarah one of the surviving daus. and heirs of William Bennett and John Scholah of Burlington Co. and his wife Rebecca, the other surviving dau. of William Bennett, 440 acres of 1000 acres released to William Bennett in 1682 who in his will dated 19 Aug 1683 devised 200 acres of said tract to his dau. Elizabeth and 200 acres to his dau. Rebecca and 200 acres to his dau. Ann and 200 acres to his dau. Sarah and made his wife Rebecca his extx. - for £80 paid by Ezra Croasdell. Ackn: 27 March 1702. Wit: Christopher Wetherell, Mathew Thompson and Edward Hunloke. Rec: 15/12/1702.

P. 105. Deed, John Town, Bristol Township, Bucks Co. for £10 paid by Ezra Croasdale, Middletown, Bucks Co., yeoman, 78 acres adjoining land of Ralph Ward and Philip Alphone. Ackn: 8/7/1702. Wit: Thomas Stackhouse, John Cutler. Rec: 5/12/1702/3.

P. 105. Deed. John Griffith, Southampton Township, Bucks Co., yeoman, to his dau, Mary Griffith and son in law Samuel Griffith land adjoining land of Ralph Draykett and containing 50 acres, part of 290 acres conveyed from Israel Taylor to said John Griffith by deed 22/1/1696/7. The said 290 acres being part of 500 acres conveyed from Christopher Taylor, to his son Israel, deed dated 7/2/1685. Ackn:

8/7/1702. Wit: Thomas Baynes and John Cutler. Rec: 16/2/1702/3.

P. 107. Deed. Lawrence Paxson, Bucks Co., eldest son of Edward Paxson, to John Burgess, Bucks Co. yeoman, and Sarah his wife, sister and only heir to Thomas Wolf, late of said county, 130 acres for £100. Ackn: 9/10/1702. Wit: Samuel Burgess, Daniel Atkison and William Paxson. Rec: 19/1/1702.

p. 108. Deed. John Burgess, Bucks Co., yeoman, and Lawrence Pearson of same county. Samuel Carpenter of city of Philadelphia, merchant and executor of last will of Frances Rossell, late of Bucks for consideration of said Frances Rossell's will dated 5/8/1794 gives unto the sons of Samuel Burgess of Bucks Co., 200 acres of land bought from Richard Lundy, Bucks Co. Ackn: 7/10/1702. Wit: Samuel Burgess, Daniel Atkison and William Paxson. Rec: 10/12/1702/3.

p. 112. Deed. Samuel Baker, Makefield Township, Bucks Co., yeoman for £22 paid by George Hayworth, Bristol Township, laborer, a parcel of land adjoining Peter Worrel's land containing 250 acres. Ackn: 16/1/1702/3. Wit: John Rowland, Henry Hartley, John Cutler.

P. 112. Deed. John Rowland, Bristol Township, Bucks Co., yeoman, 200 acres to George Hayward, Bristol for £12. Ackn: 10/1/1702. Wit: Samuel Baker, Henry Hartley, John Cutler. Rec: 5/3/1703.

P. 112. Deed. Samuel Carpenter, Philadelphia merchant, to Willoughby Warder, late of the isle of Wight, Kingdom of England but now of Bucks Co., yeoman, a tract of land on the Delaware River for £50. Ackn: 10/1/1702/3 Wit: Abigail Pemberton, Israel Pemberton, Richard Hough, William Beakes, George Browne, John Turkett. Rec: 8/3/1703.

P. 114 or 116. Deed. Bartholomew Thatcher and Joseph Thatcher, Bucks Co., carpenters, joint executors of last will of Richard Thatcher, their father, dec'd., for £100 paid by Robert Heaton of Middleton town, yeoman, 100 acres. Ackn: 1/1/1702/3. Wit: Henry Nelson, James Heaton. Rec: 22/3/1703.

P. 115 or 117. Deed. Rebecca Doyle, Bucks Co., widow and sole executrix of Edward Doyle, late of same county, 50 acres, part of land granted to Clement Dungan on 7/11/1692 and granted by said Clement

Dungan to Edward Doyle on 9/4/1696 - for £20 paid by Tobias and Sarah Dumock. Ackn: 24/3/1703. Wit: Thomas Dungan, Ezra Knight. Rec: 6/8/1703.

P. 117. Deed. John Sirkett of Bucks Co., yeoman, 536 acres and 35 perches in Bristol Township, adjoining land of Phineas Pemberton and land of William Duncan, for £300 - to William Atkinson. Ackn: 8/7/1703. Wit: William Biles, John Biles and Jane Biles. Rec: 7/8/1703.

P. 119. Deed. Samuel Coate, Springfield Township, Burlington, New Jersey, husbandman, for £80 paid by Shadrack Walley, Newtown, Bucks Co. yeoman, 200 acres adjoining land of William Snead and land of Thomas Constable, part of 500 acres granted to Christopher Taylor on 7/11/1683 and conveyed to Israel Taylor, son of said Christopher and conveyed from Israel to John Coate, father of said Samuel Coate by deed dated 13/11/1689 and assigned to son of Samuel Coate 6th mo, 1699. Ackn: 10/1/1702/3. Wit: William Beakes, William Buckman, John Cutler, Rec: 7/5/1702/3.

P. 121. Joseph Kirkbride of Falls Township, yeoman, for £30, to Mathew Kirkbride of Makefield, tailor, beginning at a post by Delaware River, the corner of John Lust's land. 103 acres.

P. 124. Deed. William Stevenson of William Stevenson, Burlington Co., West New Jersey, and Thomas Stevenson of Bucks Co., 2500 acres, on a branch of Neshaminy River, which said land was granted to aforesaid William Stevenson and Thomas Stevenson By Thomas Revell of Burlington Co., admr. of the estate and ex. in trust of the last will of Elizabeth Latham of Burlington, dec'd., relict of John Grey alias Latham of Burlington, dec'd. Now for £340, paid by John Rodman, Junr. of Flushing, Queens Co. on Nassau Island and Thomas Richardson of the town and county of West Chester, New York, shipwright. 8th of 7th month 1703. Wit: Jonathan Scaife, ---. Rec: 29th of 8th month 1703.

P. 126. Mary Giles and Dorothy Giles, both of Burlington Co., West New Jersey, spinsters, heirs of Alexander Giles, late of Bucks Co., yeoman, dec'd., a tract in Middle Township beginning by Neshaminy Creek at the corner of a tract laid out to Robert Holgate adjoining land of John Bond, 246 acres, laid out to Alexander Giles as part of 1500 acres which William Penn conveyed to Henry Baly who sold the same to said

Alexander Giles - to Robert Heaton of Bucks Co., yeoman. Wit: Benj. Wheate, Joshua Tompkins, Wm. Biles. 8/7/1703.

P. 128. John Smith of Burlington Co., West New Jersey, blacksmith, 4 lots in town of Bristol, one adjoining the lot of Thomas Musgrove on south side of Mill Street and adjoining the corner of Richard Burgis lot and John White's land, 4 1/4 acres, part of a moiety of 37 acres granted to John Smith - to Charles Levalle of the town of Bristol, cooper. 20 May 1703. Wit: Joseph White, James Carter, Joseph Wood. Rec: 20 May 1703.

P. 131. Anthony Elton of Raucocao Creek, Burlington Co., West New Jersey, yeoman, whereas Gov. Wm. Penn by lease and release dated 1 and 2 Aug 1681 granted to Anthony Elton [now dec'd.], father of the said Anthony, 500 acres - to Robert Wheeler. 23rd of 1st month 1701. Wit: Tho. Revell, John Robardes, Thomas Stokes. Rec: 8th of 7th month 1703. Rec: 5th of 9th month 1703.

P. 132. Robert Wheeler of Burlington, West New Jersey, shopkeeper, for £10, by John Large of Bucks Co., tailor, a parcel of land in Buckingham Township, beginning at the corner of Richard Lundy's and adjoining James Heaton's land, 100 acres which is part of 500 acres granted to Anthony Elton of West New Jersey by lease and release. 24/2/1703. Wit: Wm. Biddle, Jun., William Bustell. Deliver 8/7/1703. Rec: 6/9/1703.

P. 133. Samuel Smith to Solomon Warder. Whereas Edmond Lovett and Joseph Kirkbride by this indenture dated 20th of this month March convey to Samuel Smith 2 tracts, one beginning at a corner post on the Delaware River [boundary] by Joseph Large's land and the land of Phineas Pemberton, 200 acres; the other tract adjoining and containing 100 acres. Samuel Smith for £300 paid by Solomon Warder conveys same to Warder, excepting one of the messuages and 100 acres. 20/1/1703. Wit: Joseph Kirkbride, Solomon Levett, ... Kirkbride. Samuel Smith acknowledged receiving payment 7/2/1703. Rec: 8/7/1703.

P. 135. Indenture 20 March 1702/3. Edmond Lovett and Joseph Kirkbride, Bucks Co., yeoman, to Samuel Smith of the same co., Tillmonger(?). Whereas Abraham Cox late of said county, yeoman, was seized of two tracts, one beginning at a post by the Delaware River adjoining Joseph Large's land and the land of Phineas Pemberton, 200 acres, being the land which Thomas Williams and Rebecca his wife sold to Abraham Cox on 2 Nov 1695. The other tract adjoining and containing 100 acres which Edmond Lovett sold to said Abraham Cox, deed dated 8/4/1685. Abraham Cox in his will of 26/8/1687 made his wife Sarah sole extx. and gave her ⅓ his estate, real and personal and the residue to his two sons, Abraham and Thomas and appointed Edmond Lovett and Joseph Kirkbride to be trustees for his children. Wit: Pentecost Teague, Solomon Warder. Received partial payment 8/7/1703. Rec: 24/8/1703.

P. 138. Solomon Warder, yeoman, to Jacob Janney. Whereas there is a parcel of land beginning at the back end of Joseph Large's granted to Samuel Smith by Edmond Lovett and Joseph Kirkbride on 20 March last past. For £50. Also 6 ½ acres of meadow next to Edward Ratclife's line. 8 Sep 1703. Wit: George Biles, John Biles, Wm. Atkinson, Wm. Beakes. Received 8 Sep 1703 the consideration. 8/7/1703 delivered in open court. Rec: 30/9/1703.

P. 140. Deed. Jacob Janney, yeoman, to Abel Janney, blacksmith. Indenture 30 May 1700. Tract in township of Makefield, beginning at a corner tree of Richard Hough's land and adjoining land formerly belonging to Thomas Tuniclift - land granted by warrant on 12/6/1682 and laid out on 9th day of the 7th month next, 250 acres to Thomas Janney, purchaser but since by a resurvey is found to contain 365 acres and 12 perches and Thomas Janney by his last will dated 21/3/1695, devised the tract and plantation to Jacob Janney and (eldest son of the said Thomas Janney dec'd.) whereby Jacob Janney became lawfully seized of the land. For £200. Wit: Saml. Beakes, John Biles, Wm. Atkinson, Wm. Beakes. 10/1/1702/3 delivered. Rec: 30/9/1703.

P. 142. Deed. Nehemiah Blackshaw son of Randall Blackshaw, yeoman, to Peter Wood. A tract on the chief branch of Neshaminy, 300 acres, which was laid out to Randall aforesaid as part of his land purchased from James Harrison late of Bucks Co., dec'd. 2/12/1701. Wit: Joseph Hacock, John Rowland. Conveyance delivered 10/1/1702/3 Rec: 10/10/1703.

P. 143. Deed. Jacob Clowes to Richd. Hough, yeoman. Whereas John Clowes, father of the said Joseph Clowes by his last will 29/11/1686 devised to his son Joseph Clowes, 500 acres, by the River Neshaminy, bounded on the northwest by Randle Blackshaw's land, to the southeast by John Tatham's land, to the northeast by the Society's land. For £60. 10/1/1702. Wit: Samuel Beaks, Wm. Beaks. Conveyance delivered 10/1/1702. Rec: 4/10/1703.

P. 144. Deed. Thomas Sison of Philadelphia Co., yeoman, and Priscilla his wife, dau. and sole extx. of the last will of Samuel Allen late of Philadelphia Co., cordwainer, dec'd., to Henry Paxson, yeoman, Bucks Co., a tract in Newtown, beginning at a corner of William Bennett's land ... by Israel Morris's land ... 100 acres, for the use of Charles Plumly in right and as part of the purchase of said Samuel Allen from William Penn. Whereas William Plumly, son and heir of the said Charles Plumly granted the said 100 acres to Henry Paxson with another 100 acres adjoining to James Boyden's in exchange for 125 acres on Neshaminy Creek adjoining Nicholas Waln's land. Whereas said Samuel Allen by his last will dated 14/10/1699 made no mention of the said 100 acres; however he devised to his son in law Thomas Sisom "all the rest of his estate..." and gives to his son in law Thomas Sisom and his dau. Priscilla Sisom, they paying out of the same 40 shillings to Martha Dawson. Wit: Nathaniel Poole, Abraham Roe. 9/10/1705. Rec: 30/10/1703.

P. 147. Deed. Mary Plumley relict and extx. of James Plumley, yeoman, dec'd., of the first part and Wm. Budd of Burlington Co., West Jersey, Yeoman and Charles Plumly of city of Philadelphia, joyner of the second part and John Plumly of Bucks Co., yeoman, of the third part. Indenture 10 March 1702. Whereas Henry Paxson of Bucks Co., yeoman, and Margery his wife and Elizabeth Burgess of the said county, widow, dau. of the said Henry and Margery Paxson, since dec'd., did by indenture dated 10 Dec 1698 for the consideration therein, sell to said James Plumley and John Plumley of the said county of Bucks (brother of the said James), a tract beginning at a corner marked tree standing by Neshaminy Creek adjoining Henry Pawlin's land ... by the land formerly William Carter's - 500 acres. And whereas said James was seized of said land and made his last will and ordered that all his estate should be sold; that his wife Mary should have 100 acres for the breeding up of his son John Plumley and the remaining part to be improved for his said son; he appointed his wife extx. and his brother Charles Plumley and Uncle William Budd his overseers thereof - will dated 16 Oct 1702. Now by this indenture Mary Plumly by virtue of the last will of said James Plumly and with the consent of Charles Plumley and William Budd, for £150, conveyed to John Plumly all that moiety of half part of said 500 acres. Wit: Moore, C.(?), John Bouchier. Conveyance was delivered on 9/10/1703. Rec: 1/11/1703.

P. 148 (149?). Deed. Richd. Hough, yeoman, to Peter Webster, yeoman. A tract beginning at a corner tree of Robert Lucas' land [boundary] by John Sidal's land ... by Joseph Kirkbride's, part of a tract granted to Richard Hough by Edward Shippen, Thomas Story and James Logan, commissioners for granting lots and lands in Pennsylvania. For £80 and £40. 200 acres. Wit: John Cutler, Abel Janney. Conveyance delivered 9/10/1703. Received 20 Oct 1703 of Peter Webster aforementioned consideration. Rec: 13/11/1703.

P. 149. Deed. James Yates of Newtown, husbandman, to Daniel Done of Newtown for £21, a parcel of land in Newtown, beginning at a sapling in Thomas Constable's line ... Newtown Creek ... Second Hollow ... 28 acres, part of a tract granted to Israel Taylor on 18 Jan 1692/3 and sold by Taylor to said James Yates 14/2/1793. Signed 4/4/1702. Wit: James Heaton, John Cutler. Received consideration 4/4/1702. Rec: 14/11/1703.

P. 152. Deed. Robt. Heaton, Middle Township, yeoman, to Bernard Christian and Peter Lawrence, both of Bergen Co., of East Jersey, yeoman. Parcel of land beginning at a corner post by Neshaminy Creek ... land belonging to Edward Brooks ... Anthony Tomkins's land ... 500 acres, granted to Christopher Taylor by patent on 6/2/1686; also another parcel of land beginning at a post by Neshaminy Creek ... by Richard Thatcher's land ... 500 acres, granted by patent to Christopher Taylor by patent 11/3/1686. Land was confirmed to Robert Heaton by Israel Taylor, Joseph Taylor, John Buzby and his wife Mary, heirs of said Christopher Taylor. For £825. Wit: Robert Heaton, Jr., Jer. Langhorne. Signed 15 May 1703 and received within mentioned consideration. Rec: 26/11/1703.

P. 154. Release. Edmond Cowgill to Israel Morris. Whereas Edmond Cowgill and Israel Morris, both of Newtown, husbandman, jointly purchased a tract in Newtown containing 300 acres, laid out to Richard Burgess in right of Henry Pawlin first purchaser and conveyed to said Edmond Cowgill and Israel Morris from said Richard Burgess and his wife Elizabeth by deed Poll dated 11/10/1697. And whereas said Edmond

Cowgill hath sold to Thomas Hillburn 130 acres out of his moiety of the said tract confirmed jointly by said Israel Morris with Edmond Cowgill by deed dated 13/6/1702. And a release of 20 acres from Israel Morris. 1/4/1702. Wit: William Buchanan, John Hayhurst. Conveyance delivered 7/10/1703. Rec: 3/12/1703/4.

P. 155. Release Israel Morris to Edmond Cowgill. [*See above.*]

P. 156 Deed. Wm. Biles, yeoman, to Henry Paxson. Tract beginning at a corner of the land late of John White ... by the land sometime of George White's ... Neshaminy Creek ... 100 acres, part of 500 acres granted to William Carter of Philadelphia on 9/5/1686. And by William Carter conveyed to Robert Carter of Bucks Co., dec'd. on 23/5/1686 and since granted to said William Biles being admr. to Edward Carter, eldest son of afsd. Robert Carter, by John Rowland (ex. of John White), Robert Carter afsd. unto whom it legally descended after the said Robert Carter died intestate. For £80. Wit: John Rowland, Henry Bowen, Wm. Beakes. Received 10/12/1703 the sum of £80. Conveyance delivered 9/1/1793/4. Rec: 23/1/1703/4.

P. 157. Deed. John Rowland, yeoman, to Edmond Lovett, Wm. Atkinson and Nehemiah Blackshaw. Whereas a parcel of land near the house of Thomas Watson the elder, 5 perches by 5 perches formerly laid out for a burying place by said John Rowland and still reserved and used for the same purpose, now John Rowland for 6 shillings paid by Edmond Lovett, William Atkinson and Nehemiah Blackshaw, conveys the same. Wit: Tho. Watson, Wm. Beakes. 10/1/1703. Rec: 24/1/1704.

P. 158. Deed. Mary Baker, widow, to Wm. Paxson, yeoman, for £58, a parcel of land, part of which William Paxson, Junr., now lives on, viz., all the land lying on the westerly side of a run of water commonly called Paxsons Run or Creek bounded on the north by land of William Paxson, Senr., on the south by land of Jeremiah Langhorne, on the westerly side by land of Aden Harker and Thomas Stackhouse, Junr. 40 acres. Land which William Paxson, Junr. conveyed to John Scarborough by deed poll dated 14/4/1699 and said Scarborough conveyed same to Mary Baker by deed poll dated 12/12/1700. Wit: John Watson, Samuel Hanson, George Clough. Ackn: 10/1/1703/4. Rec: 24/1/1704.

P. 159. Deed. Joseph Growdon of Trevose in the township of Bensalem to Margaret Stackhouse, wife of Thomas. For £30, a parcel of land in Bensalem Township beginning at a small hickory in Southampton line being the corner of Stephen Sand's land, 100 acres, granted to Joseph Growdon on 24/25 Oct 1681. 8 March 1703. Wit: John Dunkan, Jer. Langhorne. Ackn: 10/1/1703/4. Rec: 25/1/1704.

P. 161. Deed. John Rowland, yeoman, ex. of John White; John Carter, yeoman; Henry Bowen, husbandman, and Jane his wife - to Wm. Biles, a tract beginning at the corner of John White's land ... by the land of George White's ... Neshaminy Creek ... Henry Paxson's land ... 100 acres, part of a tract of 500 acres that was granted to William Carter of Philadelphia by patent 9/5/1686 and later conveyed to Robert Carter of Bucks Co., yeoman, dec'd., father of John Carter and Jane Bowen afsd., on 23rd of month and year afsd., recorded in the Rolls Office in Book A, vol. 1, page 56. For £5 paid by William Biles, admr. of Edward Carter, dec'd., another son of Robert Carter afsd. Wit: William Croasdale, Edward Mayos, Wm. Beakes. Delivered 9/1/1703/4. Rec: 25/1/1704.

P. 162. Deed. William Biles, admr. of Edward Carter, John Carter, yeoman, Henry Bowen, husbandman and his wife Jane Bowen, to John White, a tract beginning at the corner of Francis White's land ... by land sometime of George White, 100 acres, part of 500 acres granted to William Carter [*see above*], conveyed to Robert Carter, father of Edward Carter and Jane Bowen afsd. For £5 paid by John White. Wit: William Croasdiel, Edward Mayos, Wm. Beakes. Delivered 9/1/1703/4. Rec: 29/1/1704.

P. 164. Deed. John White of Bristol, Bucks Co., to Bartoll Jacobs. Whereas John White was granted on 12/4/5th year of James 2nd, confirmed by patent to John White 500 acres by patent, beginning at a corner post of the land of Richard and William Amor's land ... by George White's land not including a piece of meadow on Neshaminy Creek granted to John Glawson. And whereas John White was granted 250 acres by patent beginning at a corner of William Carter's land. And whereas Elizabeth White, relict and extx. of George White, yeoman, dec'd., Peter White, Francis White, Joseph White and Benjamin White son of the said George and Elizabeth White, by a deed poll dated 29/4/1698 conveyed to John White 200 acres beginning at a tree on Neshaminy Creek ... a line of the land formerly of Robert Hall ... For £400, 500 acres in Middletown Township. Wit: John Jewell, Hn. Huddy,

Page Clark, Charles Huddy. Received 13 March 1702/3. Ackn: 9/1/1703/4. Rec: 6/2/1704.

P. 166. Deed. Wm. Plumly, yeoman, to Henry Paxson. In consideration of 125 acres of land adjoining Neshaminy Creek and the land of Nicholas Waln, being the upper moiety of 250 acres of land granted to Margery Plumly now wife to Henry Paxson and mother of afsd. William Plumly by patent dated 18/3/88 conveyed by Henry Paxson father in law to afsd. William Plumly of Bucks Co., yeoman, 100 acres fronting on Neshaminy Creek and adjoining land of James Boyden which land was conveyed by Samuel Allen to Charles Plumly, father of the afsd. William Plumly dec'd. by deed dated 13 Oct 1682 as also 100 acres in the wood as yet untaken up or unlaid out. Wit: Wm. Paxson, James Paxson, James Plumly. 10/12/1688. Rec: 23/5/1704.

P. 167. Deed. William Paxson, Junr., to William Paxson, Senr., for £300, a tract beginning at a post of the land of William Paxson, Senr., 286 acres, granted to James Paxson, father of above said William Paxson, Junr., on 28/11/1693 and conveyed by deed by James Paxson on 8/4/1693 to his son William Paxson, Junr. 4 April 1704. Wit: Tho. Watson, Wm. Beakes, Willoughby Warder. Received 4 April 1704 £300. Ackn: 15 June 1704. Rec: 30 Sep 1704.

P. 169. Deed. Henry Nelson of Newtown, laborer, to Henry Cooper of Newtown, blacksmith, for £75, a parcel of land in Newtown beginning at a corner of Joseph Ward's land, 154 acres, part of 564 acres conveyed to Samuel Hough by Israel Taylor and Joseph Taylor by deed poll dated 2 June 1702 which 154 acres was conveyed to said Henry Nelson by Samuel Hough 7 March 1703/4. Wit: Jonathan Cooper, Israel Langhorne, Jer. Langhorne. 1 May 1704. Ackn: 15 June 1704. Rec: 18 Nov 1704.

P. 170. Deed. Wm. Croasdell to Henry Paxson, for £4.10, a tract in Salisbury Township, beginning at a corner post in the line of Stephen Beak's land ... at a corner of Richard Burges' land, 250 acres, which was granted to said William Croasdale in right of his father's purchase from the Proprietary. Wit: Wm. Biles, Jun., Jer. Langhorne. 1 Sep 1704. Received 15 Sep 1704. Rec: 21 Nov 1704.

P. 171. Deed. Amy Scott of Bensalem Township, widow and relict of

Thomas Scott, to her eldest son, Saml. Scott, for affection and £10. Whereas there is a tract in Bensalem Township beginning at a rivulet Poquessin ... William Duncan's land ... Francis Searle's land ... other lands of Thomas Scott, 80 acres which land Thomas Knight conveyed to afsd. Thomas Scott as by assignment on the back side of his deed from Joseph Growdon. Thomas Scott by his will dated 27/12/1702/3 gave said tract to his wife Amy Scott to disperse to his children at her discretion. Wit: James Harrison, Joseph Growdon, John Dunkan, Geo. Dunkan. 28 Aug 1704. Ackn: 15 Sep 1704. Rec: 21 Nov 1704.

P. 173. Deed. Ralph Dracott of Southampton, yeoman, to Thos. Stackhouse, Junr., of Middle Township, yeoman, for £45, tract in township of Southampton, beginning at a birch tree by Neshaminy Creek ... by Evan Griffith's land ... Samuel Griffith's land ... 122 acres laid out on 1/2/1704 which is part of 250 acres granted on 4 July 1704 to Henry Walmsley and Thomas Walmsley and by them granted to said Ralph Dracott 12 Sep 1704. Wit: Wm. Rakestraw, John Naylor, Jer. Langhorne. 13 Sep 1704. Ackn: 15 Sep 1704. Rec: 22 Nov 1704.

P. 174. Deed. Henry Walmsley, yeoman, and Thos. Walmsley, yeoman, to Ralph Dracott, for £112, a parcel of land beginning at Neshaminy Creek ... by Evan Griffith's land ... by the land of Thomas Stackhouse ... land of John Swift ... by the land laid out to Israel Taylor, 250 acres, which was granted to said Henry Walmsley and Thomas Walmsley by patent. Wit: William Rakestraw, John Naylor, Jer. Langhorne. 12 Sep 1704. Received payment 12 Sep 1704. Ackn: 15 Sep 1704. Rec: 23 Nov 1704.

P. 176. Deed. Thomas Stackhouse, Jun., of Middle Township, yeoman, for £20, to Ralph Dracott, a tract in Southampton Township beginning at a corner of Ralph Dracott's land ... by Evan Griffith's land, 50 acres granted to said Thomas Stackhouse by Nicholas Walne of Philadelphia Co., yeoman, on 1/4/1686. Wit: Wm. Rakestraw, John Naylor, Jer. Langhorne. 12 Sep 1704. Payment received on 12 Sep 1704. Ackn: 15 Sep 1704. Rec: 23 Nov 1704.

P. 177. Deed. Solomon Warder, yeoman, to Wm. Biles, Jr., for £300, a tract of land beginning at a corner tree by the land sometime of John Rowland ... by Anthony Burton's land ... by William Bile's land ... by Randall Blackshaw's land ... by the land formerly of William Duncan's,

300 acres which land was first surveyed to Thomas Atkinson dec'd. but not being paid for it was purchased by William Biles, yeoman, and by William Biles and his wife Jane, sometime widow and relict of aforementioned Thomas Atkinson and by deed dated 10/4/1696 conveyed to George Biles, son of said William Biles and by George Biles conveyed on 10 June 1702 to afsd. Solomon Warder. Wit: Willoughby Warder, Wm. Beakes. 10 April 1704. Received payment 10 April 1704. Ackn: 15 June 1704. Rec: 26 Nov 1704.

P. 179. Deed. Thomas Williams of Burlington, West New Jersey, and his wife Rebecca, extx. of the last will of her former husband, William Bennett sometime of Harmondworth in the county of Middlesex, England, but late of Bucks Co., yeoman, dec'd., and Robert Edwards of Burlington, cooper, and his wife Sarah, one of the surviving daus. and heirs of said William Bennett, and John Scolah of Annanican in said county of Burlington, yeoman, and his wife Rebecca the other surviving dau. and heir of said William Bennett, for £10, 200 acres, to Ezra Croasdale of Bucks Co., yeoman. Whereas on 19-20 March 1682, Governor Wm. Penn granted to said William Bennett 1000 acres who by his last will dated 9 Aug 1683 amongst other things devised 200 acres to his dau. Elizabeth and 200 acres to his dau. Rebecca and 200 acres to his dau. Anne and 200 acres to his said dau. Sarah and made his wife Rebecca sole extx. and the residue 200 acres being vested in said Sarah and Rebecca by survivorship. Wit: Christopher Wetherill, John Cowgill, Joseph Smith. 11 May 1702. Received payment 11 May 1702. Ackn: 10/?/1702. Rec: 4 Dec 1704.

P. 181. Deed. Lawrence Pearson, yeoman, to Enoch Pearson, 100 acres, for £220, one moiety of 200 acres, that Samuel Carpenter, ex. of last will of Francis Rossell, released and confirmed to John Burgess, son of Samuel Burgess of Bucks Co., yeoman, on 17/12/1701, and later John Burgess conveyed on 9/10/1702 to afsd. Lawrence Pearson. Wit: Daniel Jackson, Saml. Burgess, Junr., Wm. ---?. 8 March 1703/4. Received payment 8 March 1703/4. Ackn: 9/1/1703/4. Rec: 5 Dec 1704.

P. 182. Deed. Edward Mayos to Jona. Greaves, for £20, a lot in the town of Bristol, beginning at a post by the side of Mill Street at the corner of John Large's lot near Lemuel Oldale's lot, confirmed to Samuel Oldale, father of said Lemuel Oldale by deed dated 1/7/1699 from Thomas Brook and by Samuel Oldale to his son by deed of gift dated 14 March

1701/2 and by Lemuel Oldale to Edward Mayos 5/12/1703. Wit: John Jackson, Wm. Gabilas. 2 Sep 1704. Ackn: 16 Sep 1704. Rec: 5 Dec 1704.

P. 183. Deed. Joseph Growdon of Trevose in Bensalem, Bucks Co., Gent., to Thomas Walmsley of Bensalem, for £58, a tract in Bensalem beginning at Samuel Allen's corner oak adjoining Clause Johnson's land ... Henry Mitchell's land, 300 acres being part of Joseph Growdon's mammoth or great tract called Bensalem. Wit: Evan Griffith, Lawrence Growdon, Eliz: Growdon. 7/1/1703/4. Conveyance delivered 10/1/1703/4. Rec: 5 Dec 1704.

P. 185. Deed Andrew Elliot of Makefield, yeoman, to John Hiett, late of same town, Bucks Co. on 1 May 1704. Patent on 26 Sep 13th year of Wm. and Mary, a tract in township of Makefield, 320 acres, whereas Andrew Elliott in 1703 granted to his brother William Elliot, 100 of the 320 acres and [now] the remaining part beginning at the Delaware River adjoining Henry Margerum's land ... land of Richard Hough, for £250. Wit: George Biles, Saml. Burges. Payment received 1 May 1704. Ackn: 15 Sep 1704. Rec: 6 Dec 1704.

P. 187. Deed. Charles Lavalle of town of New Bristol to William Silverstone of Bristol, laborer, for £125, a parcel of land in the town of Bristol beginning on the north side of Mill Street, part of 37 acres granted to John White, late of New Bristol, dec'd., by patent dated 10/12/1690 who confirmed same to Charles Lavalle by deed dated 9 June 1703. Wit: Tho. Brook, Richard Radcliffe, Jer. Langhorne. 10 Dec 1704. Ackn: 14 Dec 1704. Rec: 7 Jan 1704.

P. 188. William Hayhurst of Middletown, to John Cutler of Middletown, schoolmaster, for £50, a parcel of land in Middletown, beginning at a post in Matthew Wildman's line [boundary] by Robert Heaton's land ... Henry Huddleston's ... by the land laid out to Richard Thatcher - 50 acres which is part of 250 acres laid out to Cuthbert Hayhurst, father of said William and confirmed to him by patent dated 20/10/1685. Wit: Joseph Wildman, James Wildman. 9/10/1704. Ackn: 14 Dec 1704. Rec: 7 Jan 1703/4.

P. 190. Deed. Thomas Stevenson, yeoman, to Harman Vansandt, a tract in Bensalem Township, for £200, beginning at a corner of Johanes Vansant's land ... Joseph Growdon's land - 250 acres, part of 1000 acres which was conveyed to said Thomas Stevenson by Thomas Revel of Burlington of West New Jersey, admr. of the estate and ex. in trust of the last will of Elizabeth Tathem of Burlington, dec'd., relict of John Grey alias Tathem of Burlington by deed dated 20 Jan 1701. Wit: A. Wibardlis Vansant, Jonas Vansandt. 1 Aug 1704. Ackn: 14 Dec 1704. Rec: 8 Jan 1704.

P. 191. Deed. Thomas Stevenson, yeoman, to Johannes Vansandt, a tract in Bensalem Township, 125 acres [*part of the same tract as above*]. Wit: A. Wibardlis Vansandt, Jones Vansandt, Adalfas Bruer. 1 Aug 1704. Ackn: 14 Dec 1704. Rec: 12 Jan 1704.

P. 193. Deed. Edmund Lovett of Bristol Township, to John Adington, for £53, husbandman, a parcel of land in the place and county afsd., beginning at a tree in John Headley's line ... land laid out to George White ... by Daniel Jackson's land ... Thomas Watson's land ... an ash in Thomas Terry's line - 100 acres, being part of 300 acres and 87 perches granted to said Edmund Lovett by patent dated 2/12/1702. Wit: John Hutchinson, Thomas Watson. 9/10/1704. Ackn: 14 Dec 1704. Rec: 15 Jan 1704.

P. 195. Deed. Henry Paxton, James Plumly, Charles Plumly, John Plumly, George Plumly heirs of Charles Plumly, to Henry Tomlinson, for £30, a parcel of land beginning at Neshaminy Creek ... land of James Boyden ... land of Samuel Carpenter ... land of John Baldwin, 100 acres which part of the land that Samuel Allen conveyed to Charles Plumly, father to the afsd. James, Charles, John and George Plumly, by deed dated 13 Oct 1682 and was sold by William Plumly, eldest son of said Charles Plumly, to said Henry Paxton by deed dated 10/12/1688, acknowledged in open court 7/7/1689. Signed by Henry Paxton, Charles Plumly, George Plumly, George Hamond, John Budd. 29 Jun 1704. Ackn: 15 Sep 1704. Rec: 15 Jan 1704.

P. 196. Deed. Jonathan Eldridge, Burlington Co., cordwainer, to Shadrack Walley, for £30, tract in Newtown Township, beginning by the side of the Common adjoining Thomas Hillborn's town lot ... by Mary Haworth's land - 50 acres, part of a tract granted to Jonathan Eldridge by patent dated 15/12/first year of his majesty's reign. Wit: W. Heulings(?), Wm. Beakes. 20 June 1704. Payment received 21 June 1704. Ackn: 15 Sep 1704. Rec: 29 Jan 1704.

P. 197. Deed. William Snead of Philadelphia, innkeeper, to Shadrach Walley, land which by warrant ca. 1684 there was laid out to said William Snead, 200 acres, for £20, adjoining the lands of John Hough, Israel Taylor and Shadrach Walley's 409 acres and the land of Thomas Janney which said 200 acres the said William Snead formerly sold to said Shadrach Walley but no conveyance or deed as yet made. Wit: Richard Heath, Tho. Grey, Tho. Fairman. 21 Dec 1703. Ackn: 15 June 1704. Rec: 29 Jan 1704.

P. 198. Deed. Thomas Walmsley of Bensalem, yeoman, to Evan Griffith of Southampton, cordwainer, for £150, a parcel of land near Southampton beginning at a corner post at Neshaminy Creek being a corner of Nicholas Waln's land - 125 acres, conveyed to Thomas Walmsley by Henry Paxon and his wife Margery, Abel Hinchstone and his wife Elizabeth and James Plumly by deed dated 8/7/1699; also another parcel beginning at Neshaminy Creek adjoining former land of Elizabeth Walmsley - 200 acres being part of a tract granted to Nicholas Waln to Edmund Cutler on 6/4/1686 and by Isabel Cutler relict and admx. of Edmund Cutler to William Paxson by deed dated 10/8/1698 and from Paxon to afsd. Thomas Walmsley. Wit: Margaret Cutler, John Cutler, Henry Nelson. 7/1/1703/4. Conveyance delivered 10/1/1703/4. Rec: 30 Jan 1704.

P. 200. Deed. Margaret Atkinson of Bellmount in Bensalem Township, widow, to William Cooper of Buckingham Township, husbandman, a tract in Buckingham Township, for £30. Whereas on 18 March 1698, William Penn demised to Christopher and John Atkinson, late of Scotforth, Lancaster Co., England, dec'd., 1500 acres in the Province. And whereas the said Christopher Atkinson by his last will dated 1 July 1699 devised to Margaret Atkinson then his wife, 500 acres of the said land, to be disposed of for their younger children. The parcel beginning at a tree in Thomas Parson's line and adjoining Mercy Phillips' land ... Richard Tucker's corner ... surveyed and laid out for William Cowper in right of said Christopher Atkinson 5/6/1700. Wit: Robert Hollis(?). 8/1/1702/3. Conveyance delivered 10/1/171702/3. Rec: 30 Jan 1704.

P. 202. Deed. Samuel Smith, yeoman, to John Large, tailor, for £35, a tract beginning at the Delaware River at a corner of Tobias Dimock's land adjoining a corner of Jacob Janney's land ... post in Joseph Large's line - 104 acres, and is the moiety of a tract granted to Abraham Cox by deed from Thomas Williams and his wife Rebecca on 2(?)/9/1695 and by the will of Abraham Cox it was confirmed to above said Samuel Smith by Joseph Kirkbride and Edward Lovett, trustees on 20 March last past. Wit: Daniel Jackson, George Biles, Wm. Beakes. 24/12/1703. Payment received 24/12/1703. Ackn: 9/1/1703/4. Rec: 5 Feb 1704.

P. 203. Deed. William Biles, yeoman, admr. of estate of Edward Carter, dec'd., and John Rowland, yeoman, ex. of John White, brewer, dec'd., and John Carter, yeoman, and Henry Bowen, husbandman, and his wife Jane, to Francis White, a tract beginning at a corner of afsd. John Carter's land adjoining land formerly of George White ... by Henry Paxton's land - 100 acres, part of 500 acres granted to William Carter of Philadelphia dated 9/5/1686 and later by William Carter conveyed to Robert Carter, father of Edward Carter, John Carter and Jane Bowen. Wit: Willi Croasdale, Edward Mayos, Wm. Beakes. 10/12/1703. Conveyance delivered 15 Sep 1704. Rec: 5 Feb 1704.

P. 205. Deed. William Biles, yeoman, admr. of estate of Edward Carter and John Rowland, yeoman, ex. of John White, and Henry Bowen, husbandman, and his wife Jane, to John Carter, a tract of 200 acres, part of 500 acres granted to William Carter [see above]. Wit: Jere Howes, Stephen Mills. 2 July 1678. Rec: 7 Feb 1704.

P. 207. Release. Richard Cashbeard, citizen and wax chandler of London, to Gilbert Wheeler of Fruillerer(?). 2 July 1678. Wit: Jere Howes, Stephen Mills, Scr. Rec: 7 Feb 1704.

P. 207. Deed. Isaac Atkinson, cordwiner, 200 acres by the land of William Biles, granted on 31/5/1684 to Samuel Dark and by him conveyed to 18/6/1683 [sic] granted to John Radly and by him confirmed to Edward Guy who died intestate and the land descended to his son John Guy and to his son Edward Guy, and Edward Guy dying intestate the land descended to his sons John Guy and Edward Guy and to his dau. Ester Guy. John Guy, eldest son of the above named Edward Guy granted same to said Isaac Atkinson by his deed dated 9/10/1700. Now for £50, to Jonathan Taylor. Wit: Jer. Langhorne, T. Clarke, Wm. Biles, Jr. 10/10/1702. Conveyance delivered 11/10/1702. Rec: 26 Feb 1704.

P. 209. Deed of gift. Samuel Oldale, free mason, to his son Lemuel Oldale, all his houses, lands, lots of land, goods, chattels, etc. 14 March

1705. Wit: Samuel Beakes, Tho. Brook(?), Wm. Beakes, Rec: 2 May 1705.

P. 210. Deed. Henry Paxson, yeoman, to James Verrier, Burlington, New Jersey, mason, for £105, a tract at a corner of the land of the late John White's and adjoining land sometime of George White - 100 acres, part of 500 acres that was granted to William Carter of Philadelphia on 9/5/1686 and by William Carter conveyed to Robert Carter and later conveyed to William Biles, admr. of Edward Carter, eldest son of said Robert Carter, by John Rowland, John Carter, Henry Bowen and his wife Jane on 10/12/1703 and by William Biles to Henry Paxson. Wit: William Mead, Jer. Langhorne. 12 March 1704/5. Ackn: 15 March 1704/5. Rec: 2 May 1705.

P. 212. Deed. William Croasdale to John Headly, yeoman, for £15, a lot in Bristol, beginning at a corner of John Large's land, part of 11 acres which was confirmed to Anthony Burton and Thomas Brock by deed from Joseph English on 20/12/1695 and since laid out to the said Burton as part of his moiety as by indentures of partition made between said Brock and Burton dated 8/4/1696. Wit: Anthony Burton, Daniel Jackson, Jeremiah Langhorne. Ackn: 10 June 1705. Rec: 5 Oct 1705.

P. 214. Deed. Joseph Growdon of Trevose, Gent., to Claus Johnson, a tract in Bensalem Township, beginning at Neshaminy Creek [boundary] by the land of Michael Fredrickson - 120 acres, part of the overplus of Danl. Williams and Francis Walker's old purchase from Gov. Andrews, for £45. Wit: John Biles, John Cutler. 15 March 1704/5. Ackn: 15 March 1704/5. Rec: 5 Oct 1705.

P. 215. Deed. Joseph Growdon of Trevose, Gent., to Michael Fredrickson, yeoman, a tract in Bensalem Township, beginning at the mouth of Neshaminy Creek, 77 acres, part of the overplus of Dunk Williams and Francis Walker's old purchase from Gov. Andrews, for £35. Wit: John Biles, John Cutler. 15 March 1704/5. Ackn: 15 March 1704/5. Rec: 9 Oct 1705.

P. 217. Deed. Robert Heaton of Middle Township, yeoman, to George Hulme, Sr., and George Hulme, Jr., for £80, a parcel of land beginning at a forked maple being a corner of Jonathan Scaife's land ... by James Sutton's land ... 200 ½ acres and 20 perches, being part of a tract purchased of Robert Holgate and also part of the tract purchased of Mary and Dorothy Biles, heirs of Alexander Biles and later confirmed to said Robert Heaton by patent dated 12 March 1704. Wit: Jonathan Scaife, Tho. Stevenson, Wm. Atkinson. 12 Sep 1705. Ackn: 13 Sep 1705. Rec: 10 Oct 1705.

P. 218. Deed. Nathan Baker of Chester Co., yeoman to Thomas Hillborne, a tract in Newtown, beginning at a corner post of Jonathan Eldridge's land [boundary] by Arthur Cook's land - 225 acres together with 25 acres in the village of Newtown, granted by patent pursuant to the warrant to John Otter who by his deed dated 4/4/1694 sold the land to Henry Baker, father of afsd. Nathan Baker who devised the land to his son Nathan Baker by his last will but before Henry died he sold 250 acres to Thomas Hillborn (then of Shrewsberry of East Jersey) and died without making alterations in his will and whereas Samuel Baker, son and heir of the said Henry Baker (at the special instance of said Nathan who was then a minor between 16 and 17 years of age) was paid £60 for the use of the said Nathan. Wit: John Cowgill, Rachel Cowgill. 23/3/1705. Conveyance delivered. Ackn: 14 June 1705. Rec: 12 Oct 1705.

P. 221. Power of attorney by Margery Jennings, widow and extx. of the last will of William Jennings of Alton in the county of Southampton, schoolmaster, appoints Peter Chamberlane as her attorney. Wit: Albertus Brandt, John Swift, Junr. 19 April 1701. Rec: 12 Oct 1705.

P. 221. Deed. Joseph Kirkbride of Falls Township, yeoman, to Thomas Kirkbride, his brother, for £50, a parcel in Makefield Township, beginning at a white oak in the line of John Snowdon's land formerly laid out to William Beaks then by Matthew Kirkbride's land ... land laid out to John Luffe - 188 acres and 128 perches being part of a tract sold and conveyed to Joseph Kirkbride from John Parsons by deed dated 1/10/1701. Wit: Jer. Langhorne, John Shaw, John Cutler. 13/4/1705. Ackn: 10 June 1705. Rec: 12 Oct 1705.

P. 223. Deed. Samuel Smith of Burlington, New Jersey, Fellmonger, to Lemuel Oldale of New Bristol, cowper, for £160, a tract beginning at Pigeon Swamp - 200 acres, part of 500 acres that was surveyed to Thomas Rudyard in 1684 and later confirmed to Andrew Robeson by patent 10/6/1685 and by him conveyed by deed on 2 Aug 1686 to Daniel Jones and by Jones conveyed to Daniel Smith by an assignment on the back of the deed dated 11 Oct 1696 and by Daniel Smith conveyed to said Samuel Smith on 12 May 1702. Wit: Anthony Burton, Ralph Cowgill. 14 June 1705. Payment received 14 June 1705. Ackn: 14 June 1705. Rec: 13 Oct 1705.

P. 224. Deed. Robert Heaton of Middle Township, yeoman, to Henrich Johnson Vandike, late of Stratton Island, New York, yeoman, 4 tracts, for £692, beginning at a beach tree on Neshaminy Creek ... corner of William Hayhurst's land ... land of William Paxson ... lands of Adam Harker, Henry Huddlestone, Thomas Bayns and John Stackhouse - 280 acres which land was granted by patent to Robert Heaton dated 22 May 1705; the second tract contains 183 3/4 acres, part of 500 acres granted to James Dilworth by indenture of lease and release dated 14 April 1682 and confirmed to Robert Heaton by James Dilworth by deed on 12 Oct 1697; the third tract ... to a post by the land of William Dark ... by the land of Giles Lucas ... 66 1/4 acres which is part of 1000 acres granted to Thomas Croasdale by indentures of lease and release dated 21-22 April 1682 and whereas 250 acres of the 1000 acres was purchased with the money of Thomas Stackhouse and included in the said indenture and sold but not conveyed to Nicholas Walne who sold his interest to Robert Heaton and was conveyed to Robert Heaton by William Croasdale and John Croasdale, heirs of Thomas Croasdale, dec'd., on 8 April 1702; the 4th tract is a moiety of the north side of a tract beginning at Neshaminy Creek, 340 acres of which land is part of the land granted to Edward Bennett by patent and by Elizabeth Bennett, relict and extx. of the last will of Edward Bennett granted to Nicholas Waln on 2 Nov 1692 and by him confirmed to said Robert Heaton 1 Dec 1697.   Wit: Robert Heaton, Junr., Christian Carensen(?), Jer. Langhorne. 5 Jun 1705. Payment received 5 June 1705. Ackn: 14 June 1705. Rec: 5 Dec 1705.

P. 228. Deed. Francis White, Solsbury Township, to James Carter of Southampton, blacksmith, for £16.12 beginning at a white oak in William Croasdale's line ... William Beakes's land ... Jeremiah Langhorne's land ... 250 acres, laid out to Francis White of Middletown, yeoman, by a warrant dated 18/3/1703 in right of George White, father of the said Francis, as part of his original purchase of 2500 acres, the 250 acres devised to Francis White by the last will of said George White. Wit: Charles(?) Levalley, Ruben Pownall. 29/8/1704. Ackn: 10 June 1705. Rec: 5 Dec 1705.

P. 229. Deed. Joseph Growdon of Bensalem, Gent., to Thomas Stackhouse, Junr., yeoman, of Middle Township, for £20, a lot in the town Bristol, beginning at William Croasdale's lot on Mill Street ... Mill Creek ... part of a greater parcel of land granted to Joseph Growdon 8 Dec 1696. Wit: Jer. Langhorne, Saml. Bulkley, Law. Growdon. 26 July 1705. Ackn: 13 Sep 1705. Rec: 6 Dec 1705.

P. 231. Deed. Edward Mayos of the town of Bristol, shopkeeper, to Robert Smith of Burlington, New Jersey, cooper, for £30, a lot in the town of Bristol, beginning at a post on Ratcliffe Street, part of a greater lot conveyed to Thomas Brock on 18/8/1699, conveyed to Joseph Kirkbride and by him confirmed to Edward Mayos. Wit: John Smith, Luke Guyon. 28 June 1705. Ackn: 13 Dec 1705. Rec: 6 Dec 1705.

P. 232. Deed. William Brown of Chichester, Chester Co., Pennsylvania, and his wife Esther, extx. of Thomas Yardley of the town of Bristol, dec'd., to John Rowland of the town of Bristol, yeoman, for £140. 3 May 1705. Whereas Israel Taylor, son and heir of Christopher Taylor, Joseph Taylor the other son of said Christopher and Isaac Noms and David Lloyd, exs. of the last will of Thomas Loyd, dec'd., by their deed dated 2 Feb 1701/2, conveyed to said Thomas Yardley a tract beginning at a post by the Delaware River ... marked trees of William Hough ... land of Francis Richardson's children ... 562 acres and Thomas Yardley dated 7/11/1703/4 in which he directed his wife to sell the land with remainder of money after debts were paid to go to wife and son. Wit: David Lloyd, Edward Evans, Richard Heath. Ackn: 14 June 1705. Rec: 7 Dec 1705.

P. 234. Deed. Peter Webster, yeoman, to John Hutchinson, 2 small lots, for £20, one beginning at a post on Ratcliffe Street and the other beginning at a post on the other side of Ratcliffe Street, part of two larger lots granted to Peter Webster by Peter White and his wife Elizabeth on 11/2/1700. Wit: Jacob Janney, Wm. Beakes. 12/7/1705. Payment received 12/11/1705. Ackn: 12 Dec 1705. Rec: 13 Dec 1705.

P. 236. Deed. Robert Heaton, for 5 shillings, to Joseph Growdon, Ezra Croasdale, William Paxson, Thomas Hillborn, John Cutler and Thomas Stackhouse, Junr., all of Bucks Co., land in Middletown, beginning at a post at Henry Huddleston's corner ... post in William Hayhurst's line ... 2 acres. Wit: John Croasdale, John Cowgill. 1 Dec 1704. Ackn: 15 March 1704/5. Rec: 2(?) Dec 1705.

P. 238. Deed. William Hayhurst to Joseph Growdon, Ezra Croasdale, William Paxson, Thomas Hillborn, John Cutler and Thomas Stackhouse, for 5 shillings, land in Middletown Township, beginning at a post at Henry Huddleston's corner ... Middletown Meeting House land ... William Hayhurst's land - 1 acre, being land which on 29/10/1685 was conveyed to Cuthbert Hayhurst and after his death the land descended to William Hayhurst as eldest son of Cuthbert Hayhurst. Wit: John Cowgill, John Croasdill. 1 Dec 1704. Ackn: 10 March 1704/5. Rec: 2 Dec 1705.

P. 240. Deed. William Silverstone of the town of New Bristol, Bucks Co., laborer, to James Borradale, for £135, a lot in town of Bristol, beginning at a post on the north side of Mill Street, part of 37 acres which was granted to John White, late of New Bristol, dec'd., by patent dated 10/12/1690 and by John White granted to Charles Levalle of Bristol, cooper, and by deed dated 9 June 1703 conveyed by him to William Silverstone. Wit: Tobias Dymocke, Saml. Darke. 10 June 1705. Payment received 14 June 1705. Ackn: 14 June 1705. Rec: 3 Dec 1705.

P. 242. Deed. John Rowland of Bristol, Bucks Co., Yeoman, and his wife Priscilla Rowland, late Priscilla Shepperd, to William Buckman of Newtown, yeoman, for £20, a parcel of land in Newtown, beginning at a post Neshaminy Creek [boundary] by Stephen Twining's land - 200 acres, being part of 500 acres granted on 20 Aug 1681(1687?) to Priscilla by her then name Priscilla Shepperd. Wit: Daniel Doane, Samuel Hough, Martha White. 12/1/1704/5. Ackn: 13 Sep 1705. Rec: 3 Dec 1705.

P. 243. Deed. Joseph Growdon of Bensalem, Bucks Co., to William Croasdale, for £11, a lot in the town of Bristol fronting on Mill Street and Mill Creek which Joseph Growdon purchased from Peter White and his wife Elizabeth on 8/10/1696. Wit: John Borrodaille, Jer. Langhorne. 12 Sep 1704. Ackn: 13 Sep 1705. Rec: 3 Dec 1705.

P. 244. Deed. Enoch Pearson of Bucks Co., carpenter, to Robert Sanders, of Bucks Co., laborer, a tract, 100 acres, for £25, the moiety of 200 acres that Samuel Carpenter, executor of the last will of Francis Rossell, dec'd., conveyed to John Burges on 7/12/1701 which he conveyed on 9/12/1702 to Lawrence Paxson and by him conveyed to Enoch Paxson on 8 March 1703/4. Wit: 12 Dec 1705. Ackn: 12 Dec 1705. Rec: 4 Dec 1705.

P. 246. Deed. John Smith, late of Bucks Co., now of Burlington in West Jersey, blacksmith, to Mathew Hughes, Bucks Co., yeoman, for £105, land which was patented by John Smith on 13 April 1703, beginning at a corner of the land formerly laid out to Francis Rossell, 200 acres and 40 perches and John Smith by virtue of a deed executed by Thomas Brock of Bucks Co., yeoman, dated 10/8/1700, had land conveyed to him beginning at the top of Lahaskick Hill, 300 acres, part of 1000 acres formerly conveyed to Jacob Telnor and by him to Richard Lundy on 12/2/1688 and Richard Lundy conveyed 500 acres of the 1000 acres to Francis Rossell who by his last will devised the same said 300 acres to Ralph Boone and William Smith who after the death of Francis Rossell conveyed the same to afsd. Thomas Brock on 1/5/1698. Wit: Samuel Carpenter, Daniel Lloyd, Thos. Brock. 12/4/1705. Ackn: 14 June 1705. Rec: 4 Dec 1705.

P. 248. Deed. Peter Chamberlain of Philadelphia Co., yeoman, to William Gregory, of Southampton, yeoman, for £33, land granted by patent on 9 July last past to Margery Jennings, located in Southampton Township beginning at a corner of John Morris's land and in the line of George Willard's land - 225 acres which she conveyed to Peter Chamberlain on 22 Oct last. Wit: Rowland Hughes, John Shaw, Robert Heaton, Richd. Heath. 17 Nov 1705. Ackn: 12 Dec 1705. Rec: 4 Dec 1705.

P. 250. James Streater of Buckingham of Bucks Co., yeoman, for 40 shillings, paid by John Scarborough, John Bye, Tobias Dimock, Samuel Baker, Francis Hange, and Nemiah Blackshaw, all of Bucks Co., 10 acres, being part of 500 acres granted to said James Streater on 5/1/1700. Wit: Willoughby Varder, William Atkinson, Abel Janney. 12/7/1705. Ackn: 12 Dec 1705. Rec: 14 Dec 1705.

P. 252. Deed. Lemuel Oldale of Bucks Co. to Edward Mayos, for £10, a lot in the town of Bristol, beginning on Mill Street at a corner of John Large's lot, being part of a tract granted to Samuel Oldale, father of said Lemuel Oldale, 1/7/1797 and by him conveyed to his son Lemuel Oldale on 14 March 1702. Wit: William Croasdale, John Carter, William Beakes. 5/12/1705. Conveyance delivered 1 March 1703/4. Rec: 14 Dec 1705.

P. 253. Deed. Henry Pawlin of Bucks Co., yeoman and his wife Sarah, to Stophel Vansandt, for £350, a parcel of land beginning on Neshaminy Creek adjoining land of John Plumly and land of William Paxson, Senr. - 300 acres, part of 1000 acres conveyed to Henry Pawlin by William Penn, on 27-28 Nov 1681 and part of 500 acres that was laid out by warrant to Henry Pawlin. Wit: John J. Will(?), James Collings, Cornelius Vansand. 23 May 1706. Ackn: 23 May 1706. Rec: 7 June 1706.

P. 255. Deed. Robert Heaton, Sr. of Middle Township, yeoman, to Thomas Stackhouse and Robert Heaton, Jr. Whereas by articles of agreement made between Robert Heaton, Sr. of the one part and Thomas Stackhouse and Robert Heaton the younger of the other part, both of Middletown, hath sold to them, the Thomas Stackhouse and Robert Heaton, the younger, a parcel of land in Middletown, bounded by Neshaming Creek on the south and on the northwest side by Core Creek, for 30 shillings per acre, for building a mill with the power to dam Core Creek. Wit: James Heaton, Bartholomew Longstreth, Henry Comly, Thomas Thwaites. 3/2/1706. Ackn: 8 June 1706.

P. 256. Deed. Stophell Vansand, Cornelius Vansand, Harman Vansand, Albert Vansand, Johanes Vansand, all of Bucks Co., sons of Garret Vansand, late of Bucks Co., dec'd., and Jezina Vansand and Garret Vansand, younger children of said Garret Vansand, dec'd., for £150 paid by Jacobus Vansand and George Vansand, a tract beginning at a birch tree by Neshaminy River and against the house formerly belonging to Edward Carter - 150 acres which is part of a tract of 5000 acres granted to Joseph Growdon on 24/25 Oct 1681 and the 150 acres was granted by Joseph Growdon to Garrat Vansand by deed dated 10 Feb 1698 and Garrat Vansant dying intestate the land descended to all his children. Wit: Mary Paxson, Jer. Langhorne. 20 June 1706. Rec: 26 July 1706.

P.261 Deed. Evan Griffith, Southhampton, Bucks Co. a parcel of land lying at corner of Ralph Dracols's land adjoining land of Joseph Growdon and land of John Naylor - 125 acres, part of the land which Thomas Walmsley granted to said Evan Griffith - for £63 paid by Joseph Tomlinson. Ackn: 30/3/1706. Wit: Joshua Hoops, Thomas Watson, Henry Felson. Rec: 4/Nov 1706.

P. 263 Deed. Evan Griffith, Southhampton, Gucks Co., cordwainer, a parcel of land near the corner of John Swift's land ... to land of Ralph Draycot ... to land of Joseph Tomlinson - 120 acres, for £63, part of 325 acres granted to Thomas Walmsley, Benselam and by him conveyed to Evan Griffith. Ackn: 13/2/1706. Wit, Joshua Hoops, Thomas Watson, Henry Nelson. Rec: 4 Nov 1706.

P. 265. Mortgage. 17 April 1706. James Streater Bucks Co., practictioner of physic to James Logan, City of Philadelphia, a parcel of land lying by the land of Richard Lundy, William Say, Robert Wheeler and Margaret Atkins containing 500 acres for £50. Ackn: 17 April 1706. Wit: John Jonston, Benjamin Chambers, and John Chersman(?). Rec: 18 Nov 1706.

P. 268. Deed. David Lloyd, Philadelphia, gent., Griffith Jones of Philadelphia, merchant, 2616 acres in Richland Township, adjoining land of George Palmer, for £100. Ackn: 20 Feb 1706. Wit: Thomas England, Richard Heath, Griffith Owen. Rec: 13 Nov 1706.

P. 270 Deed. Thomas Yardley, the elder, of Buches, Parish of Horton, County of Stafford, England, yeoman and Samuel Yardley, of Heath House, Parish of Horton, miller, eldest son of said Thomas Yardley. Said Thomas Yardley, the elder to Thomas Yardley, the younger, late of Birches, now of the city of Philadelphia, cooper, and Samuel Carpenter, Richard Hough and Robert Heath, 500 acres for the consideration of a yearly rent. Ackn: Said 20 Jan 1706. Wit: Thomas Brown, Z. Fulton, Jr. Rec: 18 Nov 1706.

P. 272. Deed. Robert Heaton, of Middletown, Bucks Co., yeoman, James Heaton, son of said Robert Heaton and Henry Comley, of the Manor of Moreland, Philadelphia Co., yeoman, 182 acres in Middletown adjoining land formerly of Henry Huddlestone, dec'd., and land of Robert Heaton ... Henry Johnson Vandike's corner, being part of 432 1/2 acres granted to Robert Heaton by patent on 24/7/1705 and granted by deed of gift with other lands to James Heaton and Henry Comley - for £176 to Thomas Thwaits. Ackn: 13/9/1706. Wit: Ezra Croasdell, Christian Cavenson VandHorne, John Cutler. Rec: 18 Nov 1706.

P. 274. Deed. John Ellet, of Carcus Hook, Philadelphia Co., tailor, and William Marshall, of said county, tailer to John Cozens, Bucks Co., husbandman. John Ellet having sold unto William Marshall 200 acres for £18 but not conveyed to him. Said William Marshall conveyed unto John Couzens a parcel of land containing 50 acres lying near land of Ezra

Bowers being part of 200 acres granted to Peter Groom on 25/4/1690 who sold same to Hugh Marsh who sold the same to Anthony Morgan and said Anthony Morgan granted to Josias Hill who sold the same to John Ellet. Ackn: 27 Nov 1706. Wit: Ezra Bowen, Joseph Hill. Rec. 16 Dec 1706.

P. 276. Deed. John Ellet, of Carcus Hook, Co. of Phila, tailor and William Marshall, of said county, tailor, to Ezra Bowen, Bucks Co., husbandman, John Ellet having sold unto said William Marshall 200 acres for £18 but not conveyed to him and he conveyed same to said Ezra Bowen - a parcel of land beginning at land of Joseph Hill ... land of John Cousens ... containing 50 acres. Ackn: 27 Nov 1706. Wit: John Cousens, Joseph Hill. Rec: 27 Nov 1706.

P. 278. Deed. John Ellet, of Carcus Hook, Co. of Phila, tailor and William Marshall, of said county, tailor, and Ezra Bowen, Bucks Co., husbandman, John Ellet having sold unto said William Marshall 200 acres for £19 but not conveyed to him - 100 acres to Josias Hill. Ackn: 27 Nov 1706. Wit: Ezra Bowen, John Cousens. Rec: 17 Dec 1706.

P. 281. Deed. Nehemiah Blackshaw, Bucks Co., yeoman a parcel of land lying in Bucks Co., containing 112 acres, said land granted by Randall Blackshaw, decd. father of Nehemiah by will dated 2/1/1698 - for £100 paid by Joseph Kirkbride. Ackn: 11 Dec 1706. Wit: Roger Moone, James Moone, Jeremiah Langhorne. Rec: 18 Dec 1706.

P. 283. Deed. James Moon, Sr. Bucks Co., yeoman and his wife, Joan Moon, to Roger Moon, son of said James Mooon for love and affection - 125 acres lying by line of Samuel Dark. Ackn: 11 Dec 1706. Wit: Jonathan Cooper, Joseph Kirkbride and William Paxson. Rec: 10 Dec 1706.

P. 285. Deed. Edward Mayos, Bristol, Bucks Co., merchant, a parcel of land lying by land of John Large and the land of Samuel Oldalis - for £20 paid by John Rowland, Bristol, aforesaid county, yeoman. Ackn: 21/6/176. Wit: John Bulenson(?), Jeremiah Langhorne, Joseph Kirkbride. Rec: 24 Dec 1706.

P. 287. Deed. John Rowland, Bristol, Bucks Co., yeoman, for £100 paid by Edward Mayos, of Bristol, aforesaid county, a parcel of land lying in

Bristol township adjoining land of Francis Richardson ... to land of Samuel Carpenters... land of William Houghes ... land of Samuel Burgess, Jr. - 307 acres. Ackn: 21/6/1706. Wit: John Beeson, Jeremiah Langhorne, Joseph Kirkbride. Rec: 24 Dec 1706.

P. 289. Deed. 13 March 1705 between John Rowland, Bristol, Bucks Co., PA, yeoman, and Samuel Burgess, carpenter, Daniel Burgess and John Burgess, yeoman, Bucks Co., PA. Whereas Israel Taylor, son and heir of Christopher Taylor, dec'd. and Joseph Taylor, other son of Christopher Taylor, Isaac Morris and David Lloyd, exs. of last will of Thomas Lloyd dec'd., dated 2 Feb 1701/2, granted and conveyed unto Thomas Yardley, a tract of land contain 562 acres. Said Thomas Yardley in his will dated 27/11/1703/4 directs that land be sold. Whereas William Bown, of Chester Town, Chester Co., yeoman, and Esther his wife, sole extx. of will of Thomas Yardley, granted to William Bown and Esther his wife, dated 3 May 1705 who did convey to John Rowland above tract of land, dated 14 June 1705. This indenture of John Rowland for £40 paid by Samuel Burgess, Daniel Burgess and John Burgess brothers - a parcel of land containing 100 acres. Ackn: 13 March 1705/6. Wit: William Paxson, Nehemiah Blackshaw, John Snowden, Rec: 26 Dec 1706 Book C, Vol 1, page 289.

P. 292. Deed. Joseph Kirkbride, Bucks Co., PA, yeoman two lots of land lying in Bristol, aforesaid county, one on Ratclif Street, granted to Jeremiah Dungan dated 20/6/1701 and by him granted to said Kirkbride; the other lot fronting Ratclif street and adjoining corner of Thomas Brook's lot, conveyed to said Kirkbride by deed recorded in Book B, Vol 1, page 261 - for £200, paid by Edward Mayos, of Bristol, weaver. Ackn: 5/3/1704. Wit: Thomas Brock, Mahlon Stacy, William Beakes. Rec: 20 Dec 1706.

Pg 294. Deed. Samuel Burgess, Bucks Co., carpenter, and Daniel Burgess and John Burgess, both of Bucks Co., PA, yeoman. Whereas Israel Taylor, son and heir of Christopher Taylor and Joseph Taylor, other son of said Christopher and Isaac Morris and David Lloyd, exs. of Thomas Lloyd, dec'd., by deed dated 2 Feb 170-, 500 acres sold to him by Thomas Yardley - for £14 paid by Edward Mayos a parcel of land containing 33 acres. Ackn: 11/5/1706. Wit: Thomas Rowland, Roger Moone. Rec: 27 Dec 1706. [*See deed page 289.*]

P. 298. Deed. William Cowper, Bucks Co., a tract of land lying in Bucks Co. by land of Thomas Bayne ... to land formerly Thatcher ..., the tract granted to John Scarborough, of London, blacksmith, dated 4 July 1682 - 80 acres, for £121 paid by Henry Johnson Vandike, of said county, yeoman. Ackn: 20 Dec 1706. Wit: Thomas Watson, Peter Lester, Jonathan Cowper. Rec: 28 Dec 1706.

P. 300. Deed. Thomas Watson, Jr. Bucks Co., yeoman. Whereas Abraham Cox and his wife Sarah, sister and heir of Thomas Wolfe, decd. by deed dated 5/1/1693 did convey to Edward Pearson, late of Bucks Co., a piece of land adjoining land formerly of Christopher Bennett and land of Anthony Burton, granted by patent dated 27/11/1684 to Thomas Wolfe, and after Thomas Wolfe's death the land descended to his dau. Sarah wife of Abraham Cox and the land then became the possession of Edward Pearson, father of Lawrence Pearson whereas Lawrence by his indenture conveyed to John Burgess and said Burgess conveyed to Thomas Watson by deed - 120 acres for £165 paid by Anthony Burton, carpenter. Ackn: 27 Dec 1706. Witn: Enoch Pearson, Jeremiah Langhorne, Joshua Terry. Rec: 27 Dec 1706.

P. 303. Deed. Michael Frederick, late of Philadelphia Co., and now of Bucks Co., yeoman, for £25 paid by Joshua Nichols, Philadelphia, planter, 86 acres. Land granted to said Frederick by Thomas Fairman, Philadelphia Co., gent., attorney for Robert Fairman, London, brewer dated 24 Jan 1699. Ackn: 29 May 1702. Wit: Thomas Wooddell, William Williams. Rec: 23 Jan 1703. Book C, Vol 1, page 303.

P. 305. Deed. Sarah Dimock, Bucks Co., widow and relict of Tobias Dymock, late of said county, two tracts adjoining land formerly of William Bennett ... land formerly of Edward Doyle - 100 acres confirmed to Thomas Dungan by warrant dated 22/5/1795 and from Thomas Dungan to John Scot by will dated 17/8/1700 and by him to Tobias Dyumock and Sarah, his wife by deed dated 15/2/1706 and the same conveyed to Robert Willson. Ackn: 17 Nov 1706. Wit: Joseph Kirkbride, William Bowling, Edward Mayos. Rec: 28 Jan 1706.

P. 308. Deed. William Hayhurst, of Middletown, Bucks Co., yeoman, eldest son of Cuthbert and Mary Hayhurst, of said county, dec'd, 135 acres, lying by the land of William Hayhurst's meadow ... to land by Christopher Wetherill ... land of Cuthbert Hayhurst ... to land of Robert

Heaton, Jr. - 135 acres, part of the land granted to Mary Hayhurst by warrant on 21/2/1685 which land descended to her eldest son William who now conveys same to John Hayhurst, his brother for a certain sum of money. Ackn: 27/11/1706. Wit: Stephen Sands, John Penquite. Rec: 15 Feb 1706.

P. 310. Deed. William Hayhurst, of Middletown, Bucks Co., eldest son of Cuthbert Hayhurst and Mary Hayhurst, late of said county, a piece of land lying next to the land of Christopher Wetherill ... land of Robert Heaton, Jr. and ... land of John Hayhurst - 100 acres, part of the land granted to Mary Hayhurst on 21/2/1685 which said land after decease of Mary descended to William Hayhurst as heir and eldest son. For a certain sum of money paid by Cuthbert Hayhurst, his brother for good cause and valuable consideration. Ackn: 27/11/1706. Wit: Stephen Sands and John Penquite. Rec: 27 Jan 1706.

P. 312. Release. John Hayhurst, Bucks Co., batchelor and Cuthbert Hayhurst, his brother, for several sums of money paid by William Hayhurst, their eldest brother and for several other good causes and valuable considerations have granted and released claim to William Hayhurst 250 acres. Ackn: 26/11/1706/7. Wit: Stephen Sands and John Penquite. Rec: 20 Feb 1706/7.

P. 313. Release. Jeffery Hawkins, Philadelphia Co., PA, batchelor for a certain sum of money paid by Elizabeth Darbey, widow and sole extx. of William Darby, late of the Falls, Bucks Co., grants and releases all his right to a parcel of land containing 100 acres late in the possession of William Darby, part of the land granted to Jeffery Hawkins, father of Jeffery Hawkins dated 14/7/1684 and granted unto Roger Hawkins, his brother on 2/1/1685. Ackn: 1/1/1706. Wit: Joseph Kirkbride, Joseph Kirkbride, Jr. and Mary Kirkbride. Rec: 15 April 1706.

P. 314. Deed. Elizabeth Darby, widow of William Darby, of Falls, Bucks Co. dec'd. a parcel of land lying in Falls township adjoining land of Samuel Dark and land of George Biles - 100 acres for £70 to Thomas Kirkbride. Ackn: 17/1/1706. Wit: Joseph Kirkbride, John Large. Rec: 16 April 1706.

P. 317. Deed. Thomas Dure, Bucks Co., weaver, a certain tract of land by the land of Randall Blackshaw - 103 acres, formerly of Richard Lundy which he conveyed to Samuel Burgess who conveyed same to Thomas Dure - for £80 to Joseph Kirkbride. Ackn: 1/2/1706. Wit: John Hutchinson, Samuel Finelly. Rec: 1 Sep 1706.

P. 319 Deed. Paul Wolf of Germantown, Co. of Philadelphia, weaver, to Thomas James of Haverford, Chester Co., husbandman a parcel of land granted by warrant to Spike Aukus of Freeland containing 300 acres on 14 April 1683 and on 5 Sept 1687 conveyed to Riner Jansen who on 10 Aug 1700 conveyed same to Paul Wolf. 300 acres conveyed to Thomas James for £5.30. Ackn: 22/7/1706. Wit: Pauline Reiner, Andres Cramer and John Reeve. Rec: 17 March 1707.

P. 322. Deed. Samuel Allen, Chue Magne(?), Somerset Co., Kingdom of England, shoemaker, and now of Neshaminy Creek, for £6 paid by Charles Plumly, now of Newshaminy Creek, - 100 acres lying by land of James Boyden and land of Samuel Allen. Ackn: 13 Oct 1682. Wit: Joseph Stones, Benjamin Weekes, Thomas Powell. Rec: 3 Oct 1707.

P. 323. Deed. John Swift, of Southhampton, Bucks Co., a certain parcel of land lying in township of Warminister, Bucks Co., adjoinin land of Abel Nobles - 150 acres, part of 500 acres conveyed to William Bingley dated 6 Sep 1681 and conveyed to John Swift - to William Stockdale for £30. Ackn: 18/7/1707. Wit: Arthur Ottoson and Henry Michell. Rec: 3 Oct 1707.

P. 325. Deed. Robert Heaton, Jr. of Middletown, Bucks Co., yeoman, for £50 paid by John Cutler, of said province, 6 acres, part of the land confirmed to Robert Heaton dated 9/5/1705. Ackn: 1/1/1705/6. Wit: Robert Heaton and Samuel Hough. Rec: 1 Oct 1707.

P. 327. Robert Priestmall, formerly of Southhampton, Bucks Co., for consideration of £7 paid to John Baldwin, Philadelphia Co. from John Swift, a certain parcel of land lying in said township adjoining land of George Jackson and land of said Priestmall - 125 acres. Ackn: 11 March 1706/7. Wit: Samuel Beakes, William Biles, Jr. Rec: 10 May 1707.

P. 328. George Clough, Bucks Co., miller, and Mary, his wife, formerly Mary Hayworth, 220 acres for £100 in Newton adjoining land of Jonathan Eldridge and land of Robert Bond - paid by John Hough, Bucks Co., husbandman. Ackn: 2 March 1706/7. Wit: John Cutler, Jacob

Janney, William Beakes. Rec: 11 March 1706/7.

P. 331 Deed. John Hough, the younger, Bucks Co., husbandman, 270 acres adjoining the corner of Jonathan Eldridge's land, part of land granted to Mary Hough, wife of George Hough - for £100 paid by Shadrack Walley. Ackn: 7 March 1707. Wit: John Cutler, Jacob Janney, George Clough and William Beakes. Rec: 12 May 1707.

P. 333. Deed. Shadrack Walley, Newton, Bucks Co., yeoman, for £100 paid by John Hough, the younger, of Middletown, yeoman, a parcel of land lying by the land of Thomas Janney, land of Thomas Musgrove, land of Shadrack Walley and the land of Thomas Ashton. Ackn: 7/1/1705/6. Wit: John Hough, Sr., John Cutler, and William Beakes. Rec: 12 May 1707.

P. 335. Indenture. Samuel Carpenter, city of Philadelphia, merchant, to Benjamin Collins, Bristol, formerly called Buckingham, Bucks Co., a parcel of land lying in Bristol adjoining land of Samuel Carpenter - for £18 paid to said Samuel Carpenter. Ackn: 25 Feb 1705/6. Wit: George Clough, William Silverston, James Moon. Rec: 13 May 1707.

P. 337. Deed. Samuel Carpenter, city of Philadelphia, merchant, and George Clough, Bristol, formerly called Buckingham, Bucks Co., 8 acres adjoining land of Benjamin Collins and land of Thomas Brock - for £18. Ackn: 25 Feb 1705/6. Wit: William Silverston, Benjamin Collins, and James Moon. Rec: 18 March 1707.

P. 339. Deed. Samuel Carpenter, city of Philadelphia, merchant, and John Baldwin, Bristol, formerly called Buckingham, Bucks Co., a certain parcel of land lying near the land of Mary Beaks for £10. Ackn: 25 Feb 1705/6. Wit: George Clough, William Silverstone, Benjamin Collins, James Moon. Rec: 11 March 1706/7.

P. 341. Deed. Samuel Carpenter, city of Philadelphia, merchant, and Mary Baker, widow, Bristol, formerly called Buckingham, Bucks Co., a piece of land lying in Bristol adjoining the land of Samuel Carpenter, along Pond Street and adjoining the land of Thomas Brock - for £10. Ackn: 20 Feb 1705/6. Wit: George Clough, Benjamin Collins, William Silverstone and James Moon. Rec: 14 May 1707.

P. 343. Deed. Jeremiah Langhorne, Province of PA, yeoman, a certain tract of land lying in Solebury Township by the Delaware River at a corner of Henry Paxson's land adjoining land of William Croasdale and land of Francis White - 150 acres for £50 paid by Henry Paxson. Ackn: 25 April 1707. Wit: Francis White, John Plumly. Rec: 7 June 1707.

P. 345. Deed. Edward Shippen, of Philadelphia, merchant, and John Clark, of Hopewell, Burlington Co., West Jersey, yeoman, a parcel of land confirmed by indenture on 4 June 1702, made between Gilbert Wheeler of Bucks Co., and Edward Shippen, a parcel of land lying by the land of William Biles - 280 acres for £161 paid by John Clark. Ackn: 4/2/1707. Wit: Griffith Jones, William Biles, David Lloyd and Richard Heath. Rec: 18/4/1707.

P. 348 Deed. Joseph Kirkbride, Bucks Co., yeoman, a certain tract of land lying in Bristol, Bucks Co., adjoining land of Joseph Burgess and land of Anthony Burton - for £10 to Samuel Burgess. Ackn: 13/2/1707. Wit: Willoughby Warder, Thomas Stevenson. Rec: 11 June 1707.

P. 352. Deed. James Streater, of Buckingham, Bucks Co., and Anne, his wife, relict and extx. of Joseph Ward, late of said county, dec'd. and John Ward, only son and ex. of said Joseph to Stephen Twining, of said county, yeoman, a parcel of land lying in Newton adjoining the line of Thomas Revell's land - 300 acres for £100. Ackn: 2/3/1707. Wit: Thomas Barnes. Rec: 19 June 1707.

P. 354. Deed. Thomas Kirle, Bucks Co., Pa, carpenter, 100 acres beginning at the land of William Houge adjoining land of George Gwinop and land confirmed to Andrew Robeson - 100 acres for £22.6.8 paid by William Dowdney, Bucks Co., weaver. Ackn: 10/6/1707. Wit: Francis White, John Cutler. Rec: 24 Oct 1707.

P. 356. Deed. Thomas Groom, Philadelphia Co., a parcel of land lying at the corner of the land of Robert Turner and adjoining land of Edward Pennington and land of Griffith Jones - to Barnard Christian, Bergen Co., East Jersey, yeoman, for £290. Ackn: 29 Sep 1707. Wit: William Stevenson, Arthur Otherson. Rec: 29 Sep 1707.

P. 359. Deed. Edward Cowgill, late of Newton, husbandman, 20 acres lying in Newton beginning at town common and adjoining the land of

Thomas Hillborn and Jonathan Elridge, part of the land conveyed to Thomas Hillborn by Margaret and John Cook - 20 acres to Henry Cooper, Newton for £100. Ackn: 9 Sep 1707. Wit: Willoughby Warden, Thomas Stevenson. Rec: 29 Sep 1707.

P. 361. Deed. Samuel Carpenter, city of Philadelphia, merchant for £37 paid by Robert Shaw, of Bristol, Bucks Co., 7 acres in Bristol. Ackn: 14/6/1707. Wit: John Baldwin, George Clough. Rec: 31 Oct 1707.

P. 364. Deed. Robert Shaw, Bristol, Bucks Co., yeoman, for £37 paid by Samuel Carpenter, city of Philadelphia, merchant, 8 acres in Bristol lying by land of Thomas Brock. Ackn: 26 Oct 1707. Wit: John Baldwin, George Hough. Rec: 31 Oct 1707.

P. 366. Deed. Samuel Baker, Bucks Co., 437 acres for £100, in Wrightstown, Bucks Co. adjoining land of Thomas Coleman, land of William Derrick and land of William Parker. Ackn: 31 Oct 1707. Wit: Samuel Carpenter, Ed Mayos. Rec: 31 Oct 1707.

P. 368. Deed. Robert Shaw, Bristol, Bucks Co., yeoman, for £65 paid by Edward Mayos, Bristol, of aforesaid county, yeoman, 2 lots on Cedar Street. Ackn: 31 Oct 1707. Wit: Samuel Carpenter, Samuel Baker. Rec: 31 Oct 1707.

P. 370. Deed. Joseph Growden, City of Philadelphia, merchant for £46 paid by Thomas Walmsley, Bensaleum, Bucks Co. 46 acres. Ackn: 10/10/1707. Wit: Wm. Croasdale, John Stocker. Rec: 10/10/1707.

P. 372. Deed. John Rowland, New Bristol, formerly called Buckingham, Bucks Co., yeoman, for £40 paid by William Silverstone, of said county, 1 lot of land adjoining the line of John Rowland. Ackn: 22 Nov 1707. Wit: Francis White, John Chenoweth, John Large. Rec: 10 Dec 1707.

P. 374. Deed. Samuel Baker, Bucks Co., yeoman, a certain parcel of land lying in Bristol, Bucks Co. adjoining the land of John Sotcher, land of Anthony Burton and land of Edward Mayos, for £15 paid by Jacob Janney, of said county, yeoman. 10 Dec 1707. Wit: Willoughby Warder, Solomon Warder, Sarah Pemberton. Rec: 5 Feb 1707.

P. 376. Deed. John Rowland, Bristol, Bucks Co., yeoman, for £30 paid by John Large, of said township and county, tailor, 100 acres next to the land of William Houges, land of Samuel Burgess and land of Edward Mayos - 100 acres. Ackn: 22/9/1707. Wit: Francis White, John Chenoweth, Lemuel Oldale. Rec: 10 Dec 1707.

P. 378. Deed. Joseph Kirkbride, Bucks Co., yeoman, a certain parcel of land lying near the land of Richard Lundy conveyed by Randall Blackshaw ... conveyed by Samuel Burgess to Richard Lundy on 24 May 1689 and by him conveyed to Thomas Dure on 9 June 1700 and by him conveyed to Joseph Kirkbride - 103 acres for 5 shillings paid by John Hutchinson, and his wife, Phebe, of said county and also other valuable considerations. Ackn: 8 Dec 1707. (3 acres which are enclosed in said parcel which were conveyed by Richard Lundy to Ralph Sutton.) Wit: Thomas Stevenson, Wm. Croasdale. Rec: 8 Dec 1707.

P. 381. Deed. Robert Shaw, Bucks Co., husbandman, 200 acres in Wrightstown, Bucks Co., running to line of town park and adjoining land of Thomas Coleman, land of William Derrick and land of William Partlits, part of 494 acres granted to Samuel Baker by patent on 14 Jan 1706 who confirmed same to Robert Shaw - 200 acres to Richard Mitchell for £45. Ackn: 18 Dec 1707. Wit: John Shaw, James Cooper. Rec: 11 June 1707.

P. 383. Deed. Charles Levally, Bucks Co., cooper, to John Hall, for £200, a lot lying in Bristol, Bucks Co. adjoining land formerly of John Town, part of which was confirmed to Samuel Carpenter by William Hillborn, of Philadelphia, merchant and the other part said Samuel Carpenter purchaed from Rebecca Hardiman, and Samuel Carpenter confirmed the lot to Charles Levalley on 19 April 1706. Ackn: 10 Dec 1707. Wit: John Swift, Samuel Beakes, Thomas Harding. Rec: 10 Dec 1707.

P. 385. Deed. 29 June 1707 between Cesar Gisling, of Philadelphia, goldsmith on the one part and Samuel Marmiom (Marmion), of same place, merchant, 150 acres for £150, near land of Dunck Williams. Ackn: 29 June 1707. Wit: Mary Starney, Elizabeth Evens, Thomas Grey. Rec: 29 July 1707.

P. 387. Deed. Samuel Burgess, Jr., Bristol, Bucks Co., carpenter, two lots of land along Ratclife Street to Delaware River, conveyed to Samuel Burgess by Anthony Burton on 14 March 1704/5 - for £10, paid by

Joseph Burgess. Ackn: 10 Dec 1707. Rec: 10 Dec 1707.

P. 389. Deed. Thomas Murray, City of Philadelphia, merchant, and Rebecca, his wife to Francis Richardson of same place, silversmith, (the said Francis and Rebecca being the only survivors of Francis Richardson late of New York, merchant dec'd.), conveying a certain parcel of land lying in Philadelphia containing 1200 acres to Francis Richardson, a part of the land containing 50 acres lying in township of Wrightstown. Whereas the will of Francis Richardson dated at New York 7/5/1688 did devise ---- As for the remaining land after all debts are paid bequeath to wife, Rebecca Richardson 1/3, 2/3 divided among my three children: Francis Richardson, Rebecca and John Richardson. Francis Richardson, son of Francis Richardson died without issue and under age bequeathed to Rebecca Richardson. Whereas said Rebecca, mother since intermarried with Edward Shippen, of Boston, now of Philadelphia, merchant ... mother is since deceased ... land granted to Samuel Powell, of Philadelphia 1/3 of lot ... said Thomas Murray and Rebecca, his wife convey to said Francis Richardson 1200 acres of land in exchange of remaining right to land after death of Edward Shipppen ... for £35. Ackn: 13/7/1707. Wit: Edward Shippen, Jr., Joseph Anthrobus. Rec: 2/11/707.

P. 393. Release. Barnard Christian, of Bergen, East Jersey, yeoman for consideration of making a writing of release of moiety for two tracts of land from Peter Lawrence of the said county, yeoman, 280 acres along Neshaming Creek. Ackn: 18 Sep 1707. Wit: Henry Johnson Vandike, John Cutler. Rec: 26 Feb 1707.

P. 394. Release. Peter Lawrence, of Bergen Co., East Jersey, yeoman, for consideration of making a writing release of moiety or one half of two tracts mentioned from Barnard Christian, of said county quit claim to said Barnard Christian 200 acres, conveyed jointly from Robert Heaton of Middletown beginning at the corner of land of Richard Thatcher and adjoining land of Edward Brooks. Ackn: 18 Sep 1707. Wit: Henry Johnson Vandike, John Cutler. Rec: 6 Feb 1707.

P. 399. Deed. Barnard Christian, Bergen Co., East Jersey, yeoman, 294 acres for £200, adjoining land of Peter Lawrence, land of Peter Barnson and land of Edward Pennington to Christian Barnson. Ackn: 20 Sep 1707. Wit: Henry Johnson Vandike, John Cutler. Rec: 26 Feb 1707.

P. 401. Deed. Barnard Christian, Bergen Co., East Jersey, yeoman, to his son Peter Barnson, 257 acres, for £190, part of 500 acres granted to Christopher Taylor by patent on 6/2/1686 who granted same to Robert Heaton who granted same to Barnard Christian and Peter Lawrence and the land was divided by deeds of partitiion on 18 Sept 1707. Ackn: 20 Sep 1707. Wit: Henry Johnson Vandike, John Cutler. Rec: 26 Feb 1707.

P. 403. Release. Samuel Atkinson, Bucks Co., carpenter, for £50.8, paid by William Biles, father in law to said Samuel and for other valuable considerations, release and quit claim unto William Paxson to a certain parcel of land formerly in possession of George Biles, son of said William Biles and sometime in possession of Solomon Warder but now William Paxson, bounded by land of Thomas Watson ... land of Gabriel Baynes ... land of Nehemiah Blackshaw ... formerly Charles Brighams' land. Ackn: -- 1707/8. Wit: Thomas Watson, John Smith, Abel Janney, William Biles and William Croasdale. Rec: 9 March 1707.

P. 406. 18/10/1707 between John Cowgill, of Trusoe, Bensalem, Bucks Co., yeoman and Rachel, his wife (relict and sole extx. of Job Bunting, late of said county, decd.) to Edward Ratclife, Bristol, yeoman, a certain parcel of land lying in said township, adjoining land of Joseph Large - 200 acres for £250. Ackn: 18/10/1707. Wit: Solomon Warder, John Cutler. Rec: 18 Dec 1707.

P. 407. Deed. Edward Ratclife, Bristol, Bucks Co., yeoman, for --- paid by Solomon Warder of said township, yeoman, a certain parcel of land, lying by land of Solomon Warder and land of Edward Ratclife - 50 acres. Ackn: 11/1/1707. Wit: John Cowgill and John Cutler. Rec: 11 March 1707.

P. 410. Deed. James Radclife, Wrightstown, Bucks Co., dec'd. was seized of a parcel of land containing 200 acres lying in Wrightstown adjoining land of Phenas Pemberton and land laid out to Riger Logwood. Whereas Mary Baker, of Bristol, relict of James Radclife, Richard Radclife and Edward Radclife, sons of said James, William Hayhurst and Rachel his wife and Rebecca Radclife, daus. of said James for £46 conveyed the land to Joseph Cooper. Ackn: 15/12/1707. Wit: Edmond Cowgil and James Wildman. Rec: 21 March 1707.

P. 412. Deed. Jacque or James Verrier, Middletown, Bucks Co., mason, and his wife Warbet, 100 acres lying in Middletown adjoining land of John White, land formerly George White's and formerly Henry Paxson's. Whereas Henry Paxson of Middle Township, yeoman, conveyed same to said James Verrier on 12 March 1704/5 - for £130 paid by Vaudine, late of East Jersey and now of Bucks Co., yeoman. Ackn: 26 March 1708. Wit: John Taylor. Rec: 26 March 1708.

P. 416. Deed. 11/9/1704, Tobias Dynmock of New Bristol, Bucks Co., yeoman, and Sarah his wife to Joshua Nickhoils, of Bensalem, yeoman, for £10, 200 acres. Ackn: 11/9/1704. Wit: Jacob Usher and Maurice List. Rec: 12/2/1708.

P. 417. Deed. John Large, Bucks Co., tailor, a certain parcel of land lying in said county adjoining land of Tobias Dymock, decd., land of Jacob Janney and land of Joseph Large, part of the land confirmed to Abraham Cox, then executed to Thomas Williams and Rebecca his wife, confirmed to Samuel Smith by Joseph Kirkbride and Edmond Lovett, trustees of said Cox, then to John Large. Conveyed to Esther Willson, Bucks Co., widow - for £45. Ackn: 25 April 1708. Wit: William Croasdale and John Chenoweth. Rec: 25 April 1708.

P. 420. Deed. Samuel Oldale and Lemuel Oldale, of New Bristol, formerly called Buckingham, Bucks Co., for £40 paid by John Rowland of said county, a certain parcel of land lying by land of William Croasdale near land now of John Rowlands. Ackn: 3 Nov 1707. Wit: Daniel Doane, Francis White and John Chenoweth. Rec: 12 June 1708.

P. 421. Deed. Francis Richardson, City of Philadelphia, silver smith, a parcel of land granted to his father, Francis Richardson, dec'd., a tract of land containing 1200 acres lying by a line of Wrightstown near land of Joseph Amber and land of John Chapman - for £240 paid by Thomas Stackhouse, Bucks Co., yeoman. Ackn: 19 Nov 1707. Wit: Robert Heaton, Jr., Henry Nelson, John Bourchires. Rec: 17/3/1708.

P. 423. Deed. John Swift, of Southampton, Bucks Co., yeoman, for £800 paid by Lawrence Johnson, Kings Co., Long Island, and Charles Hufteen, Richmond Co., Staten Island, New Jersey, yeomen, a parcel of land lying by land of Peter Groome adjoining land of Nicholas Randall and land of John Jones in Philadelphia Co. ... land of Henry Painter -

containing 580 acres, part of a tract of 680 acres granted by patent to John Swift on 20 Dec 1690, 200 acres therof in right of Thomas Fairman in part of William Stanley's purchase of 5480 acres in right of John Swift's own purchase of 500 acres. Ackn: 15/4/1708. Wit: Nicholas Randall, Stoffel VanSaul, John Cutler. Rec: 15 June 1708.

P. 428. Release. John Baldwin, of Makefield Township, Bucks Co., yeoman, has released and quitclaimed unto Thomas Heed, of Solebury, Township, yeoman, all claims of any money owed. Ackn: 13/11/1707. Wit: Joshua Chessman and Matthew Durham.

P. 428. Deed. Daniel Doan, Jr. of Middletown, Bucks Co. carpenter, for £53 paid by James Ray of Middletown, Monmouth Co., East New Jersey, bachelor, 150 acres lying by the land of Charles Brigham, land of Joseph Doan, land of Joseph Hampton ... to line of Abraham Chapman. Ackn: 13 March 1723. Wit: John Chapman, Joseph Hampton, Abraham Chapman, Elizabeth Routledge. Rec: 13 March 1723.

Bucks Co. SS: Recorder's Office, Doylestown, Pa, November 21, 1901. transcribed and recopied by Burrough Nichsner.

INDEX

-A-
ABRAHAM, ---, 27, 28
ACCERMAN, John, 6
ACERMAN, James, 76
John, 76
ACKERMAN, John, 1, 37
Widow, 10
ACREMAN, James, 89
John, 42
ADDINGTON, John, 68
ADINGTON, John, 107
ADKINSON, Jean, 14
Thomas, 52
ADKISON, Isaac, 51
Samuel, 51
Thomas, 51
William, 51
ADLER, Mark, 35
ALASH, Hugh, 86
ALDRICH, Peter, 54
ALFORD, Philip, 50, 62
ALLEN, Elinor, 43
Jane, 74
Jedediah, 9
John, 27, 28
Nathan, 90
Nathaniel, 43
Nehemiah, 43, 50
Samuel, 12, 27, 28,
29, 30, 36, 37, 46, 63, 74, 99, 103, 106, 107, 122
ALLRICKS, Peter, 24
ALPHONE, Philip, 94
ALSOP, John, 4, 6, 80
ALTON, John, 27
AMBER, Joseph, 129
AMOR, Richard, 102
William, 102
AMOS, Richard, 7
ANDERSON, John, 20
ANDREWS,
Edmund, 55
Elizabeth, 65
Francis, 65, 75
ANTHROBUS,
Joseph, 127
ANTILL, Edward, 29, 37
ARMOR, Richard, 12
ATKINS, Margaret, 117
ATKINSON,
Christopher, 91, 108
Daniel, 85
Isaac, 84, 86, 89, 109
Jane, 17, 92
John, 86, 108
Margaret, 91, 108
Samuel, 128
Thomas, 7, 14, 85,
92, 105
William, 84, 88, 94, 96, 98, 101, 111, 115
ATKISON, Daniel, 95
AUKUS, Spike, 122
AUSTIN, John, 12, 38

-B-
BAINBRIDGE, John, 90
BAKER, Henry, 15, 17, 29, 36, 37, 38, 42, 51, 52, 53, 56, 64, 66, 71, 72, 74, 78, 86, 111
Joseph, 32
Mary, 88, 101, 123, 128
Nathan, 86, 111
Samuel, 86, 89, 95, 111, 115, 125, 126
William, 80
BALDWIN, John, 11, 36, 37, 107, 122, 123, 125, 130
BALL, Joseph, 76
BALY, Henry, 96
BANNOR,
Lawrance, 3
Lawrence, 1
BARBER, Elizabeth, 62
James, 68
BARCLAY, John, 37
BARKER, Thomas,

INDEX

27
BARNARD, Thomas, 77
BARNES, Thomas, 124
BARNSON,
  Christian, 127
  Peter, 128
BARTHOLEMEW,
  Jeremiah, 90
BASSIET, Richard, 16
BAYES, Thomas, 67
BAYLEY, Henry, 60
BAYNE, Thomas, 120
BAYNES, Gabriel, 93, 128
  Thomas, 92, 95
BAYNS, Thomas, 76, 112
BEAKES, Abraham, 43, 44
  Daniel, 69, 76
  Henry, 51
  Mary, 14, 42, 43
  Samuel, 20, 33, 36, 37, 38, 40, 43, 51, 53, 67, 71, 73, 76, 77, 78, 79, 80, 84, 89, 98, 110, 122, 126
  Stephen, 14, 17, 22, 43, 53, 56, 57, 58, 66, 70, 75, 89
  W., 31
  William, 14, 18, 24, 29, 32, 33, 42, 43, 44, 88, 92, 93, 94, 95, 96, 98, 101, 102, 103, 105, 107, 109, 110, 112, 113, 115, 119, 123
BEAKS (BEAK),
  Daniel, 44
  Elizbeth, 42
  Mary, 42, 123
  Samuel, 48, 53, 99
  Stephen, 77, 81, 103
  William, 2, 31, 42, 92, 99, 111
BEAL, William, 25, 75, 78
BEALE, William, 25
BECKER, Mary, 34
BECKMAN, John, 62
BEESON, John, 119
BENNET, Ann, 46
  Christopher, 41
  Edmond, 1
  Edmund, 39
  Elizabeth, 39
  Rebecca, 15, 46
  Sarah, 46
  Thomas, 41
  William, 15, 92
BENNETT, Anne, 105
  Christopher, 4, 120
  Edmond, 2
  Edmund, 8, 57, 68, 75
  Edmund B., 21
  Edward, 112
  Elizabeth, 57, 68, 105, 112
  Mary, 41, 44
  Rebecca, 94, 105
  Sarah, 105
  Thomas, 41, 44
  William, 1, 46, 70, 81, 94, 99, 105, 120
BETEREY, Mark, 13
BETRIDGE, Marke, 46
  Prudence, 46
BIBB, Thomas, 55
BIDDLE, William, 97
BILES, Alexander, 111
  Charles, 11, 12, 20, 30, 33, 36, 37, 45, 53, 57, 82, 86
  Dorothy, 111
  George, 51, 76, 77, 78, 80, 81, 84, 85, 91, 92, 98, 105, 106, 109, 121, 128
  Jane, 51, 84, 88, 92, 96, 105
  John, 96, 98, 110
  Mary, 111
  Sarah, 60, 78
  William, 1, 2, 5, 8, 9, 10, 12, 13, 15, 16, 17, 18, 20, 22, 25, 26, 29, 32, 33, 34, 36, 37, 44, 47, 48, 49, 51, 53, 55, 56, 57, 60, 62, 65, 68, 69, 70, 71, 72, 74, 76, 78, 79, 80, 81, 82, 84, 85, 86, 87, 88, 91, 92, 94, 96, 97, 101, 102, 103, 104, 105,

INDEX

109, 110, 122, 124, 128
BILLING, Edward, 45
BILLIS, Thomas, 55
BILLS, Thomas, 55
BILTERT, Joseph, 91
BINGLEY, William, 122
BIRCHAM, Henry, 27, 54
  Margaret, 54
BIRCHER, Michael, 76
BLACKSHAW,
  Nehemiah, 59, 76, 98, 101, 118, 119, 128
  Nemiah, 115
  Randal, 59, 64, 75, 76
  Randall, 91, 98, 104, 118, 121, 126
  Randel, 49, 52
  Randle, 3, 51, 84, 86, 87, 99
  Randolph, 22, 31
BLACKWELL, John, 32
  Robert, 4
BLEEKER, John, 83
BOARD, Joshua, 47, 48
BOARE, Joshua, 20
  Margaret, 3
BOERDAILL, John, 60
BOLTON, Edward, 81

BOND, John, 96
  Robert, 122
  Thomas, 41, 78, 87
BOONE, Ralph, 69, 84, 115
BORDALE, Arthur, 12, 13
  John, 12
  Sarah, 12
BORDEN, Joseph, 23
  Mordecai, 13
  Samuel, 16, 23, 24
BOREMAN, Peter, 19
  Thomas, 19
BORRADALE,
  James, 114
BORRODAILLE,
  John, 114
BOSMAN, Thomas, 7
BOUCHIER, John, 100
BOUNDS, John, 83
BOURCHIRES,
  John, 129
BOWDEN/
  BOWDON,
  Mordecai, 46, 48, 69, 79, 82, 93
BOWEN, Ezra, 118
  Henry, 101, 102, 109, 110
  Jane, 102, 109, 110
  John, 64
BOWERS, Ezra, 118
BOWIN, Henry, 75
BOWLING, William, 120

BOWMAN, Thomas, 6, 8, 84
BOWN, Esther, 119
  John, 80
  Samuel, 51
  William, 119
BOWNE, John, 53, 80
  Samuel, 53
BOYDEN, James, 28, 30, 50, 99, 103, 107, 122
BOYEN [BOWEN],
  Henry, 91
  Jane, 91
BOYER, Jane, 91
BRADFORD,
  Thomas, 43
BRANDT, Albertus, 111
BRASSEY, Thomas, 27
BREMMAN,
  Edward, 61
BRIAN, William, 1
BRIDGMAN, Walter, 48, 56, 62, 75
BRIGHAM, Charles, 51, 84, 128, 130
BRINCLAE, John, 88
BRINDLEY, Luke, 2, 11, 18, 19, 29
BRINGHAM,
  Charles, 7
BRINSON, Daniel, 5, 6, 10, 42, 76
BRITTAIN, Leonel, 1
  Lyonel, 3

BRITTAN, Lyonel, 21
BRITTON, Lionel, 22
BROCK, Anthony, 66, 70
  Burton, 51, 85
  John, 11, 33, 60, 80
  Thoams, 50
  Thomas, 18, 20, 35, 36, 39, 42, 44, 47, 49, 51, 52, 53, 58, 65, 66, 69, 70, 71, 78, 84, 85, 88, 89, 93, 110, 113, 115, 119, 123, 125
BROCKET, Thomas, 52
BROOK, Thomas, 105, 106, 110, 119
BROOKS, Charles, 83
  Edward, 27, 100, 127
  Thomas, 58
BROWN, Esther, 113
  George, 22
  John, 84
  Thomas, 117
  William, 113
BROWNE, George, 95
BRUER, Adalfas, 107
BRYAN, George, 33
  William, 4
BUCHANAN, William, 101
BUCKMAN, Robert, 62
  William, 38, 46, 61, 96, 114
BUCKMASTER, Edward, 29
BUD, James, 34
BUDD, John, 41, 44, 107
  William, 99, 100
BULENSON, John, 118
BULKLEY, Samuel, 14, 113
BULL, Richard, 87
  Sarah, 87
BUNTING, James, 21
  Job, 37, 38, 45, 46, 49, 68, 93, 128
  Samuel, 21
BURCHEN, Henry, 55
  Margaret, 55
BURGES, Isaac, 11
  John, 114
  Richard, 103
  Samuel, 21, 32, 106
BURGESS, Daniel, 66, 119
  Elizabeth, 68, 71, 93, 99, 100
  John, 90, 95, 105, 119, 120
  Joseph, 124, 127
  Richard, 57, 58, 68, 71, 93, 100
  Samuel, 3, 31, 54, 86, 90, 94, 95, 105, 119, 122, 124, 126
  Sarah, 95
BURGIS, Richard, 97
BURKETT, Jospeh, 55
BURLING, John, 44, 45
BURTON, Anthony, 21, 39, 41, 47, 49, 50, 51, 52, 53, 58, 63, 65, 70, 78, 85, 88, 89, 91, 104, 110, 112, 120, 124, 125, 126
  Peter, 50
  Stanley, 50
BUSTELL, William, 97
BUTTE, Thomas, 76
BUZBY, John, 73, 100
  Mary, 73, 100
BYE, John, 115
BYLLYINGS, Edward, 34

-C-
CADDER, John, 68
CAMBLE, Daniel, 71
CARBROW, John, 31
CARENSEN, Christian, 112
CARPENTER, Abraham, 65
  Samuel, 23, 24, 38, 46, 48, 49, 52, 58, 60, 62, 65, 71, 79, 83, 90, 95, 105, 107, 114, 115,

INDEX

117, 119, 123, 125, 126
Samuell, 69
CARTER, Edward, 7, 18, 79, 81, 86, 101, 102, 109, 116
James, 97, 112
Joan, 73
John, 20, 58, 76, 84, 102, 109, 110, 115
Margaret, 88, 89
Robert, 7, 12, 58, 59, 72, 73, 84, 88, 89, 91, 101, 102, 109, 110
William, 58, 71, 73, 84, 88, 89, 91, 99, 101, 102, 109, 110
CARTER(CHARTER), William, 7
CASHBEARD, Richard, 109
CHAMBERLAIN, Peter, 115
CHAMBERLANE, Peter, 111
CHAMBERLIN, Lucy, 77
Peter, 77
CHAMBERS, Benjamin, 117
CHANDLER, John, 14
CHAPMAN, Abraham, 130
Jane, 79
John, 79, 93, 129, 130
CHARLEY, Joseph, 36
CHARTER, William, 7
CHENOWETH, John, 125, 126, 129
CHERRY, Edward, 68
CHERSMAN, John, 117
CHESSMAN, Joshua, 130
CHILD, Amey, 71
CHORLEY, Joseph, 42, 76
Mary, 42, 76
CHRISTIAN, Barnard, 124, 127, 128
Bernard, 100
CIRCUIT, John, 55
CLARK, Ann, 27
Anne, 75
John, 15, 33, 56, 124
Page, 103
William, 28, 75
CLARKE, Sell, 35
CLAWSON, John, 27, 50
CLAYPOOL, James, 5, 9, 10, 11, 60
CLAYPOOLE, James, 3, 7, 13, 27
John, 7
Nathaniel, 22
CLEFT, Samuel, 4
CLIFF, Samuel, 89
CLIFFE, Samuel, 88
CLIFT, Samuel, 11, 35, 47, 50, 57, 69, 88, 89
CLOUGH, George, 90, 101, 122, 125
Mary, 122
CLOWES, Jacob, 98
John, 1
Joseph, 80, 98, 99
William, 33
CLOWS, John, 17, 19, 34, 59
Joseph, 19, 33, 34, 90
Margery, 19, 34
Sarah, 74
William, 19, 34, 74
COATE, John, 33, 96
Samuel, 96
COATES, John, 31
COATS, John, 5
COCKS, Abraham, 1, 21
CODERY, William, 72
COKES, Arthur, 52
COLBOURN, Richard, 81
COLE, Edward, 67
COLEMAN, Thomas, 60, 125, 126
COLLINER, Ursula, 10
COLLINGS, James, 116
COLLINS, Benjamin, 123
John, 2, 6, 15, 28
Richard, 65

Susanna, 6
Thomas, 12
COLLS, William, 29
COLMAN, Thomas, 20
COLSON, John, 28
COMLEY, Henry, 17, 117
COMLY, Henry, 16, 116
CONDON, John, 70
CONSTABLE,
  Thomas, 31, 38, 45, 96, 100
CONWAY, Philip, 2, 3, 5, 24, 54, 61, 86
COOK, Arthur, 5, 24, 25, 55, 58, 61, 63, 64, 68, 79, 82, 84, 86, 89, 111
Elizabeth F., 44
Francis, 61, 83, 84
John, 14, 48, 49, 55, 79, 82, 84, 89, 125
Margaret, 55, 82, 84, 89, 125
Mary, 55, 83, 84
COOKE, Arthur, 14, 16, 17, 36, 41
Francis, 70, 73, 81
John, 17, 31, 36
Mary, 70
Thomas, 65
COOPER, Henry, 103, 125
James, 126
Jonathan, 118
Joseph, 128

Joshua, 51
William, 108
CORASDELL,
  William, 77
CORDEREY,
  William, 92
CORSADELL,
  William, 76
COUSENS, John, 118
COVERDALE, Jane, 28
  Thomas, 4, 28
COVET, Edward, 1
COWGIL, Edmond, 128
COWGILL,
  Abraham, 59
  Edmond, 100, 101
  Edmund, 62
  Edward, 92, 93, 124
  John, 46, 48, 75, 91, 105, 111, 113, 114, 128
  Nehemiah, 59
  Rachel, 111, 128
  Ralph, 49, 56, 59, 62, 112
COWPER, Jonathan, 120
  William, 108, 120
COX, Abraham, 38, 41, 46, 61, 63, 83, 97, 98, 108, 109, 120, 129
  Abraham A., 58
  Daniel, 34
  Sarah, 41, 83, 98, 120

Thomas, 22, 23, 25, 26, 30, 31, 98
William, 33
COXE, Thomas, 4, 71
COZENS, John, 117
CRAMER, Andres, 122
CRAPP, John, 31
CRASH, Sell, 26
CRASKE, Sell, 26, 71
CRISPIN, Silas, 5
CROADELL, John, 48
CROASDALE,
  Agnes, 10
  Ezra, 17, 31, 62, 105, 113, 114
  John, 10, 78, 112, 113
  Thomas, 23, 112
  Widow, 4, 9
  William, 10, 21, 36, 51, 80, 102, 109, 110, 112, 113, 114, 115, 124, 125, 126, 128, 129
CROASDALL,
  William, 77
CROASDELL, Ezra, 48, 50, 94
  John, 56
  Thomas, 48
  William, 48, 49, 61, 85, 103
CROASDIEL,
  William, 102
CROASDILL, John, 114

INDEX 137

CROP, Joseph, 22, 50
CROSDALE, John, 56
Thomas, 56
William, 52
CROSDALL, Thomas, 62
CROSDEL, William, 45
CROSDELL, John, 62, 75, 94
Thomas, 75, 94
William, 46, 52, 53, 62, 66, 75, 94
CROSLEY, James, 21, 42, 74
CROSSDELL, Thomas, 75
William, 64
CROSSLY, James, 19
CROW, Mary, 83
CUFF, Edward, 56
John, 12, 33, 51
CUFT, John, 33
CUPS (OR CUFFS), John, 32
CURTIS, Abigail, 72
Thomas, 89
CUTLER, Edmond, 4
Edmund, 9, 74, 108
Isabel, 74
John, 9, 27, 54, 74, 85, 91, 92, 93, 94, 95, 96, 100, 106, 108, 110, 111, 113, 114, 117, 122, 123, 124,
127, 128, 130
Margaret, 108

-D-
DARBE, William, 48, 68
DARBEY, Elizabeth, 121
DARBY, William, 54, 77, 121
DARK, John, 53
Samuel, 22, 35, 65, 66, 67, 70, 75, 76, 80, 84, 85, 109, 118, 121
William, 1, 12, 45, 51, 53, 59, 67, 82, 112
DARKE, Samuel, 34, 58, 87, 114
William, 30, 33, 86
DARKS, William, 11
DAUGAN, Widow, 46
DAVE, Robert, 12
DAVID, Lloyd, 60
DAVIDS, Richard, 75
DAVIES, David, 2, 4
DAVIS, Richard, 65
DAWSON, John, 75
Martha, 75, 99
DEACON, George, 90
DERRICK, William, 125, 126
DICKERSON, Alice, 15, 54
Thomas, 5, 15, 28, 54

DICKINSON, Jonathan, 73
DILLWORTH, James, 30
DILWORTH, James, 5, 9, 10, 24, 30, 45, 67, 68, 85, 112
DIMOCK, Sarah, 120
Tobias, 108, 115
DOAN, Daniel, 130
Joseph, 130
DOANE, Daniel, 87, 114, 129
DOLE, John, 53
DONE, Daniel, 100
Francis, 15, 16, 40, 41
Robert, 14, 15, 18, 21
DONSEY, John, 29
DOWDNEY, William, 124
DOYAL, Edward, 49
DOYLE, Edward, 48, 54, 70, 95, 96, 120
Rebecca, 95
DOYLS, Edward, 81
DRACOTT, Ralph, 104
DRAKE, Joseph, 81
DRAYCOT, Ralph, 116
DRAYKETT, Ralph, 94
DREWETT, Cassandra, 4
Morgan, 4

INDEX

DUEPLOVIE, John, 40
DUMOCK, Sarah, 96
Tobias, 96
DUNCAN, Jane, 52
William, 51, 54, 60, 62, 91, 93, 96, 104
DUNGAN, Clement, 16, 49, 54, 69, 81, 84, 93, 95, 96
Elizabeth, 16, 17
George, 91
Jeremiah, 46, 48, 69, 70, 78, 81, 85, 88, 93, 119
John, 69, 81, 93
Thomas, 1, 17, 48, 69, 70, 81, 84, 93, 96, 120
Widow, 54
William, 13, 16, 19, 25, 48, 55, 79, 82, 84
DUNGWORTH, Richard, 35, 57
DUNKAN, George, 104
John, 102, 104
DURE, Thomas, 54, 86, 87, 121, 122, 126
DURHAM, Matthew, 130
DYMOCK, Sarah, 88
Tobias, 88, 120, 129
DYMOCKE, Tobias, 114
DYNMOCK, Sarah, 129
Tobias, 129

-E-
EASTBOURN, John, 40
EASTBURN, John, 17
EDWARDS, Robert, 94, 105
Sarah, 94, 105
ELDRDIGE, Jonathan, 52, 86
ELDRIDGE, Jonathan, 21, 56, 107, 111, 122, 123
ELFORETH, Jeremiah, 8
ELFORTH, Jeremiah, 29
ELLET, Andrew, 44
John, 81, 117, 118
ELLIOT, Andrew, 106
William, 106
ELLIS, Heugh, 76
Rowland, 75
ELRED, Audry, 18
ELRIDGE, Jonathan, 33, 125
ELTON, Anthony, 97
ELY, Joshua, 37
EMLEY, Wiliam, 50
William, 6, 10, 43, 58, 76, 90
EMPSON, Cornelius, 40
ENGLAND, Robert, 69

Thomas, 117
ENGLISH, Hannah, 47
John, 18
Joseph, 19, 20, 22, 31, 34, 35, 36, 47, 49, 50, 51, 52, 53, 66, 69, 70, 78, 85, 88, 89, 110
ERICKSON, John, 50
EVANS, Edward, 65, 91, 113
EVENS, Elizabeth, 126

-F-
FAIRLAMB, Nicholas, 92
FAIRMAN, Robert, 63, 64, 74, 120
Thomas, 47, 48, 49, 50, 63, 64, 70, 73, 74, 77, 80, 108, 120, 130
FALKED, John, 92
FALKNER, Hannah, 19
John, 11
FELSON, Henry, 116
FEW, Isaac, 64
FIELD, Benjamin, 55, 81
FINELLY, Samuel, 122
FIRTH, Edward, 6
FLOWER, Enoch, 4, 29, 69
Henry, 29, 69

Mary, 29
FLOWERS, Enoch, 40
FORD, Philip, 26, 27
FORDEROY, William, 91
FORREST, Walter, 64
FOSTER, Alen, 73
  Allen, 70
  Mary, 70, 73
  Miles, 37
FOX, Thomas, 24, 25
FREDERICK, Michael, 80, 120
FREDRICKSON, Michael, 110
FREEBORN, Gideon, 52
FULTON, Z., 117
FURNISS, John, 50

-G-
GABITAS, William, 61, 106
GALT, William, 44
GARDINER, Daniel, 1, 21
  Thomas, 69
GARDNER, Daniel, 52, 54
GARNER, Daniel, 77
GARNOR, Daniel, 21
GARY, George, 80
GAY, John, 84
GERRIS, Barrent, 31
GIBBS, Elizabeth, 3, 7
GIDDON, Samuel, 83
GIFFITH, Evan, 104
  Samuel, 104
GILBERT, John, 64, 73
GILBERTS, John, 40
GILES, Alexander, 4, 9, 96, 97
  Dorothy, 96
  Mary, 96
GILL, John, 6
GISLING, Cesar, 126
GLADING, Thomas, 31
GLAWSON, John, 102
GOODSON, John, 21, 28, 30, 77, 83
GOW, Sarah, 71
GRAY, Elizabeth, 90
  John, 90
GREAVES, Jonathan, 105
GREEN, Edward, 1
  John, 13, 48, 82
  Katherine, 48
  Rachel, 39
  Thomas, 39, 48, 49
GREENE, John, 13, 25
  Katharine, 13
GREENLAW, Henry, 5
GREGORY, William, 115
GRESOE, Jonathan, 86
GREY, Elizabeth, 107
  John, 96, 107
  Thomas, 108, 126
GRIFFIN, John, 57
GRIFFITH, Abraham, 90
  Benjamin, 4, 22, 23, 30, 31
  Evan, 106, 108, 116, 117
  John, 60, 94
  Mary, 94
  Samuel, 94
GRISCOME, Andrew, 10
GROISBECK, Jacob, 64
GROOM, Peter, 47, 118
  Thomas, 124
GROOME, Peter, 38, 129
GROSBECK, Jacob, 63, 64
GROWDEN, Joseph, 25, 46, 50, 51, 53, 62, 110, 125
GROWDON, Eliza:, 106
  Elizabeth, 89
  Grace, 32
  Joseph, 10, 17, 24, 28, 30, 31, 32, 36, 40, 51, 60, 62, 63, 64, 65, 66, 73, 74, 75, 76, 77, 78, 79, 80, 81, 84, 87, 89, 90, 91, 101, 102, 104, 106, 110, 113, 114, 116

Law., 113
Lawrence, 106
Sarah, 89
Thomas, 65
GROWSON, Joseph, 21
GRUBB, Henry, 70, 72, 73, 90
GUY, Edward, 85, 86, 109
Ester, 109
Esther, 86
John, 85, 86, 109
Richard, 60
GUYON, Luke, 113

-H-
HACOCK, Joseph, 98
HAIG, William, 25
HAIGE, William, 6, 7
HAIGHT, Samuel, 53
HAIGUE, William, 8
HALL, Elizabeth, 92
Jacob, 15, 18, 20, 26, 35, 36, 62, 68
John, 92, 126
Robert, 5, 6, 11, 12, 13, 16, 61, 72, 92, 102
HAMOND, George, 107
HAMPTON, Joseph, 130
HANGE, Francis, 115
HANSON, Samuel, 101
HARDEN,
Nathaniel, 50
HARDIMAN,
Rebecca, 126
HARDIN, Nathaniel, 80
Thomas, 69
HARDING,
Nathaniel, 63, 64
Thomas, 29, 126
HARDMAN,
Abraham, 71
HARGROVES,
James, 90
HARKER, Adam, 93, 112
Aden, 101
Samuel, 89
HARRIOTT, Miriam, 55
Samuel, 55
HARRISON, James, 1, 6, 8, 23, 30, 34, 45, 52, 53, 59, 61, 78, 87, 98, 104
John, 64, 76
Phebe, 34
Samuel, 77
HART, John, 12
HARTLEY, Henry, 95
HARVEY, Mathias, 56
HARVIE, Mathias, 65, 72, 74
HASTINGS, Joshua, 64
HATCHER, Richard, 24
HAWIRTH, James, 60

HAWKINS, Daniel, 15, 28
Jeffery, 6, 15, 28, 67, 121
Jeffrey, 2, 3
Roger, 3, 8, 121
Roger R., 15
HAWORTH, Mary, 107
HAYDOCK, Roger, 15
HAYHURST,
Cuthbert, 24, 106, 114, 120, 121
John, 101, 121
Mary, 120, 121
Rachel, 128
William, 24, 29, 48, 74, 75, 78, 88, 91, 106, 112, 113, 114, 120, 121, 128
HAYWARD,
Nicholas, 34
HAYWOOD, James, 33
HAYWORTH,
George, 95
Mary, 122
HEADLEY, John, 71, 88, 92, 107
HEADLY, John, 110
HEALY, Robert, 73
HEARN, William, 70
HEARST, Cuthbert, 10, 70
Mary, 10
Widow, 67
William, 9
HEATH, Andrew, 58, 90

INDEX

Elizabeth, 90
Mary, 43
Richard, 108, 113, 115, 117, 124
Robert, 117
HEATHIELE,
  George, 16
HEATON, James, 60, 86, 97, 100, 116, 117
  Robert, 4, 7, 9, 10, 13, 29, 45, 48, 56, 62, 67, 68, 70, 75, 78, 85, 93, 94, 95, 97, 100, 106, 110, 111, 112, 113, 115, 116, 117, 121, 122, 127, 128, 129
HEED, Thomas, 130
HEITT, George, 7
HENGES, Ann, 55
  William, 55
HENRICK DE BROWN, John, 29
HEOUGH, John, 86
  Richard, 62, 65, 66, 72
  Thomas, 85
HERSENT, ---, 18
HERST, Cuthbert, 77
  William, 77
HEULINGS, W., 107
HEWWORTH,
  James, 19
HEYWOOD, James, 59
HEYWORTH,

James, 76
Mary, 76
HIBBS, Will, 25
HICK, James, 44
HICKET, Nicholas, 24, 25
HICKMAN, Robert, 90
HIETT, John, 85, 92, 106
HILBORN, Thomas, 92
HILBORNE,
  Thomas, 86
HILL, James, 3, 10, 20, 22, 31, 35, 60, 87
  Josias, 38, 81, 118
  Seth, 56
  Shadrick, 84
HILLBORN,
  Thomas, 111, 113, 114, 125
  William, 126
HILLBORNE,
  Thomas, 89, 111
HILLBURN,
  Thomas, 101
HILLIARD, Mary, 70
  Richard, 70
HINCHKSTON,
  Abel, 79
  Elizabeth, 79
HINCHKSTONE,
  Abel, 80
HINCHSTONE,
  Abel, 108
  Elizabeth, 108
HINCKSTONE,

Abel, 78
HINEKSTONE,
  Abel, 25
HINGES, William, 54
HINKET, Nicholas, 32
HINKSTON, Abel, 75
HIOFF, John, 85
HISCOCK, William, 1, 3
HIUKSTON, Abel, 24
HODGSON, Mary, 80
  Robert, 79, 82, 84
HODSON, Robert, 79
  Thomas, 26, 68, 72, 74, 81, 87
HOLD, Thomas, 38
HOLDEN, Joseph, 39, 40, 51
  Margaret, 39
HOLGATE, Robert, 4, 7, 9, 96, 111
HOLLIS, Robert, 108
HOLME, Thomas, 27, 74
  Tyrall, 5
HOLMS, Thomas, 3
HOLT, Obadiah, 47
HOOD, Caspar, 83, 84
HOOKES, Daniel, 58
HOOKS, Daniel, 56, 57
  Joshua, 56, 71

INDEX

HOOPES, Daniel, 44
Joseph, 32
Joshua, 21, 33, 67
Josiah, 86
HOOPS, Joshua, 116, 117
HORNER, Isaac, 45
John, 5, 45
Joshua, 45
Mary, 45
HORTON, Obadiah, 55
HOSKINS, Aurelius, 79
HOUGE, William, 124
HOUGES, William, 126
HOUGH, Francis, 11
George, 123
John, 41, 68, 81, 84, 108, 122, 123
Mary, 123
Richard, 17, 19, 32, 33, 37, 39, 44, 49, 51, 52, 53, 54, 56, 57, 71, 74, 78, 80, 82, 83, 84, 95, 98, 100, 106, 117
Samuel, 92, 93, 94, 103, 114, 122
William, 91, 113
HOUGHE, William, 119
HOUGHTON, John, 68
HOUGS, Richard, 18
HOWELL, Jacob, 61
Job, 61, 76
Jobe, 14

Joseph, 52
Philip, 70
Stephen, 87
HOWERTZ, James, 56
HOWES, Jeremiah, 109
HOWEYTE, Jamey, 56
HOWIE, Mathias, 56
HUDDLESTON, Henry, 106, 113, 114, 117
HUDDLESTONE, Henry, 112
HUDDY, Charles, 103
Hn., 102
HUDLESTON, Henry, 24, 76, 77
Valentine, 60
HUDSON, Robert, 7, 12
Thomas, 26, 36, 41, 55, 56, 65, 71, 78
William, 82
HUFF, Joan, 16, 20
Mary, 69
Michael, 16, 20
HUFTEEN, Charles, 129
HUGHES, Mathew, 115
Rowland, 115
HULME, George, 110
HUMPHARY, Walter, 78
HUMPHREYS, John, 75
HUNLOKE,

Edward, 94
HURELEY, Edward, 85
HURST, William, 10
HUTCHINSON,
George, 55
John, 90, 107, 113, 122, 126
Joyce, 90
Phebe, 126
Robert, 77

-I-
INGENY, Henry, 26

-J-
JACKMAN, George, 11, 69
JACKSON, Daniel, 84, 105, 107, 109, 110
George, 122
John, 106
JACOB, James, 70
JACOBS, Bartoll, 102
JAMES, Thomas, 122
JANEY, Abel, 56
Jacob, 56
JANNEY, Abel, 45, 57, 80, 82, 98, 100, 115, 128
Abell, 88
Jacob, 9, 32, 34, 44, 57, 59, 93, 98, 108, 113, 123, 125, 129
Thomas, 2, 4, 8, 9, 14, 16, 17, 32, 33,

39, 80, 98, 108, 123
JANSEN, Riner, 122
JEFFES, Robert, 20
JEFFS, Mary, 18
  Robert, 19
JELSON, Joal, 77
JENKINS, Jere, 35
JENNER, Thomas, 50, 62, 65
JENNEY, Joseph, 77
  Thomas, 78
JENNINGS,
  Margery, 111, 115
  William, 111
JEWELL, John, 102
JOHNSON, Britain, 50
  Claus, 63, 110
  Clause, 106
  Claws, 31
  Katerine, 50
  Lawrence, 129
JONES, Daniel, 6, 7, 8, 67, 68, 111
  Griffith, 3, 4, 11, 14, 117, 124
  Henry, 91
  Jnieolls Rich., 37
  John, 52, 70, 91, 129
  Joseph, 38, 77
JONSON, Elizabeth, 50
JONSTON, John, 117

-K-
KEEN, Francis, 93
  Jonas, 93
  Matts, 50
KELLEY, Patrick, 5
KEMPE, Edward, 92
KENERLY, William, 53
KENWAY, Mary, 6
KINGSTON,
  Elizabeth, 74
KINLOW, John, 93
KIRBRIDE, Joseph, 59
KIRK, Joseph, 63, 65
  Thomas P., 50
KIRKBRIDE,
  Joseph, 14, 16, 45, 46, 49, 51, 52, 53, 58, 60, 65, 67, 71, 75, 76, 78, 83, 86, 87, 88, 89, 92, 96, 97, 98, 100, 109, 111, 113, 118, 119, 120, 121, 122, 124, 126, 129
  Mary, 121
  Mathew, 96
  Matthew, 111
  Thomas, 111, 121
KIRKE, Joseph, 43
KIRLE, Thomas, 124
KNIGHT, Ezra, 96
  Joseph, 48, 49
  Thomas, 60, 62, 90, 104
KNOWLES, John, 90

-L-
LAMBERT, Thomas, 22, 43
LAND, Edward, 50, 57
LANE, Will, 33
LANGHORNE,
  Grace, 17, 60, 78
  Israel, 103
  Jeremiah, 60, 75, 77, 78, 81, 87, 100, 101, 102, 103, 104, 106, 109, 110, 111, 112, 113, 114, 116, 118, 119, 120, 124
  Thomas, 13, 15, 16, 17, 60, 78
  Widow, 44, 68
LARGE, John, 97, 105, 108, 110, 115, 118, 121, 125, 126, 129
  Joseph, 46, 48, 49, 54, 69, 72, 79, 82, 83, 93, 97, 98, 128, 129
  Richard, 82
LATHAM, Elizabeth, 96
  John, 96
LAVALLE, Charles, 106
LAVALLER,
  Charles, 91
LAWRENCE, Peter, 100, 127, 128
  William, 55, 81
LEHAMMANY,
  Philip H., 9
LEILL, ----, 59
LESTER, Peter, 120

LEVALLE, Charles, 97, 114
LEVALLEY, Charles, 92, 112
Elizabeth, 92
LEVALLY, Charles, 126
LEVETT, Solomon, 97
LEWIS, Elizabeth, 75
Samuel, 75
LISLE, Maurice, 88
LIST, Maurice, 129
LITTLE, Francis, 74
LITTLETON, Peter, 6
LLOYD, Da., 60
Daniel, 115
David, 11, 47, 65, 66, 68, 73, 75, 79, 86, 91, 93, 113, 117, 119, 124
Thomas, 42, 91, 119
LLYOD, Thomas, 11
LOGAN, James, 100, 117
LOGWOOD, Riger, 128
LONGSHORE, Robert, 27
LONGSTRETH, Bartholomew, 116
LONGWORTH, Roger, 34
LOVER, John, 16
LOVET, Edmond, 1
LOVETS, Edmund, 82

LOVETT, Edmond, 2, 7, 19, 38, 97, 98, 101, 129
Edmund, 61, 63, 72, 79, 82, 83, 85, 107
Edward, 109
Elizabeth, 85
LOYD, Da., 15, 19, 22
Thomas, 3, 113
LOYKE, Dance, 50
LUCAS, Edward, 18, 67, 89
Elizabeth, 18, 67
Giles, 18, 67, 112
Robert, 1, 2, 6, 8, 11, 12, 13, 16, 29, 60, 67, 100
Widow, 65
LUFF, Edward, 22
John, 1, 6, 70, 77
LUFFE, John, 111
LUFT, Edward, 21, 33
LUGG, Bartholomew, 6
LUNDY, Elizabeth, 15
Richard, 1, 2, 15, 16, 18, 19, 39, 64, 66, 71, 86, 90, 95, 97, 115, 117, 121, 126
Richrd, 31
LUST, John, 96
LVYKEN, Elner, 80
Michael, 80

-M-
MCCOMB, John, 49
MACKLIER, John, 91
MCVAGH, Edmond, 5
MAGOO, Steward, 85
MAJORAM, Henry, 44
MALLOWS, Henry, 71
MARGARAM, Henry, 2
MARGEREUM, Henry, 19
MARGEROM, Henry, 1, 80
MARGERUM, Henry, 5, 22, 32, 33, 87, 106
MARJORAM, Henry, 51
MARJORUM, Henry, 56, 66
MARJORUN, Henry, 62
MARKES, Joseph, 16
Joseph A., 16
MARKHAM, William, 21, 28, 30, 38, 54, 62, 77, 83
MARMIOM (MARMION), Samuel, 126
MARSH, Anthony, 38
Hugh, 24, 38, 39,

40, 118
Robert, 29, 40
Sarah, 40
MARSHALL,
 William, 117, 118
MARTIN, George, 9,
 10
MASLEY, Moses, 27
MASSLEY, Moses,
 27
MASTERS, Thomas,
 71, 89
MATHER, Joseph,
 15
MATHIS, Joseph, 56
 Richard, 45
MATTHEWS,
 Margaret, 81
MAUBIE, Richard,
 15
MAYES, Edward, 63,
 66
MAYLEIGH,
 Thomas, 19
MAYOS, Edward,
 61, 88, 89, 93,
 102, 105, 106,
 109, 113, 115,
 118, 119, 120,
 125, 126
MEAD, William, 110
MEREDITH, John,
 38
MICHELL, Henry,
 122
MILFORD, Joseph,
 10
MILLCOME, Anne,
 2, 3, 5
 Annie, 5

MILLS, Stephen,
 109
MILNER, Joseph,
 14, 56
MILNOR, Joseph,
 11, 36, 56, 59, 65,
 66, 67, 74
MITCHELL, Henry,
 106
 Richard, 126
MOON, James, 18,
 19, 22, 85, 86, 87,
 123
 Joan, 22, 118
MOONE, James, 87,
 118
 Roger, 118, 119
MOONES, John, 41
MOORE, James, 18,
 35, 65
 Nicholas, 27
MOORES, John, 40
MORGAN, Anthony,
 38, 81, 118
 Elizabeth, 81
MORREY,
 Humphrey, 83
MORRIS, Anthony,
 73, 82, 83, 91
 Isaac, 119
 Israel, 68, 92, 93,
 99, 100, 101
 John, 73, 115
MOW, Xooll, 10
MURRAY, Rebecca,
 127
 Thomas, 127
MUSGRAND,
 Widow, 81
MUSGRAVES,

 Thomas, 50
MUSGROVE,
 Thomas, 58, 60,
 66, 97, 123

-N-
NAUSAND, Garrett,
 78
NAYLOR, John, 50,
 104, 116
NEILD, John, 51
NELSON, Henry,
 95, 103, 108, 117,
 129
NEWBOULD,
 Michael, 47
NEWEL, Stephen,
 60
NEWELL, Steven,
 53
NICHOLLS, Elias, 6,
 42
 John, 5, 6, 10, 12,
 42
 William, 37
NICHOLS, Elias, 74,
 76
 John, 74, 76
 Joshua, 120
NICHSNER,
 Burrough, 130
NICKHOILS,
 Joshua, 129
NIELD, John, 56
NOBLE, Richard, 27,
 28, 54
NOEL, Stephen, 24
NOMS, Isaac, 113
NORRIS, Isaac, 91
NOWELL, Stephen,

25, 89
Steven, 24
NUTT, William, 87
NUTTBY, John, 16

-O-
OGDEN, David, 4
OLDALE, Lemuel,
  105, 106, 109,
  111, 115, 126, 129
Samuel, 66, 105,
  109, 115, 129
OLDALIS, Samuel,
  118
OLDDEL, Samuel,
  80
OTHERSON,
  Arthur, 124
OTTER, John, 1, 8,
  31, 36, 52, 57, 86,
  111
OTTOSON, Arthur,
  122
OVERTON, Hannah,
  14
Samuel, 5
OWEN, Griffith, 17,
  75, 117

-P-
PAIL, Joseph, 70
PAINE, John, 43
PAINTER, Henry,
  129
PALMER, George,
  117
John, 44
PARBELBERT,
  Jacob Clark, 84
PARKER, William,

125
PARNALL, Ruben,
  44
PARSINS, John, 61
PARSON, Thomas,
  108
PARSONS, John, 92,
  111
PARTLITS, William,
  126
PASCHEL, Thomas,
  43
PAUL, Joseph, 61
PAULK, Phil, 69
PAULLIN, Henry,
  68
PAWLIN, Henry, 7,
  8, 18, 21, 45, 58,
  99, 100, 115, 116
Sarah, 115
PAWLINGS, Henry,
  71
PAXON, Henry, 108
James, 61
Margery, 108
William, 49
PAXSON, Abigail, 76
Edward, 95
Enoch, 114
Henry, 7, 18, 28,
  45, 58, 68, 71, 79,
  87, 99, 101, 102,
  103, 110, 124, 129
James, 28, 58, 60,
  68, 87, 103
Lawrence, 95, 114
Margery, 71, 79,
  87, 99
Mary, 116
Thomas, 91

William, 28, 44, 45,
  60, 68, 71, 74, 76,
  81, 86, 95, 101,
  103, 108, 112,
  113, 114, 116,
  118, 119, 128
PAXTON, Henry,
  21, 107, 109
William, 7, 21
PEARL, Mary, 70
Thomas, 70
PEARSON, Edward,
  41, 63, 120
Enoch, 90, 105,
  114, 120
Lawrence, 95, 105,
  120
PECKER, Philip, 86
PEDECOCK, John,
  87
PEGG, Daniel, 36
Elizabeth, 36
PEIRCE, Edward, 27
Richard, 32, 78
PELLISON, Jacob,
  27
PEMBERTON,
  Abigail, 56, 59,
  60, 74, 75, 80, 95
Alice, 85
Isaac, 90
Israel, 75, 95
Joseph, 93
Phebe, 22, 45
Phenas, 128
Phineas, 1, 3, 27,
  42, 45, 46, 47, 49,
  50, 51, 52, 55, 56,
  59, 60, 63, 64, 66,
  68, 69, 70, 72, 73,

INDEX

74, 75, 76, 78, 80, 82, 83, 84, 85, 87, 88, 89, 91, 96, 97, 98
  Phinehas, 2, 6, 7, 8, 9, 11, 12, 14, 15, 16, 17, 18, 19, 20, 21, 22, 33, 34, 35, 36, 37
  Ralph, 15
  Sarah, 125
  Thomas, 83
PENINGTON,
  Edward, 81
PENN, William, 2, 3, 4, 5, 19, 20, 22, 23, 25, 26, 30, 31, 35, 39, 40, 53, 62, 65, 67, 71, 73, 77, 96, 97, 99, 105, 108, 116
PENNINGTON,
  Edward, 124, 127
  John, 75
PENQUITE, John, 18, 91, 121
PENQUOIT, John, 17
PERSONS, John, 43
PETER, Thomas, 20
PETTISON, Jacob, 27
PHILLIPS, Mercy, 108
  Thomas, 82
  William T., 6
  William F., 6
PICKERING,
  Charles, 9, 12, 22, 46
  William, 18
PIDCOCK, John, 1, 4
PIDECOCK, John, 86
PIERCE, Richard, 85
PLUMBLY, James, 100
PLUMBY, Charles, 71
  James, 77
PLUMLEY, Charles, 28, 99, 100
  James, 28, 99
  Margery, 28
  Mary, 99
  Widow, 4
  William, 28, 99
PLUMLY, Charles, 103, 107, 122
  George, 107
  James, 70, 71, 73, 79, 87, 100, 103, 107, 108
  John, 71, 79, 107, 116, 124
  Margery, 21, 103
  Widow, 74
  William, 58, 79, 103, 107
PLUMSTEAD,
  Clement, 91
POINTER, Henry, 13
POOLE, Nathaniel, 99
POWALL, Widow, 17
POWELL, Ann, 3
  David, 3, 5, 10, 11, 62, 73
  Samuel, 92, 127
  Thomas, 20, 122
POWNAL, Ruben, 80
POWNALL, Reuben, 57
  Ruben, 34, 56, 112
PRALLWORTH,
  John, 1
PRESSINALL,
  Robert, 11
PRIEST, Thomas, 17
PRIESTMALL,
  Robert, 122
PULMER, John, 86
PUMPHARY,
  Wallen, 72
  Walter, 69, 70
PUMPHREY,
  Walter, 93

-R-

RADCIFF, James, 34
RADCLIFE, James, 128
  Rebecca, 128
  Richard, 128
RADCLIFFE,
  Richard, 106
RADLEY, Daniel, 86
  John, 85
RADLY, John, 109
RAKESTRAW,
  William, 104
RANDALL, Nicholas, 70, 129, 130
RATCLIFE, Edward, 98, 128
RATCLIFF, Richard,

INDEX

73
RAY, James, 130
READ, Amey, 71
  Anne, 61
  Charles, 60, 61, 71
READMAN, John, 70
REALE, William, 24
REDMAN, John, 12
REEVE, John, 122
REINER, Pauline, 122
REOUDY, Peter, 67
RESTOENE, Ben, 33
REVEL, Thomas, 11, 19, 27, 28, 107
REVELL, Thomas, 90, 92, 93, 96, 97, 124
REVELLS, Thomas, 62
REYNOLDS, William, 32
RICHARD, Thomas, 55
RICHARDS, Philip, 40
RICHARDSON,
  Fancis, 127
  Francis, 91, 113, 119, 129
  John, 127
  Rebecca, 127
  Samuel, 82, 84
  Thomas, 96
RIDGWAY, Abigail, 77
  Elizabeth, 18
  Richard, 1, 3, 5, 6, 10, 12, 15, 17, 18, 20, 21, 31, 35, 36, 37, 42, 48, 77
RIDWAY, Richard, 37, 77
RIGGE, Robert, 12
ROBARDES, John, 97
ROBERTS,
  Benjamin, 41, 44, 83
  Hannah, 41, 44
ROBERTSON,
  Thomas, 20
ROBESON, Andrew, 6, 7, 8, 111, 124
  Pat, 6
  Samuel, 8
ROBINSON,
  Andrew, 67
  Pat, 14
  Pat., 3, 7, 8, 12, 24
  Smauel, 67
ROCKFORD, Denis, 55
RODMAN, John, 53, 96
ROE, Abraham, 99
  Robert, 57
ROGERS, Thomas, 44, 60, 61
ROOTLIDGE,
  William, 12
ROSILL, Francis, 39
ROSSEL, Francis, 19, 20
ROSSELL, Frances, 95
  Francis, 1, 58, 69, 105, 114, 115
  Michael, 1
ROSSIL, Frances, 14
  Francis, 19, 31
ROSSILL, Frances, 66, 71, 90
  Francis, 21, 69, 71
ROUTELEDGE,
  Elizabeth, 130
ROUTLEDGE, John, 86
ROW, Robert, 1
ROWLAND, ----, 59
  John, 2, 3, 4, 7, 10, 11, 13, 14, 19, 30, 31, 33, 36, 37, 41, 51, 61, 63, 64, 66, 78, 82, 85, 87, 91, 92, 95, 98, 101, 102, 104, 109, 110, 113, 114, 118, 119, 125, 129
  Priscilla, 63, 82, 85, 114
  Thomas, 1, 3, 10, 11, 12, 13, 24, 25, 31, 33, 36, 41, 46, 61, 66, 78
ROWLING, John, 92
  Priscilla, 92
RUDLEY, Daniel, 44
RUDYARD, Thomas, 8, 82, 84, 111
RUMFORD, John, 81
RUSH, John, 70

-S-
SALTER, Anna, 11, 64
  Hannah, 4

SAMUEL, Beakes, 61
SAMWAY, Edward, 40
SAMWAYS, Edward, 15, 16
SAND, Stephen, 102
SANDERS, Robert, 82, 114
SANDFORD, William, 54
SANDS, Stephen, 81, 121
SANFORD, William, 55
SAXBY, John, 6, 13, 15, 18, 19, 74
SAY, William, 19, 39, 91, 117
SCAIFE, Jeremiah, 69
　Jonathan, 3, 13, 45, 46, 48, 51, 56, 57, 62, 68, 69, 71, 76, 78, 79, 81, 96, 110, 111
　Mary, 45
SCAIFF, John, 82
SCARBOROUGH, Jhon, 77
　John, 31, 67, 70, 71, 75, 76, 87, 101, 115, 120
SCARBORROW, John, 39
SCARBROUGH, John, 69, 88
SCARFE, Jonathan, 34
SCHOLAH, John, 94
　Rebecca, 94
SCOLAH, John, 105
　Rebecca, 105
SCOT, Jane, 88
　John, 88, 120
SCOTT, Amy, 103
　John, 81
　Samuel, 104
　Thomas, 62, 90, 104
SCOVEY, Guit, 26
SEARLE, Francis, 60, 62, 79, 104
SENIOR, Abraham, 86
SHARP, Joseph, 31
SHAW, John, 61, 76, 81, 111, 115, 126
　Robert, 125, 126
SHEPPERD, Priscilla, 114
SHINN, Joseph, 55
　Samuel, 55
SHIPPEN, Edward, 100, 124, 127
　John, 20
　Rebecca, 127
SHIRE, John, 81
SHORLOE, William, 27
SIDAL, John, 100
SIDDAL, Henry, 45
SIDDALL, Henry, 18, 28
SIDEWELL, Henry, 17
SILVERSTON, William, 123
SILVERSTONE, William, 106, 114, 125
SIRKETT, John, 96
SISON, Priscilla, 99
　Thomas, 99
SKATIGER, Richard, 39
SMART, Lydia, 43
SMITH, Daniel, 67, 111, 112
　Edward, 60, 75
　Elizabeth, 85
　Emanuel, 90
　John, 21, 33, 34, 44, 49, 50, 57, 58, 64, 66, 78, 84, 97, 113, 115, 128
　Joseph, 105
　Joshua, 77
　Priscilla, 63
　Ralph, 1, 4, 6, 61, 63, 82
　Robert, 113
　Samuel, 85, 93, 97, 98, 108, 109, 111, 112, 129
　Thomas, 59
　William, 24, 66, 69, 79, 84, 115
SNEAD, William, 96, 108
SNODEN, Christopher, 37
SNOWDEN, Christopher, 90
　John, 42, 43, 87, 119
SNOWDON, Christopher, 37
SNOWDWON, Christopher, 78

INDEX

SONMANS, P., 19
SOTCHER, John, 125
SPENCER, James, 8, 17
  John, 8, 17, 27
  Samuel, 8, 17
SPRINGETT,
  Anthony, 26, 35
  Habt., 35
  Haibs, 71
  Harbt., 4, 22, 23, 25, 26, 30, 31
STACKHOUSE,
  John, 92, 93, 112
  Margaret, 102
  Robert, 116
  Thomas, 5, 9, 13, 24, 33, 60, 62, 67, 77, 78, 79, 94, 101, 102, 104, 112, 113, 114, 129
STACY, Mahlon, 42, 63, 64, 73, 74, 75, 119
  Robert, 47
STAKEHOUSE,
  John, 46
  Thomas, 50
STANLEY, Hugh, 10
  William, 47, 130
STANTON, Annie, 60
  Edward, 6, 60, 61, 71
STAPLES, Thomas, 18
STARNEY, Mary, 126
STEVENS, Francis, 22, 31
STEVENSON,
  Thomas, 90, 91, 96, 106, 107, 111, 124, 125, 126
  William, 81, 90, 96, 124
STEWARD, Joseph, 32, 44, 61
STEWART, Joseph, 44
STOCKDALE,
  William, 122
STOCKER, John, 125
STOCKTON,
  Abigail, 35, 36
STOKES, Thomas, 97
STONE, George, 56, 78, 87
  Phebe, 78
  Thomas, 88
STONES, Joseph, 122
STORRY, Thomas, 89
STORY, Thomas, 22, 84, 100
STOUT, George, 74
STRAITON, James, 91
STREATE, James, 117
STREATER, Anne, 124
  James, 115, 124
SURKEL, John, 79
SURKET, John, 82, 83

William, 82
SUTTON, James, 110
  Ralph, 86, 126
SWAFFER, James, 21
SWATHY, John, 42
SWETT, Benjamin, 46
SWIFT, John, 13, 18, 47, 60, 73, 74, 75, 76, 77, 78, 104, 111, 122, 126, 129, 130
SWINTON, James, 25
  Js., 26
SYMOCK, John, 27

-T-

TALLMAN, John, 81
TALMAN, John, 55
TALTHUR, John, 79
TATHAM, Elizabeth, 90
  John, 34, 90, 99
TATHEM, Elizabeth, 107
TAYLOR,
  Christopher, 2, 39, 47, 59, 73, 91, 92, 93, 94, 96, 100, 113, 119, 128
  Israel, 2, 6, 7, 8, 11, 31, 38, 39, 40, 45, 47, 58, 59, 60, 73, 91, 92, 93, 94, 96, 100, 103, 104, 108, 113, 119
  John, 18, 21, 129

Jonathan, 109
Joseph, 73, 91, 92, 93, 100, 103, 113, 119
Will, 66
William, 65
TEAGE, Penticost, 83
TEAGUE, Penetecost, 98
TELLNOR, Jacob, 2
TELNER, Jacob, 19
TELNOR, Jacob, 115
TERRY, Joshua, 120
Thomas, 44, 107
THATCHER, Amos, 70
Bartholomew, 70, 95
Joseph, 70, 95
Ricahrd, 75
Richard, 29, 70, 87, 95, 100, 106, 127
THOMPSON, Mathew, 94
THORN, Joseph, 81
Samuel, 81
THWAITES, Thomas, 116
THWAITS, Thomas, 117
TOMEKIN, Anthony, 83
TOMKINS, Anthony, 9, 14, 100
TOMLINSON, Henry, 107
Joseph, 116
TOMPKINS, Joshua, 97

TOOKER, Arthur, 16
TOWN, John, 49, 50, 58, 67, 72, 74, 85, 91, 94, 126
Joseph, 58
TOWNE, John, 52, 66
TOWNSEND, Richard, 74
TUCKER, Arthur, 16
Richard, 108
TULY, John, 19
TUNICLIFT, Thomas, 98
TUNNECLIF, Francis, 80
TUNNICLIF, Susannah, 80
Thomas, 80
TUNNICLIFFE, Thomas, 32
TUNNICLIFT, Thomas, 6, 13
TUNNISCLIFT, Thomas, 14
TURKETT, John, 95
TURNER, Robert, 3, 5, 7, 9, 10, 11, 13, 14, 32, 53, 54, 77, 83, 84, 124
TWINING, Stephen, 45, 46, 69, 78, 114, 124

-U-

URHER, Jacob, 92
USHER, Jacob, 129

-V-

VAN SANDS, Cornelius, 92
VANDEGRIFT, Frederick, 73
Johannis, 63
Leonard, 73
Nicholas, 63, 73
VANDER BURIKS, Cornelius, 29
VANDERGRIFT, Frederick, 63, 64
Johannes, 64
Leonard, 64
Leondert, 63
Nicholas, 64
VANDHORNE, Christian Cavenson, 117
VANDIKE, Henrich Johnson, 112
Henry Johnson, 117, 120, 127, 128
VANSAND, Albert, 116
Cornelius, 79, 116
Garrat, 116
Garret, 116
George, 116
Harman, 116
Jacobus, 116
Jezina, 116
Johanes, 116
Stophell, 116
VANSANDT, Harman, 106
Johanes, 106
Johannes, 107
Stophel, 116
VANSANT, Jonas,

107
Wibardlis, 107
VANSAUL, Stoffel, 130
VARDER,
   Willoughby, 115
VAUDINE, ---, 129
VENABLES,
   Francis, 90
   Joyce, 90
   William, 43, 90
VENEABLES,
   Orphans, 44
VERRIER, Jacque, 86
   James, 110
   James (or Jacque), 129
   Warbet, 129
VIRKIRK, Bardnt, 63
   Barndt, 64, 73

-W-
WALKER, Francis, 30, 37, 93, 110
   John, 70
WALLER, Nicholas, 68
   Richard, 68
WALLEY, Lydia, 15
   Shadrach, 34, 44, 108
   Shadrack, 7, 15, 83, 96, 107, 123
WALLN, Nicholas, 11, 12, 15, 16, 17, 21, 25, 29
WALLNE, Nicholas, 5

WALMSLEY,
   Elizabeth, 4, 5, 74
   Henry, 104
   Thomas, 74, 86, 87, 104, 106, 108, 116, 117, 125
WALMSLY, Thomas, 79
WALN, Nicholas, 2, 4, 9, 10, 24, 27, 28, 38, 39, 46, 63, 64, 68, 74, 79, 99, 103, 108
   Richard, 67
WALNE, Nicholas, 9, 94, 104, 112
WALTER, Joseph, 55
WARD, John, 124
   Joseph, 103, 124
   Ralph, 50, 62, 94
WARDE, Solomon, 104
WARDEN,
   Willoughby, 125
WARDER, Solomon, 91, 92, 94, 97, 98, 105, 125, 128
   Willoughby, 95, 103, 105, 124
WATERMAN, Isaac, 60
WATSON, John, 82, 101
   Thomas, 92, 101, 103, 107, 116, 117, 120, 128
WEBB, Elizabth, 62
   Robert, 62
WEBSTER, John, 14, 38, 54, 76
   Peter, 65, 67, 76, 85, 100, 113
WEEKES, Benjamin, 122
WEEKS, Benjamin, 18
WETHERILL,
   Christopher, 2, 60, 94, 105, 120, 121
WHARLEY,
   Abraham, 21, 44
WHARMLY, Lydia, 6
WHEALEY,
   Abraham, 83
WHEARLY,
   Abraham, 8, 14, 17
WHEATE,
   Benjamin, 97
WHEATH,
   Benjamin, 31
WHEELER, Gilbert, 1, 4, 12, 13, 29, 32, 33, 54, 66, 67, 87, 109, 124
   Richard, 41, 44
   Robert, 19, 39, 91, 97, 117
   Sarah, 41, 44
WHERLY, Abraham, 9
WHITE, Ann, 72
   Benjamin, 72, 86, 88, 102
   Elizabeh, 85
   Elizabeth, 49, 50, 52, 53, 72, 73, 77, 102, 113, 114

INDEX

Francis, 69, 72, 73, 86, 102, 109, 112, 124, 125, 126, 129
George, 72, 101, 102, 107, 109, 110, 112, 129
Joan, 73, 87
John, 4, 7, 12, 16, 36, 47, 49, 52, 57, 58, 69, 72, 73, 85, 87, 89, 91, 92, 97, 101, 102, 106, 109, 110, 114, 129
Joseph, 72, 97, 102
Martha, 114
Peter, 7, 47, 49, 50, 52, 53, 71, 72, 76, 85, 102, 113, 114
William, 12, 72, 86
WHITEPAINE, John, 24
Zachariah, 24
WHITPAINE, Zechariah, 74
WHITWELL, Francis, 10
WIGGANS, William, 40
WIGGINS, William, 15, 16
WIGGLESWORTH, Alice, 9
WIGGLEWORTH, Alice, 10
WILDERLAW, Martin, 67
WILDMAN, James, 106, 128
Joseph, 106
Matthew, 92, 106

WILEFORD, Rebecca, 66
WILKENS, John, 88
WILL, John J., 116
WILLARD, George, 46, 61, 76, 115
WILLCOX, Joseph, 74
WILLETS, Abigail, 53
Hannah, 53
Richard, 53
WILLIAMS, Daniel, 110
Dunck, 126
Dunk, 93, 110
Dunken, 50
John, 93
Nicholas, 10
Rebecca, 46, 83, 94, 98, 105, 109, 129
Thomas, 46, 48, 94, 98, 105, 109, 129
William, 93, 120
WILLIS, James, 57
WILLSFORD, John, 14
WILLSON, Esther, 129
Robert, 120
WILSFORD, Joseph, 25
WILSON, Richard, 18, 19, 21, 77
Stephen, 66, 67, 78
WOLF, Paul, 122
Thomas, 10, 95
WOLFE, Sarah, 120
Thomas, 3, 4, 7, 41, 120

WOOD, Alex. A., 14
James, 65, 69
John, 3, 6, 10, 12, 15, 20, 24
Joseph, 3, 4, 8, 15, 20, 21, 29, 33, 47, 51, 52, 75, 76, 83, 97
Peter, 79, 85, 98
Richard, 65, 70
WOODDELL, Thomas, 120
WOODWORTH, Richard, 52
WOOLEY, Ezekiel, 20
WOOLF, Thomas, 21
WOOLFE, Thomas, 1, 2
WOOLIDGE, Samuel, 12
WOOLRICH, Thomas, 22, 23
WOOLRICK, Thomas, 22
WORRAL, Peter, 80
WORRALL, Peter, 29, 56, 73, 90, 93
WORREL, Peter, 95
WORRELLOW, Jane, 56
WORRILAW, Thomas, 80
WORRILEW, Elizabeth, 43
WORRILOW, Elizabeth, 32
John, 32
Thomas, 6
Walter, 31, 32

WORRLEW, John,
  43
 Wallie, 43

-Y-
YARDLEY, Enoch,
  11, 32, 45, 46, 56,
  57, 59, 66, 76, 78,
  93
 Samuel, 117
 Thoams, 113
 Thomas, 57, 71, 79,
  82, 91, 93, 117,
  119
 Will, 17, 34, 35
 William, 1, 2, 4, 7,
  8, 9, 11, 14, 16,
  17, 32, 33, 36, 57,
  93
YATES, James, 40,
  44, 100

Other Heritage Books by Charlotte Meldrum:

Abstracts of Bucks County, Pennsylvania Land Records, 1684-1723

*Early Church Records of Burlington County, New Jersey
Volumes 1-3*

Early Church Records of Chester County, Pennsylvania, Volume 2
Charlotte Meldrum and Martha Reamy

Early Church Records of Gloucester County, New Jersey

Early Church Records of Salem County, New Jersey

Early Records of Cumberland County, New Jersey

Johnston County, North Carolina Marriages, 1764-1867

Marriages and Deaths of Montgomery County, Pennsylvania, 1685-1800

www.ingramcontent.com/pod-product-compliance
Lightning Source LLC
Chambersburg PA
CBHW062227080426
42734CB00010B/2054